‖‖‖‖‖‖‖‖‖‖‖‖‖‖‖‖‖‖‖‖‖‖‖‖‖‖‖‖‖

☞ **S0-AZJ-142**

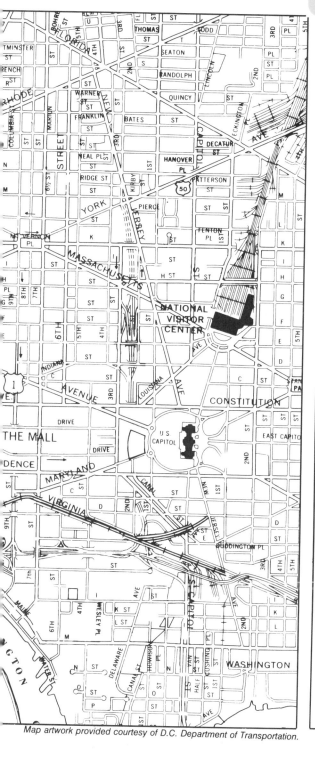

A Overseas Private Investment
   Corporation
   1615 M Street, NW
   Washington, DC 20527

B Small Business Administration
   1441 L Street, NW
   Washington, DC 20416

C Export-Import Bank of the
   United States
   811 Vermont Avenue, NW
   Washington, DC 20571

D Office of the U.S. Trade
   Representative
   600 17th Street, NW
   Washington, DC 20506

E U.S. Trade and Development
   Program
   1621 North Kent Street
   Rosslyn, VA 22209
   (Mailing Address: Washington,
   DC 20523)

F Agency for International Development
   Department of State Building
   320 21st Street, NW
   Washington, DC 20523

G Department of Commerce
   14th Street and Constitution
   Avenue, NW
   Washington, DC 20230

H Department of Agriculture
   14th Street and Independence
   Avenue, SW
   Washington, DC 20250

I The International Bank for
   Reconstruction and Development
   (World Bank)
   1818 H Street, NW
   Washington, DC 20433

J International Finance Corporation
   1850 I Street, NW
   Washington, DC 20433
   (Mailing Address: 1818 H Street)

Map artwork provided courtesy of D.C. Department of Transportation.

INSIDE WASHINGTON

INSIDE
WASHINGTON

The International Business Executive's Guide To Government Resources

Edited by
WILLIAM A. DELPHOS

Theodore Lownik Library
Illinois Benedictine College
Lisle, Illinois 60532

MADISON BOOKS
Lanham • New York • London

Copyright © 1988 by

William A. Delphos

Madison Books

4720 Boston Way
Lanham, MD 20706

3 Henrietta Street
London WC2E 8LU England

All rights reserved

Printed in the United States of America

British Cataloging in Publication Information Available

Library of Congress Cataloging-in-Publication Data

Delphos, William A. (William Arthur), 1951–
Inside Washington : the international business executive's guide
to government resources / edited by William A. Delphos.
p. cm.
Entirely new, rev., and updated ed. of: Washington's best kept
secrets. © 1983.
1. Corporations, American—Government policy—Information
services—United States. 2. International business enterprises—
Information services—United States. 3. Industrial promotion—
Information services—United States. 4. United States—Commerce—
Information services. I. Delphos, William A. (William Arthur),
1951–   Washington's best kept secrets. II. Title.
HD2785.D385   1988
353.0082'7—dc 19   88–1591 CIP
ISBN 0–8191–6934–X (alk. paper)

All Madison Books are produced on acid-free
paper which exceeds the minimum standards set by the National
Historical Publications and Records Commission.

Madison
B O O K S

CONTENTS

To President Ronald Reagan who said that Government should be run on a business-like basis and to Craig Nalen, President of OPIC, who proved it could be done.

Foreword

By Clayton Yeutter
United States Trade Representative

Until recently international trade did not attract a great deal of attention in the United States. We were rich in natural resources, the possessors of the world's largest economy and generally isolated from the rest of the industrialized world. As a result, we produced most of the goods we needed within our own borders. Indeed, as recently as 1960, our export-import trade totaled only $35 billion. Since the U.S. usually had a trade surplus or only a small deficit, the effects of trade, when considered at all, were typically viewed as benign.

All that has now changed. Imports and exports today amount to some $650 billion, accounting for over 20 percent of the U.S. gross national product. One-eighth of all manufacturing jobs depend upon exports and 40 percent of our farm production is sold abroad. The U.S. is now part of a vast global economy and if it is to retain its position of preeminence in the world, American businesses must learn to compete internationally.

The U.S. government is doing its part to establish an environment in which American producers can go head-to-head with their competitors. We support measures that will create more openness in world markets because we think most American businesses can compete with anyone in the world if given the chance. The U.S. policy for promoting open markets has three major elements: to confront agressively foreign unfair trade practices, to negotiate better bilateral and multilateral trade agreements such as the U.S.-Canada Free Trade Arrangement and the work product of GATT Uruguay Round, and to improve the international economy so that foreign consumers will be able to buy more of our products.

We are making significant progress in establishing an environment that enhances export opportunities for American business. U.S. exporters had a record 1987 and we expect overseas sales to continue rising in the years ahead. The key now is for the private sector to continue taking advantage of these new opportunities.

The first step any business executive considering overseas opportunities should take is to learn about the many and varied services available throughout the U.S. government. Numerous agencies offer programs to help exporters; I would encourage all exporters to find out about them and use them to the fullest extent possible.

PREFACE

Imagine, if you will, walking into the neighborhood grocery store to buy a jar of chunky peanut butter. As you enter the store, you're stunned to discover that the aisles have been rearranged. Instead of familiar product groups, the displays are organized by manufacturer—Procter & Gamble, General Foods, Del Monte, Beatrice Foods, and so forth.

What should have been a simple shopping excursion has now become a bizarre hunting expedition, where success rests on a combination of dogged determination and almanaclike knowledge. Who manufactures peanut butter? Which one makes chunky peanut butter? And who makes chunky peanut butter in a reusable plastic tub?

While the grocery store scenario may seem to be a bit farfetched, it is an all too realistic description of the dilemma facing American businesses today when they attempt to shop in Washington for assistance in operating overseas.

This book is designed to unscramble the scores of government programs available for American firms seeking to do business abroad—taking them off the shelves now marked Department of Commerce, Export-Import Bank, Small Business Administration, Overseas Private Investment Corporation, International Finance Corporation, and so forth, and putting them onto more logical shelves such as financing, regulations and market information.

Ten Washington-based agencies currently offer most of the key programs in this particular area of business assistance. Another half-dozen agencies provide a limited number of services for U.S. businesses seeking to enter the international marketplace. All have contributed to this guide in the desire to make information about government assistance more accessible to the American business community.

While it would be an exaggeration to suggest this publication is all-inclusive, every effort has been made to include detailed descriptions of the major government programs available for U.S. businesses considering overseas operations. It is our hope that it will make a significant contribution to strengthening the working partnership between the private sector and the government—a critical need if we are to be competitive in the international marketplace.

WILLIAM A. DELPHOS

Washington, DC
March 1988

CHAPTER ONE

WINNING OVERSEAS

Now that time and distance have been so compressed that an American can fly to Paris for lunch and return the same day, "business as usual" has a decidedly new dimension. New technologies in communication, not to mention instant access to an almost limitless supply of information, have triggered a revolution posing tremendous challenges and opportunities for the modern business executive.

Only a few years ago, a company could seek new markets by exploring opportunities in other cities and other states. Although some of the Nation's larger companies looked for growth in other nations, the majority of American businesses thought the magic of the U.S. marketplace was enough. Today, the character of the U.S. marketplace is vastly different. Investors from foreign countries are flocking to the United States in increasing numbers, while our whole structure is shifting from a "smokestack" economy to a more sophisticated, technologically oriented society. The U.S. business executive now must look for new avenues of growth, and many are facing the reality that the best opportunities may lie beyond the water's edge.

The Potential

Multinational corporations have long recognized the potential of overseas expansion, and their investments have made enormous contributions to accelerating trade and economic growth in many areas of the world. But if the United States is to maintain a competitive position in world commerce, we must broaden our effort by encouraging more small and medium-sized firms to enter international markets, especially those of the developing world, which are today's fastest growing markets for U.S. goods and services.

1

Winning at Home

The stage is now set for a new era of growth and opportunity, and the U.S. business community has an uncommon chance to restore its competitive leadership. It would be difficult to overestimate the importance of this effort. To a great extent, our success will depend on teamwork between the government and the business community. Effective use of federal services can make the difference between success and failure.

This book is designed as a ready reference manual, compiling information on the scores of government-supported business assistance programs classified by some as well kept secrets. This wall of secrecy has not been built by government alone, although government has made a significant contribution by isolating both programs and information into various departments and agencies. At least some of it can be attributed to the business community's previous lack of interest in international operations. This guide seeks to tear down that wall, putting all the pieces in one place so that the array of government programs becomes a solution rather than a puzzle.

About the Book

Virtually all of the trade and investment incentive programs designed to help American business compete overseas are administered by ten organizations: the Departments of Agriculture and Commerce, Office of the U.S. Trade Representative, Agency for International Development, Export-Import Bank, Overseas Private Investment Corporation, Small Business Administration, the U.S. Trade and Development Program, the World Bank and the International Finance Corporation. Brief descriptions of their functions as they relate to promoting international business development can be found at the end of this chapter.

Until now, businesses seeking the appropriate federal assistance program or individual to help them overseas were forced to wander through the bureaucratic labyrinth of these Washington agencies in hopes of finding an answer. With this reference guide, however, the maze of agency authority lines has been erased. In its place is a "repackaged" presentation of government programs for business, arranged according to type of assistance available rather than by agency. To further illustrate how these programs can best be used by American businesses, case studies are highlighted in each chapter.

Readers unfamiliar with the overseas marketplace should notice that the chapters logically flow from "getting started" information to the nuts-and-bolts of putting a business deal together. Chapter 2, for example, outlines the wide array of business information available to U.S. firms considering operations overseas, including market background reports, statistical profiles, country economic analyses, and international demographic data.

In Chapter 3, discussions of specific programs—data banks, search services, and contract bid notifications—are designed to help businesses and identify trade and investment opportunities that currently exist overseas.

Chapter 4 is devoted to outlining government programs that help plan for or support reconnaissance trips overseas.

Chapter 5 provides detailed descriptions of the various programs available for obtaining feasibility study funding and assistance.

In Chapter 6, the regulations and requirements of doing business overseas are explored, and programs available for obtaining foreign government approvals are discussed. At the end of this chapter is a useful consideration of taxation issues.

Chapter 7, "Financing the Deal," sets forth the dozens of loan, loan guarantee, and letter of credit programs available to U.S. businesses with sights on overseas markets, including information on eligibility, interest rates, and terms. In addition, the chapter presents useful information concerning multilateral bank contract opportunities.

Chapter 8 details how the business executive can obtain insurance or other forms of guarantee to protect an overseas venture.

Chapter 9 discusses programs for initiating actual operations overseas and for expanding such operations at a later stage.

In addition to the contact individuals noted throughout the book, a listing of key regional federal offices and U.S. embassy contacts overseas is provided in the appendix.

Obviously, no single volume could begin to describe the scope and diversity of the thousands of overseas enterprises involving U.S. firms or the hundreds of government programs that have been used to help those undertaking such enterprises. Nevertheless, every effort has been made to present as much information as possible in an easy-to-understand form that can help make business decisions more effective and productive.

The following agencies administer the bulk of programs designed to assist American businesses wishing to compete in the international marketplace.

Department of Agriculture. Through its Commodity Credit Corporation, the Department of Agriculture administers export sales and donations for foreign use through other agencies as well as providing export guarantees to foreign buyers. Its Foreign Agricultural Service gathers worldwide information through representatives stationed in 70 U.S. embassies, develops export data to support trade, and works to reduce trade barriers. Its Office of International Cooperation and Development is responsible for international and technical cooperation for development assistance programs.

Department of Commerce. The Department's International Trade Administration coordinates issues relating to trade administration, international export policies, and trade programs. It is staffed by trade specialists in 48 district offices and 19 branch offices in industrial and commercial centers nationwide.

Through commercial sections located in U.S. embassies and consulates, the Department of Commerce's U.S. & Foreign Commercial Service (US&FCS) operates in 128 cities in 67 countries, and is composed of 150 American officers and 480 nationals of the various host countries. The US&FCS is principally charged with assisting small and medium-sized U.S. businesses through counseling, supporting promotional events such as trade shows and trade missions, collecting and disseminating commercial information, representing U.S. commercial interests to host-country governments, and supporting other U.S. agencies' overseas programs.

Office of the U.S. Trade Representative. This Cabinet-level agency is responsible for the direction of trade negotiations, formulation of overall trade policy, and bilateral and multilateral negotiations pertaining to trade. It represents the United States at meetings of the General Agreement on Tariffs and Trade (GATT) and the Organization for Economic Cooperation and Development (OECD) and in negotiations with the United Nations Conference on Trade and Development (UNCTAD).

Agency for International Development. AID offers loans and grants on concessional terms to less developed countries to further development plans. Assistance sectors include agriculture, health, population control, education, human resources, housing, and private volunteer organizations. Its Bureau for Private Enterprise supports projects involving local private-sector resources. AID maintains posts at 64 U.S. embassies abroad.

Export-Import Bank of the United States. This agency provides support for facilitating exports, offers export credits and guarantees, and offers direct credit to borrowers outside the United States. Through the Foreign Credit Insurance Association, Eximbank provides credit protection for U.S. exporters; these policies insure repayment in the event of default by a foreign buyer and may be used as collateral for bank loans. The agency also guarantees repayment to commercial banks that provide financing to exporters covering service contracts, leases, and other special situations.

Overseas Private Investment Corporation. OPIC encourages U.S. private investment in developing countries by providing political risk insurance and finance services. Its insurance provides protection against the risks of inconvertibility of local currency, expropriation or nationalization, and losses resulting from war, revolution, insurrection, or civil strife. Finance services include direct loans of up to $6 million to smaller businesses and loan guarantees of up to $50 million. Programs are available for new projects or expansion of existing facilities. OPIC operates its programs in more than 90 developing countries.

Small Business Administration. SBA offers financial assistance, counseling, export workshops and training to help U.S. companies enter international markets. It provides loans and loan guarantees to U.S. companies for equipment, facilities, materials, and working capital for selected export market development activities. Export counseling services and marketing information are available at no cost from the agency's Service Corps of Retired Executives and Active Corps of Executives, and by university students who participate in the Small Business Institute Program. In addition, Small Business Development Centers based at universities offer business counseling and assistance. SBA has 79 district offices throughout the United States.

U.S. Trade and Development Program. This agency is responsible for the administration of planning services leading to reimbursable programs with U.S. agencies, or direct host-government contracts with U.S. private firms, for project implementation. The program includes support for project identification, design, feasibility studies, and design engineering.

The International Bank for Reconstruction and Development (World Bank). The World Bank, owned by more than 140 member governments and based in Washington, DC is responsible for providing both financial and technical assistance to developing countries to stimulate economic development. It also makes structural adjustment loans to help developing countries make national policy changes and institutional reforms needed to improve their balance of payments and restore economic growth.

The Bank lends funds to creditworthy countries or their agencies, generally for specific development projects. Through its procurement program, contract opportunities for suppliers of goods and services are available through international competitive bidding.

The International Finance Corporation. The IFC is a multilateral development institution established to promote productive private investment that will contribute to the economic growth of its developing member countries. Its principal objectives are to provide the financing, technical assistance and management needed to develop productive investment opportunities in its member nations. The Corporation seeks to encourage the flow of private capital, both domestically and internationally, through the establishment or expansion of local capital markets and financial institutions. It also offers technical assistance to member governments in support of their efforts to create an investment environment which will encourage productive and beneficial domestic and foreign investment.

CHAPTER TWO

THE MARKETS

Before considering an overseas venture, most businesses want to ascertain the market potential for their products or services. In many cases, the U.S. government can provide U.S. firms with important market data at little or no charge. Various federal resources for obtaining such market information are reviewed in this chapter, categorized into three major subject areas:

Global Information. International economic and demographic statistics as well as worldwide agricultural data.

Industry/Commodity Information. In-depth reports and services for analyzing the factors affecting commodity shipments, and markets for products of specific industry sectors.

Country Information. Economic and demographic reports for specific countries, country seminars, market research reports, and country risk assessment.

GLOBAL INFORMATION

General International Information

In September of each year, the Central Intelligence Agency publishes the *World Factbook*, which provides recent and projected data on the geography, people, government, economy, communications, and defense forces of every country in the world. It includes charts on the United Nations system, international organizations and their members, mathematical conversions, and regional maps. The data is provided by the CIA's Defense Intelligence Agency, Bureau of the Census, and the Department of State.

Cost
$19.00 per copy. Order no.: S/N 041-015-00163-9.

Contact
Superintendent of Documents
U.S. Government Printing Office
Washington, DC 20402
(202) 783-3238

The *Atlas of United States Foreign Relations* is a compilation of six documents on subjects that deal with foreign relations machinery, international organizations, elements of the world economy, trade and investments, development assistance, and national security. Comprehensive worldwide information on the historical perspectives and trends of U.S. foreign relations is provided, including detailed maps and charts. The 1985 edition is the most recent edition of this State Department publication; however, a 1987 reprint of the *Foreign Relations Machinery* document is available free of charge from the State Department's Bureau of Public Affairs.

Cost
$5.00 per Atlas copy. Order no.: S/N 044-000-02102-1.

Contact
Superintendent of Documents
U.S. Government Printing Office
Washington, DC 20402
(202) 783-3238

8

Current developments in trade are reported in the *United States Trade Performance in 1985 and Outlook*, published by the Department of Commerce. This edition emphasizes the following developments: United States Trade Performance with Canada; Growing United States—Japan Trade Imbalance; Who is Buying LDC Manufactures?; Industrialized West's Trade with Centrally Planned Economies; Trends in United States Petroleum Imports; Exports and United States Employment; State and Metropolitan Export Profiles; United States International Competitiveness; Harmonized Trade Data System; and Dollar Exchange Rates, Performance and Caveats. The 1986 report is expected by January 1988.

Cost
$8.50 per copy. Order no.: S/N 003-009-00481-1.

Contact
Superintendent of Documents
U.S. Government Printing Office
Washington, DC 20402
(202) 783-3238

International Demographic Data

The *World Population Profile: 1985* was published under a Resources Support Services Agreement with the United States Agency for International Development, Bureau for Science and Technology. It contains regional demographic estimates and projections for the world, including summary statistics of 205 countries and territories with 1985 populations of at least 5,000.

Cost
$4.25 per copy. Order no.: S/N 003-024-06218-6.

Contact
Superintendent of Documents
U.S. Government Printing Office
Washington, DC 20402
(202) 783-3238

The *Aging World Report* draws from statistics provided by the United Nations and the Census Bureau's International Data Base on Aging to summarize demographic and socioeconomic information on the older population of 31 countries. This report includes sections on:

life expectancy; mortality and health; gender differences; urban and rural perspectives; marital status and living arrangements; education and literacy; social support; labor force; occupations; and economics.

Cost
$5.50 per copy. Order no.: S/N 003-024-06699-8.

Contact
Superintendent of Documents
U.S. Government Printing Office
Washington, DC 20402
(202) 783-3238

International Agricultural Data

Several divisions of the Department of Agriculture provide international agricultural data.

The Economic Research Service

The Economic Research Service's International Economics Division collects and analyzes extensive information on foreign country and commodity markets for U.S. agricultural products, forecasts changes in these markets, and conducts research on longer term agricultural supply, demand, and trade issues. Regional branches study individual country markets, as well as such regional groupings as the European Community (EC) and the Association of South East Asian Nations (ASEAN). Analysts also collect and interpret current information on developments in commodity markets and foreign government policies that can influence internationally traded commodities.

The Trade Policy Branch furnishes current information on trade strategies of major agricultural trading countries and on activities of international organizations such as the Food and Agriculture Organization (FAO), Organization for Economic Cooperation and Development (OECD), General Agreement on Tariffs and Trade (GATT), and United Nations Conference on Trade and Development (UNCTAD). The Branch also analyzes alternative trade policies and their implications for U.S. agricultural trade.

The Global Analysis Branch regularly generates and distributes a wide variety of world price and quantity data for commodities of major interest to U.S. exporters, such as grains and livestock products. This Branch maintains a large data base of agricultural export and import statistics for many countries and regions.

The Agricultural Development Branch makes available analyses and data on the economic development and future market needs of the developing countries.

Contact
Director
Agricultural and
   Trade Analyses   T. Kelley White   (202) 786-1700

Branch	Branch Chief	Telephone
Agricultural and Trade Policy	Vernon Roningen	(202) 786-1662
Agricultural and Trade Indicators	Ed Overton	(202) 786-1712
Centrally Planned Economics	Ken Gray	(202) 786-1620
Developed Market Economies	Mark Newman	(202) 786-1614
Developing Economies	Gene Mathia	(202) 786-1680
U.S. Agricultural Policy	Harry Baumes	(202) 786-1668

The Economic Research Service also issues the following publications on a regular basis:

The Foreign Agricultural Trade of the United States (bimonthly)
World Agricultural Outlook and Situation (quarterly)
Outlook for U.S. Agricultural Exports (quarterly)
World Aid Needs and Availabilities (annually)
Regional Situation and Outlook Reports (annually) for the following areas:

    Western Hemisphere
    Middle East and North Africa
    Sub-Saharan Africa
    East Asia
    South Asia
    Southeast Asia
    China
    Eastern Europe
    The Soviet Union
    Western Europe

OUTLOOK for
U.S. Agricultural Exports

Approved by the World
Agricultural Outlook Board,
Economic Research Service,
and Foreign Agricultural
Service, U.S. Department
of Agriculture

August 27, 1987

U.S. AGRICULTURAL EXPORT FORECAST RAISED SLIGHTLY

The forecast for U.S. agricultural exports in fiscal 1987 has been raised to $28 billion and 129 million tons. Compared with fiscal 1986, export value is now expected to rise $1.7 billion, a $500 million increase from the May forecast. Grains account for virtually all of fiscal 1987's 18 percent expected rise in volume as lower U.S. prices, reduced competitor supplies, and the Export Enhancement Program (EEP) increase the U.S. share of world grain trade. However, with lower prices offsetting virtually all the expected volume gains in grain, increased livestock, horticultural, and cotton exports account for most of fiscal 1987's expected gain in value. U.S. high-value exports have benefited from a weaker dollar and export promotion activities under the Targeted Export Assistance Program (TEA).

The estimate for agricultural imports in fiscal year 1987 has been increased by $500 million from the May estimate to $20.5 billion, largely due to increased U.S. imports of livestock products. However, import value is still expected to fall compared with fiscal 1986 because of a substantial decline in coffee prices since last year. The U.S. agricultural trade surplus is expected to rise to $7.5 billion in fiscal 1987.

U.S. agricultural exports are expected to increase again in fiscal 1988, gaining in both value and volume. Volume will rise as the U.S. retains its larger share of world grain markets and world grain trade increases. Export value could rise faster than volume as prices improve for bulk exports and exports of high-value products continue expanding.

Table 1--U.S. agricultural trade balance, fiscal 1981/82-1986/87

Item	1981/82	1982/83	1983/84	1984/85	1985/86	Forecast 1986/87
			-- Billion dollars --			
Exports	39.1	34.8	38.0	31.2	26.3	28.0
Imports	15.5	16.4	18.9	19.7	20.9	20.5
Trade balance	23.6	18.4	19.1	11.5	5.4	7.5
			-- Million tons --			
Export volume	157.9	144.8	143.6	125.7	109.5	129.0

1

Sample pages from quarterly Outlook for U.S. Agricultural Exports, *which follows developments around the world affecting U.S. agricultural exports. Annual subscription cost is $5.00 U.S.; $6.25 foreign.*

12

Commodity Highlights

U.S. coarse grain exports are forecast at 47.8 million tons, an increase of 600,000 tons from May's forecast and 11.5 million tons above the 1986 level. The value forecast has been revised to $3.8 billion, $100 million above May's forecast, but unchanged from fiscal 1986. Strong import demand for U.S. corn accounts for the improved export prospects.

Import demand for U.S. corn has strengthened considerably due to a reduction in exportable supplies from major foreign corn exporters such as Argentina, China, Thailand, and South Africa and a subsequent shift to U.S. corn for such major foreign importers as Japan and South Korea. Some of that shift has been at the expense of U.S. sorghum as key markets like Japan and Mexico have either scaled back their import needs or shifted to corn.

U.S. wheat and flour exports for fiscal 1987 are forecast at 30.4 million tons and $3.1 billion. While the volume estimate has been changed only slightly from May's forecast, export value has been lowered by $200 million. The reduction was made to adjust for the large sales of U.S. wheat under the Export Enhancement Program (EEP) to the Soviet Union (4 million tons) and China (1 million tons). These are scheduled to be shipped before the end of fiscal 1987. The EEP has allowed exporters of U.S. wheat and products to compete more effectively in selected markets where the European Community (EC) has been undercutting U.S. exports with subsidies.

Rice exports are forecast at 2.4 million tons and $600 million, up 100,000 tons in volume and unchanged in value from May's estimate. Import demand for U.S. rice is expected to strengthen in coming months due to drought conditions in Southeast Asia brought about by this year's late monsoon season. Delayed plantings nd lower yields may curtail Thailand's production of this important food staple and export commodity.

The outlook for U.S. oilseed and product exports has improved as world soybean meal trade is greater than had been expected. U.S. oilseed and product exports have been raised to $6.2 billion from May's forecast of $5.8 billion. This revision reflects larger than expected movements of soybeans and soybean meal. Supplies in South America have tightened as Brazil closed soybean export registrations.

The forecast for U.S. exports of horticultural products has been raised to $3.2 billion from the previous forecast of $3.0 billion. The latest estimate places exports 19 percent above fiscal 1986. U.S horticultural exports continue to gain momentum as foreign import demand responds to the weakened dollar and to market promotion activities under the Targeted Export Assistance (TEA) program.

U.S. cotton exports are estimated at 1.5 million tons and $1.7 billion, unchanged in volume but down $100 million in value from last quarter. A combination of competitive U.S. prices, reduced foreign export availability, declining world stocks, and strong foreign import demand resulted in an upsurge in U.S. cotton exports to all major U.S. markets. Export volume in fiscal 1987 will triple last year's poor showing.

The estimate for U.S. tobacco exports for fiscal 1987 remains unchanged from the previous forecast of $1.2 billion and 200,000 tons. While exports of unmanufactured tobacco are forecast to be down from year earlier levels, a larger share of tobacco exports to traditional markets is being shipped in the form of manufactured tobacco. These products are reported as nonagricultural exports.

3

13

Contact

Diane Decker
Public Information Specialist
Economic Management Staff and Information Division
Room 228
1301 New York Avenue, NW
Washington, DC 20005-4788
(202) 786-1494

For information on the other listed publications:

Contact

Economic Management Staff and Information Division
Research Information Branch
Room 237
1301 New York Avenue, NW
Washington, DC 20005-4788
(202) 786-1512

Foreign Agricultural Service

The Foreign Agricultural Service (FAS) issues a variety of regularly scheduled and special publications to assist agricultural exporters.

Foreign Agriculture is a monthly magazine for business firms selling U.S. farm products overseas. It offers news and background information useful in export marketing, feature articles reporting and analyzing conditions affecting U.S. agricultural trade, and details on programs to expand agricultural exports.

Cost

Annual subscription $11 in U.S.; $13.75 foreign. Single copies $1.25 in U.S.; $1.56 foreign. Order no.: S/N 701-027-00000-1.

Contact

Superintendent of Documents
U.S. Government Printing Office
Washington, DC 20402
(202) 783-3238

Foreign Agricultural Circulars include production, trade, and other specialized reports on major commodities and monthly statistical reports on commodities in world trade. Circulars are published periodically on a subscription basis.

United States
Department of Agriculture

Foreign Agricultural Service

August 1987

Foreign Agriculture

**Exporting
Animal Products:
The Road to Success**

Cover page of Foreign Agriculture, the FAS monthly magazine for business firms selling overseas.

15

Cost

From $3 to $63; $4 to $91 foreign, depending on commodity.

Contact
Media and Public Affairs Branch
Foreign Agricultural Service
U.S. Department of Agriculture
Room 5920-S
Washington, DC 20250-1000
(202) 447-7937

Weekly Roundup of World Production and Trade is a weekly bulletin presenting current news items and statistics on various commodities. It also summarizes recent developments in world production and trade.

Cost
Free.

Contact
Media and Public Affairs Branch
Foreign Agricultural Service
U.S. Department of Agriculture
Room 5920-S
Washington, DC 20250-1000
(202) 447-7937

World Agricultural Production provides the Department of Agriculture's estimates on the production of wheat, rice, coarse grains, oilseeds, and cotton in major countries and selected regions of the world.

Cost
Annual subscription $18 in U.S.; $25.00 foreign.

Contact
Media and Public Affairs Branch
Foreign Agricultural Service
U.S. Department of Agriculture
Room 5920-S
Washington, DC 20250-1000
(202) 447-7937

World Production and Trade

United States Department of Agriculture

Foreign Agricultural Service

Washington. D.C. 20250

Weekly Roundup

WR 39-87

Sept. 30, 1987

The Foreign Agricultural Service of the U.S. Department of Agriculture today reported the following developments in world agriculture and trade.

GRAIN AND FEED

INDONESIA May Buy U.S. Feed Corn. The United States is among the countries likely to fill Indonesia's need to import 750,000 tons of feed corn over the next six months, according to a wire service report quoting an Indonesian official. The purchase would replace shortfalls in domestic production due to drought. While the Indonesian official listed Thailand and China as other likely sources, the exports of these countries are limited due to lower production and higher demand. This suggests that U.S. corn could capture the bulk of the demand. Indonesia's 1987 production is estimated at 5.3 million tons, slightly below last year's 5.4 million-ton level when only 50,000 tons of corn were imported. Indonesian corn imports have been under 100,000 tons in recent years, and the United States has not been a supplier since 1983/84.

*****

SOVIET Grain Harvest Still Plagued by Rainy Weather. The U.S. agricultural attache in Moscow reported that as of September 21, small grains and pulses were cut on 96.1 million hectares, of which 89.8 million were threshed. The latter figure represents 83 percent of the sown area. Additionally, 506,000 hectares of corn-for-grain were cut. Corn for all purposes was cut on 14.6 million hectares. The lateness of the grain harvest is indicated by comparing this year's 89.8 million-hectare-threshed figure with the 100 million in 1986 and an average of 103.6 million during 1980-85.

Soviet press reports as of September 21 indicated sunflowers were harvested from only 10 percent of the area; sugar beets from 500,000 hectares, or 15 percent of the area; potatoes were dug on 1.3 million hectares, or 48 percent of the area; and 872,000 tons of cotton were harvested.

Regarding fall fieldwork, 38.4 million hectares or 34 percent of the planned area were plowed, and fall crops were seeded on 28.5 million hectares, given as 74 percent of plan.

—more—

SALLY KLUSARITZ, Editor, Tel. (202) 447-3448. Additional copies may be obtained from FAS Media and Public Affairs Branch, 5922-S, Washington, D.C. 20250. Tel. (202) 447-7937.

Example of the FAS Weekly Roundup of World Production and Trade which follows significant developments in world agriculture and trade.

17

FAS Attaché Commodity Reports are raw data reports providing information on unexpected changes in crop production prospects, weather damage, insect infestation, tariff decisions, major policy changes, and other foreign agricultural developments. Raw data reports are available on specific countries and commodities, covering 100 markets and over 125 commodities. These include approximately 500 scheduled reports and 3500 voluntary-alert reports.

Cost
Raw data reports are available on a subscription basis or by special request. Costs vary.

Contact
James Benson, Reports Officer
Foreign Agricultural Service
U.S. Department of Agriculture
Room 6078-S
Washington, DC 20250-1000
(202) 382-8924

The Foreign Agricultural Service's International Agricultural Statistics (IAS) area has three specific divisions that provide analytical, international agricultural information.

1. The Trade and Economic Information Division develops, maintains, and analyzes trade, international financial, and macroeconomic data and information in support of expansion of U.S. export programs and trade policies.

Contact
Division Director	(202) 382-1294
Tariff and Economic Information Branch	(202) 382-1293
Trade and Marketing Information Branch	(202) 382-1295

The Export Sales Reporting Branch collects export sales and export data for selected U.S. produced agricultural commodities from exporters as required under Section 812 of the Agricultural Act of 1970, as amended. This information is compiled and published weekly in the report, *U.S. Export Sales*, reflecting outstanding sales and accumulated exports by commodity, country, and marketing year.

Contact
Branch Chief	(202) 447-9209

2. The Foreign Production Estimates Division estimates world production for crops and livestock. Computer-generated statistical reports for production-related information are available upon request.

Contact

Division Director	(202) 382-8888
Crops Branch, Chief	(202) 382-8873
Livestock Branch, Chief	(202) 382-8874

3. The Foreign Crop Condition Assessment Division develops estimates for world crop production.

Contact

Division Director	(202) 382-8888

World Agricultural Transportation Report is a monthly newsletter that highlights the role of ocean and air transportation in the international marketing of agricultural products. Each issue includes an update on current events, legislation, and the ocean freight market. The editions also include feature articles that explore topical agricultural exports.

USDA: ALERT REPORTS

A prolonged drought in Australia's wheatlands or a hurricane in Honduras can affect supply and price in the world's farm markets and change the competitive position in the United States. Consequently, accurate information on weather damage is vital to investors and the U.S. government as well. To keep the U.S. market posted, the Department of Agriculture maintains an international telex communication network in addition to a microcomputer system that allows instant contact between major U.S. embassies and the Department. The system issues about 5000 alert reports each year to keep the farm community and others abreast of unexpected changes in crop production prospects, weather damage, insect infestation and other developments that affect markets.

Cost
Annual subscription $8 (for residents of the United States, Canada, and Mexico).

Contact
Martin F. Fitzpatrick, Administrator
Office of Transportation
U.S. Department of Agriculture
Auditors Building
Room 1405
Washington, DC 20250-4500
(202) 653-6060

INDUSTRY/COMMODITY INFORMATION

Foreign Trade Reports

The Bureau of the Census' monthly *Foreign Trade Report, FT410: U.S. Exports-Commodity by Country* provides a statistical record of shipments of all merchandise from the United States to foreign countries, including the quantity and dollar value of exports to each country. It also contains cumulative export statistics from the first of the calendar year. Sales of 4500 U.S. products to 160 countries are covered. Review of the reports for three to four years can reveal the countries that are the largest, most consistent markets for specific products.

Cost

Annual subscription $112 in U.S.; $140 foreign. Single copies $24 in U.S.; $30 foreign. Order no.: S/N 703-044-00000-0.

Contact

Superintendent of Documents
U.S. Government Printing Office
Washington, DC 20402
(202) 783-3238

Commodity Reports

The annual *Market Share Report's Commodity* Series shows U.S. participation in foreign markets for manufactured products. These reports also provide basic data for exporters to evaluate overall trends in the size of import markets, measure changes in the import demand for specific products, compare the competitive position of U.S. and foreign exporters, select distribution centers for U.S. products abroad, and identify existing and potential markets for U.S. components, parts, and accessories.

Reports in the Commodity Series provide combined total exports from 14 major industrialized countries for particular products shipped to 100 countries. Each of the 1412 commodity reports also shows the value of exports from the United States and eight other major exporting countries as well as the U.S. percentage share. Commodity reports exhibit data for the years 1980-83.

TABLE 2. SCHEDULE E COMMODITY BY COUNTRY-DOMESTIC MERCHANDISE-CONTINUED

(See "Explanation of Statistics" for information on coverage, definition of f.a.s. export valuation, security restrictions, sampling procedures, sources of error in the data, OTH CTY (other countries), and other definitions and features of the export statistics. The figure preceding Canada is the number in the sample for Canada. "SC" at the end of the alphabetic commodity description identifies "Special Category" commodities. Dash (-) represents zero. Z-Less than one-half of rounded unit)

Each block gives: Country of destination | Current month: Net quantity, Value (000 dollars) | Cumulative, January to date: Net quantity, Value (000 dollars)

2482110 PINE LUMBER, EASTERN WHITE AND RED, ROUGH, NOT TREATED WITH ANY PERM. WOOD PRESERV. MBF

Country	Net quantity	Value (000 dollars)	Net quantity	Value (000 dollars)
CANADA	2 121	436	9 427	1 938
MEXICO	419	83	2 645	528
BAHAMAS	13	7	212	80
LW WW L	43	17	146	59
BARBADO	-	-	67	43
N ANTIL	46	12	505	183
U KING	96	62	373	227
JAPAN	-	-	201	103
OTH CTY	6	2	178	81
TOTAL	2 744	620	13 754	3 242

2482115 PINE LUMBER, SOUTHERN YELLOW, LONGLEAF, ETC., ROUGH, NT TRTD WITH A PERM. WOOD PRESERV. MBF

Country	Net quantity	Value (000 dollars)	Net quantity	Value (000 dollars)
CANADA	-	-	597	145
MEXICO	-	-	1 002	200
BERMUDA	22	8	504	231
BAHAMAS	14	6	246	101
JAMAICA	1 350	473	4 800	1 617
HAITI	620	320	1 798	829
DOM REP	2 843	828	15 371	4 454
LW WW L	-	-	358	163
BARBADO	6	3	735	399
TRINID	14	8	1 792	756
N ANTIL	213	67	1 048	368
F W IND	-	-	148	32
VENEZ	-	-	257	125
URUGUAY	25	16	92	39
DENMARK	166	103	1 101	629
U KING	359	231	1 901	1 175
IRELAND	-	-	52	33
NETHLDS	-	-	773	412
BELGIUM	132	66	2 054	1 176
FRANCE	42	25	262	157
FR GERM	833	478	5 819	3 436
SWITZLD	34	18	70	40
SPAIN	4 267	2 186	18 947	10 107
ITALY	2 689	1 392	11 591	6 031
GREECE	211	137	1 534	973
ISRAEL	89	53	337	170
CHINA T	55	19	136	48
JAPAN	57	32	513	284
OTH CTY	-	-	170	125
TOTAL	14 376	6 679	74 042	34 142

2482120 PONDEROSA PINE LUMBER, ROUGH, NOT TREATED WITH ANY PERMANENT WOOD PRESERVATIVE MBF

Country	Net quantity	Value (000 dollars)	Net quantity	Value (000 dollars)
CANADA	4 885	1 215	23 749	6 235
MEXICO	651	131	2 469	501
SPAIN	-	-	238	215
ISRAEL	-	-	364	157
JAPAN	64	41	528	262
OTH CTY	16	13	214	113
TOTAL	5 616	1 400	27 562	7 483

2482125 PINE, NSPF, ROUGH, NOT TREATED WITH ANY PERMANENT WOOD PRESERVATIVE MBF

Country	Net quantity	Value (000 dollars)	Net quantity	Value (000 dollars)
CANADA	1 877	346	8 066	1 511
MEXICO	539	113	2 799	603
BAHAMAS	-	-	83	31
FR GERM	226	86	357	150
PORTUGL	-	-	148	66
ITALY	48	28	148	98
JAPAN	42	15	243	56
AUSTRAL	140	33	140	33
REP SAF	-	-	241	45
OTH CTY	15	9	694	177
TOTAL	2 887	629	12 959	2 769

2482130 DOUGLAS FIR LUMBER, RGH, UNDER 2 INCHES, NOT TREATED WITH ANY PERM. WOOD PRESERVATIVE MBF

Country	Net quantity	Value (000 dollars)	Net quantity	Value (000 dollars)
CANADA	859	157	6 978	1 308
U KING	271	61	3 902	1 257
NETHLDS	-	-	159	66
BELGIUM	-	-	329	114
FRANCE	-	-	596	336
FR GERM	23	10	421	139
AUSTRIA	-	-	81	31
SPAIN	135	76	1 176	322
ITALY	29	11	1 814	619
GREECE	208	134	1 639	764
S ARAB	-	-	286	123
JAPAN	1 780	530	16 346	4 732
AUSTRAL	228	84	2 065	625
FR P IS	5	3	312	83
MOROC	-	-	423	190
REP SAF	-	-	84	31
OTH CTY	57	31	474	155
TOTAL	3 595	1 098	37 085	10 896

2482135 DOUGLAS FIR LUMBER, RGH, 2IN.-NT OV 5IN, NOT TREATED WITH ANY PERM. WOOD PRESERVATIVE MBF

Country	Net quantity	Value (000 dollars)	Net quantity	Value (000 dollars)
CANADA	1 582	995	6 597	3 740
MEXICO	47	8	266	66
DENMARK	40	28	182	153
U KING	369	292	4 406	3 278
IRELAND	6	4	45	34
NETHLDS	64	58	195	166
BELGIUM	109	79	2 666	1 352
FRANCE	52	43	1 273	783
FR GERM	326	300	3 303	3 160
AUSTRIA	-	-	190	188
ISRAEL	-	-	96	73
SPAIN	1 788	1 253	6 858	4 943
ITALY	3 621	3 110	43 442	36 528
GREECE	-	-	6 276	5 279
SYRIA	-	-	850	246
ISRAEL	54	42	336	236
S ARAB	159	93	595	371
HG KONG	128	49	319	136
JAPAN	558	352	9 180	4 112
AUSTRAL	9 240	2 857	51 151	16 457
N ZEAL	14	12	52	35
FR P IS	263	99	1 161	416
FED MIC	-	-	145	50
OPAC IS	-	-	577	185
REP SAF	99	35	505	268
OTH CTY	55	30	280	139
TOTAL	18 574	9 740	140 938	82 393

2482140 DOUGLAS FIR LUMBER, ROUGH, 5 IN. & OVER, NOT TREATED WITH ANY PERM. WOOD PRESERVATIVE MBF

Country	Net quantity	Value (000 dollars)	Net quantity	Value (000 dollars)
CANADA	1 074	478	6 421	2 813
MEXICO	-	-	130	49
PERU	-	-	63	32
DENMARK	-	-	125	79
U KING	167	71	1 380	750
NETHLDS	-	-	128	133
FR GERM	233	112	714	352
FRANCE	-	-	56	56
FR GERM	65	66	344	355
SPAIN	68	84	1 502	1 194
ITALY	309	279	3 669	3 189
GREECE	-	-	299	302
SYRIA	-	-	450	251
S ARAB	-	-	428	265
HG KONG	8 636	2 548	8 636	2 548
AUSTRAL	-	-	110	38
JAPAN	2 389	1 448	11 149	5 587
FR P IS	8 150	2 432	46 136	13 807
FED MIC	135	144	485	495
FR P IS	112	7	234	57
OTH CTY	-	-	78	40
TOTAL	21 338	7 669	82 537	30 899

2482145 FIR LUMBER, NSPF, ROUGH, NOT TREATED WITH PERMANENT WOOD PRESERVATIVE MBF

Country	Net quantity	Value (000 dollars)	Net quantity	Value (000 dollars)
CANADA	219	66	2 753	827
BAHAMAS	1	2	57	39
U KING	30	9	356	112
BELGIUM	64	19	418	133
FR GERM	-	-	109	33
SPAIN	630	188	1 234	407
GREECE	45	14	106	32
JAPAN	3 218	1 194	25 578	8 954
OTH CTY	81	30	405	133
TOTAL	4 288	1 521	31 016	10 669

2482150 HEMLOCK LUMBER, ROUGH, NOT TREATED WITH ANY PERMANENT WOOD PRESERVATIVE MBF

Country	Net quantity	Value (000 dollars)	Net quantity	Value (000 dollars)
CANADA	1 044	369	5 200	1 898
U KING	924	315	5 129	1 824
BELGIUM	12	4	432	168
FR GERM	338	118	1 828	662
ITALY	-	-	170	59
S ARAB	59	28	169	84
KUWAIT	-	-	90	53
S ARAB	-	-	397	56
SO ASIA	935	246	935	246
CHINA T	150	36	482	118
JAPAN	17 625	5 356	93 945	28 866
AUSTRAL	88	27	269	75
OTH CTY	147	49	329	108
TOTAL	21 322	6 548	109 375	34 216

2482155 LARCH LUMBER, ROUGH, NOT TREATED WITH ANY PERMANENT WOOD PRESERVATIVE MBF

Country	Net quantity	Value (000 dollars)	Net quantity	Value (000 dollars)
OTH CTY	-	-	25	3
TOTAL	-	-	25	3

2482160 WESTERN RED CEDAR LUMBER, ROUGH, NOT TREATED WITH ANY PERMANENT WOOD PRESERVATIVE MBF

Country	Net quantity	Value (000 dollars)	Net quantity	Value (000 dollars)
CANADA	358	129	2 158	759
MEXICO	247	80	1 905	627
U KING	-	-	166	81
IRELAND	30	24	62	35
SPAIN	-	-	35	33
KOR REP	744	477	4 142	1 916
CHINA T	4	4	35	33
JAPAN	194	75	1 069	504
AUSTRAL	54	30	901	536
N ZEAL	151	67	241	96
OTH CTY	11	23	185	125
TOTAL	1 793	908	10 967	4 744

2482165 CEDAR LUMBER, NSPF, ROUGH, NOT TREATED WITH ANY PERMANENT WOOD PRESERVATIVE MBF

Country	Net quantity	Value (000 dollars)	Net quantity	Value (000 dollars)
CANADA	1 523	191	2 422	572
JAPAN	133	84	2 406	1 080
AUSTRAL	395	253	873	578
OTH CTY	19	9	276	107
TOTAL	2 070	537	5 976	2 337

2482170 REDWOOD LUMBER, ROUGH, NOT TREATED WITH ANY PERMANENT WOOD PRESERVATIVE MBF

Country	Net quantity	Value (000 dollars)	Net quantity	Value (000 dollars)
CANADA	656	181	2 713	682
NORWAY	-	-	518	661
U KING	-	-	26	33
NETHLDS	72	16	87	38
FR GERM	-	-	155	118
JAPAN	18	21	178	174
AUSTRAL	12	17	74	75
N ZEAL	114	32	304	96
FR P IS	-	-	434	187
OTH CTY	-	-	78	40
TOTAL	872	267	4 489	2 064

2482175 SOFTWOOD LUMBER, NSPF, ROUGH, NOT TREATED WITH ANY PERMANENT WOOD PRESERVATIVE MBF

Country	Net quantity	Value (000 dollars)	Net quantity	Value (000 dollars)
CANADA	145	37	774	231
MEXICO	-	-	162	52

Sample page from the Bureau of the Census Foreign Trade Report, FT 410: U.S. Exports—Commodity by Country Schedule E, which provides statistical records of all merchandise shipped from the U.S. to foreign countries.

Cost
$10 per commodity report; $20 foreign.
$11 per country report; $22 foreign.
Catalog is free.

Contact
For Information:
Trade Statistics Division/OTIA/ITA
U.S. Department of Commerce
Room 2217
Washington, DC 20230
(202) 377-4211

To Purchase:
National Technical Information Service
5285 Port Royal Road
Springfield, VA 22161
(703) 487-4650

Trade Information and Analysis

The office of Trade Information and Analysis at the Department of Commerce is responsible for macroeconomic trade, finance, investment, and cross-industry assessments and analyses.

U.S. Industrial Outlook is the primary source of economic and econometric analysis, industry statistics, and trade, finance, and investment data. Special features in the 1987 edition include chapters on: economic assumptions for this outlook; highlights of the 1987 outlook; financial performance of United States manufacturing corporations; and trends in world trade and outlook for U.S. manufacturers.

Cost
$24.00 per copy. Order no.: S/N 003-009-00522-1.

Contact
Superintendent of Documents
U.S. Government Printing Office
Washington, DC 20402
(202) 783-3238

Information on Foreign Industry Sectors

Additional trade information and assistance in identifying markets for specific industrial products can be obtained by contacting either a Commerce Department district office or the appropriate industry officer at the Department of Commerce in Washington, DC.

Contact
nearest Commerce Department district office (see appendix) or appropriate Commerce officer in Washington, DC:

Industry Specialties	Officer	Telephone
Science & Electronics		
Computers and Business Equipment	John E. McPhee	(202) 377-0572
Microelectronics and Instrumentation	Jack Clifford	(202) 377-2587
Telecommunications	Roger Stechschulte	(202) 377-4466
Basic Industries		
Chemicals and Allied Products	Vincent Kamenicky	(202) 377-0128
Energy	Joseph J. Yancik	(202) 377-1466
Metals, Minerals and Commodities	Robert Reiley	(202) 377-0575
Forest Products and Domestic Construction	Chris Kristensen	(202) 377-0384
Capital Goods and International Construction		
General Industrial Machinery	William Donahoe	(202) 377-5455
Special Industrial Machinery	E.G. Smith	(202) 377-0302
Services		
Service Industries	Brant Free	(202) 377-5078
Textiles and Apparel		
Textiles and Apparel	Art Garel	(202) 377-5078
Aerospace		
Aerospace Policy and Analysis	Sally Bath	(202) 377-8228

Industry Specialties	Officer	Telephone
Aerospace Market Development	Richard Cohen	(202) 377-8228
Automotive Affairs and Consumer Goods		
Automotive Industry Affairs	Stuart Keitz	(202) 377-0554
Consumer Goods	J. Hayden Boyd	(202) 377-0337

Contact

Direct written inquiries to appropriate officer at:

Office of Service Industries
U.S. Department of Commerce
Room 1128
Washington, DC 20230
(202) 377-3575

Customized Statistical Information

United States firms can obtain trade statistics, covering imports as well as exports, custom-tailored to meet the user's specifications. The data can be provided for any product or country of interest, arrayed as desired, with figures showing dollar values, quantities, growth rates, or market share percentages.

Cost

$10 to $200 or more, depending on the amount of data needed and the complexity of the job.

Contact

nearest Commerce Department district office

Agricultural Commodity Analysis

Commodity experts and economists at the Foreign Agricultural Service (FAS) analyze U.S. embassy reports on production and trade, combining them with accumulated background information and expertise. The Deputy Directors for Analysis can provide information on consumption, trade, and stocks for their specific commodity areas. Questions regarding marketing a specific commodity should be directed to the appropriate Deputy Director for Marketing. These individuals can provide commodity-specific information concerning competition, export financing, marketing opportunities, and cooperator programs. Commodity information compiled and analyzed by the FAS is available to anyone interested in foreign trade.

Contact
appropriate FAS specialists in Washington, DC:

Office	Specialist	Telephone
Dairy, Livestock, and Poultry Division		
Deputy Director for Marketing	Thomas Hamby	(202) 447-3899
Deputy Director for Analysis	Roger Lowen	(202) 447-7217
Grain and Feed Division		
Deputy Director for Marketing	Steve Yoder	(202) 447-4168
Deputy Director for Analysis	Chris Goldthwait	(202) 447-2009
Horticultural and Tropical Products Division		
Deputy Director for Marketing	Richard Barnes	(202) 447-7931
Deputy Director for Analysis	Ed Missiaen	(202) 447-3275
Oilseeds and Products Division		
Deputy Director	Michael Humphrey	(202) 447-8809
Tobacco, Cotton, and Seeds Division		
Deputy Director for Marketing	Molly Iler	(202) 382-9518
Deputy Director for Analysis	John Reddington	(202) 382-9524

Agricultural Product Marketing Profiles

Product Marketing Profiles are a series of *International Marketing Profile* (IMP) reports that are published by the Agricultural Information and Marketing Services (AIMS) within the Department of Agriculture's Foreign and Agricultural Service (FAS). Vital information about the magnitude, growth, and distribution of 30 selected groups of agricultural products in the high-value and value-added product sectors is presented in table form. Each profile provides information on leading foreign markets, fastest growing markets, best-selling products abroad, and principal competitors. Custom marketing profiles can also be produced.

Cost
$50.00 per profile.

Contact
Philip Letarte
AIMS Coordinator
U.S. Department of Agriculture
Foreign Agricultural Service
Room 4649-S
Washington, DC 20250-1000
(202) 447-7103

Agricultural Research and Technical Assistance

The Agricultural Research Service provides exporters with information on research, publications and consultations on transportation, packaging, storage, refrigeration, animal and plant diseases, insect control, and pesticide residues.

Contact
Dr. William H. Tallent
Assistant Administrator for Cooperative Interactions
ARS/USDA
Room 358-A
Administration Building
14th and Independence Avenue, NW
Washington, DC 20250
(202) 447-3973

Forest Products Information

The Forest Service prepares periodic analyses of U.S. timber supply and demand, which can be used by the U.S. timber industry to plot overseas investment strategies.

Cost
Free.

Contact
David Darr
Branch Chief
Forest Inventory and Economics Research
U.S. Department of Agriculture, Forest Service
P.O. Box 96090
Room 4105 South
Washington, DC 20000-6090
(202) 447-2747

The Forest Products Laboratory publishes technical papers, guidelines, and books on various aspects of engineering and applications for timber products. Free mailing lists can be requested by letter or telephone.

Cost
Free.

Contact
Publications Office
Forest Products Laboratory
One Gifford Pinchot Drive
Madison, WI 53705-2398
(608) 264-5637

Solar Market Conditions and Potential

The Department of Energy conducts studies which analyze the market conditions and potential for solar energy equipment in 28 countries around the world.

Cost
Free.

Contact
Steve Rubin
Technical Assistance Service
Solar Energy Research Institute
1617 Cole Boulevard
Golden, CO 80401
(303) 231-7303

COUNTRY INFORMATION

Country Information Kits

The Overseas Private Investment Corporation (OPIC) created the Investor Information Service (IIS) to serve as a publications clearinghouse. IIS provides interested companies and individuals with easy "one-stop-shopping" for basic data and country information commonly sought when considering overseas markets.

The materials, which are gathered together into "kit" form, are obtained from various U.S. Government agencies, foreign governments and international organizations. These resource materials cover the economies, trade laws, business regulations and attitudes, political conditions, and investment incentives of specific developing countries and regions.

Each information kit generally contains the following country-specific publications: Background Notes; Foreign Economic Trends and Their Implications for the United States; Overseas Business Report; Post Report; Investment Climate Statement; Foreign Labor Trends; Travel Advisories; Map; Foreign Publications; and Foreign Investment and Licensing Checklist for U.S. Firms.

Kits are available by country or by geographic region. At present, IIS kits are available for more than 100 developing countries and 16 regions.

Cost

Country kits range from $10.00—$45.00.
Regional kits range from $35.00—$400.00.

Contact

Chris Astriab
Investor Information Service
Overseas Private Investment Corporation
1615 M Street, NW
Washington, DC 20527
(202) 457-7089

Country Handbooks

Published by the National Technical Information Service, the *Area Handbook Series* includes a number of handbooks which cover various aspects of a foreign country. Each book describes and analyzes

29

the economic, military, political and social systems and institutions of a given country, and examines their interrelationships.

Cost
Varies for each handbook.

Contact
National Technical Information Service
5285 Port Royal Road
Springfield, VA 22161
(703) 487-4650

Foreign Economic Trends

Foreign Economic Trends and Their Implications for the United States is a series of country-specific reports that provides an in-depth review of business conditions and current and near-term prospects. The reports include most recent data on the gross national product, foreign trade, wage and price indexes, unemployment rates, and construction starts. This series analyzes current developments and their implications for future U.S. trade. Reports are prepared by U.S. embassies and consulates abroad. Approximately 100 reports are issued each year.

Cost
Annual subscription $49 in U.S.; $61.25 foreign.
Order no.: S/N 803-006-00000-8.

Contact
Superintendent of Documents
U.S. Government Printing Office
Washington, DC 20402
(202) 783-3238

For single copies:
Publication Sales Branch
U.S. Department of Commerce
Room 1617
Washington, DC 20230

Country Analyses

Each of the State Department's *Background Notes* provides a survey of a nation's people, geography, economy, government and foreign policy pursuits. The publications provide economic information, including total and per capita gross domestic product, a country's annual growth rates, and percentage shares for natural resources by product, industry, and agriculture. The reports also include trade information on imports and exports, major trading partners, official exchange rates, and a country's membership in international organizations.

Background Notes are published for most countries.

Cost

Annual subscription $14 in U.S.; $17.50 foreign.
Order no.: S/N 844-002-00000-9.

Contact

Superintendent of Documents
U.S. Government Printing Office
Washington, DC 20402
(202) 783-3238

Country Consumer Information

The Census Bureau has collected international data through a formal information exchange program with the other national statistical offices around the world, which it presents in country *Executive Briefs*.

Information on consumers and their characteristics is combined with trade statistics in an effort to identify potential foreign consumer markets for U.S. exporters.

The *Executive Brief* on China is the first in a series of executive briefs that will be prepared to cover potential consumer markets in several countries, beginning with the United States' largest potential markets and largest trading partners. Briefs on Japan and Canada are being prepared.

Cost

Free.

Contact

to request Brief copies:

Jennifer Marks
U.S. Bureau of the Census
U.S. Department of Commerce
Washington, DC 20233
(301) 763-3814

for information:

Richard A. Engels
Senior Demographic Advisor
Center for International Research
U.S. Bureau of the Census
U.S. Department of Commerce
Washington, DC 20233
(301) 763-4713

background

notes Venezuela

United States Department of State
Bureau of Public Affairs

April 1987

Official Name:
Republic of Venezuela

PROFILE

Geography

Area: 912,050 sq. km. (352,143 sq. mi.); about the size of Texas and Oklahoma combined. **Cities:** *Capital*—Caracas (metropolitan area pop. est. 4.0 million). **Terrain:** Varied. **Climate:** Varies from tropical to temperate, depending on elevation.

People

Nationality: *Noun and adjective*—Venezuelan(s). **Population** (1986): 17,791,000. **Annual growth rate:** 2.7%. **Ethnic groups:** Spanish, Italian, Portuguese, Arab, German, Amerindian, African. **Religions:** Roman Catholic 96%, Protestant 2%. **Languages:** Spanish (official), Indian dialects spoken by some of the 200,000 Amerindians in the remote interior. **Education:** *Years compulsory*—9. *Literacy*—88.4%. **Health:**

Infant mortality rate—27.3/1,000. *Life expectancy*—70 yrs. **Work force** (about 6 million): *Agriculture*—15%. *Industry and commerce*—35%. *Services*—26%. *Other*—24%.

Government

Type: Federal republic. **Independence:** July 5, 1821. **Constitution:** January 23, 1961.
Branches: *Executive*—president (head of government and chief of state); 24-member Council of Ministers (Cabinet). *Legislative*—bicameral National Congress (200-member Chamber of Deputies, 47-member Senate). *Judicial*—18-member Supreme Court.
Subdivisions: 20 states, 2 federal territories, 1 federal district, and a federal dependence (72 islands).
Political parties: Democratic Action (*Accion Democratica*—AD), Social Christian (*Comite Organizador Politico pro Elecciones Independientes*—COPEI). *Other parties*—minor, which gained representation to the National Congress Dec. 1983: Movement to Socialism (*Movimiento al Socialismo*—MAS); People's Electoral Movement (*Movimiento Electoral del Pueblo*—MEP); Republican Democratic Union (*Union Republicana Democratica*—URD); New Alternative (*Nueva Alternativa*—NA); Movement of the Revolutionary Left (*Movimiento de Izquierda Revolucionaria*—MIR); Movement of National Integrity (*Movimiento de Integridad Nacional*—MIN); National Opinion (*Opinion Nacional*—OPINA); and Venezuelan Communist Party (*Partido Communista de Venezuela*—PCV). **Suffrage:** Universal and compulsory over 18.
Central government budget (1985): $13.1 billion.
Flag: Three horizontal bands—yellow, blue, and red, with a crest in a corner of the yellow band and a semicircle of seven stars in the middle of the blue band. The colors come from the banner flown by Simon Bolivar; the stars represent the seven provinces.

Economy

Real GDP (1985): $50 billion. **Real annual growth rate** (1984–85): -0.4%. **Real per capita income:** $2,629. **Avg. inflation rate** (1985): 11.4%.
Natural resources: Petroleum, natural gas, coal, iron ore, gold, other minerals, hydroelectric power, bauxite.
Agriculture (7.4% of GDP): *Products*—rice, coffee, corn, sugar, bananas, and dairy, meat, and poultry products. *Land*—4%.
Industry (19% of GDP): *Types*—petrochemicals, oil refining, iron and steel, paper products, aluminum, textiles, transport equipment, consumer products.
Trade (1985): *Exports*—$14.2 billion: petroleum ($12.8 billion), iron ore, coffee, steel, aluminum, cocoa. *Major markets*—US, Canada, Italy, Japan, Spain, FRG. *Imports*—$7.3 billion: machinery and transport equipment, manufactured goods, chemicals, foodstuffs. *Major suppliers*—US, Japan, Canada, FRG, France, Italy, Brazil.
Official exchange rate: *Preferential*—14.5 bolivars = US$1. In February 1983, Venezuela adopted a multitiered exchange rate system. In December 1986, the government decreed an official exchange rate of 14.5 per US$1 for specified products and transactions.
Fiscal year: Calendar year.

Membership in International Organizations

UN and some of its specialized and related agencies, including membership in the Security Council (1986–87); Organization of American States (OAS); International Coffee Agreement; Latin American Integration Association (ALADI); Andean Pact; Rio Pact; Organization of Petroleum Exporting Countries (OPEC); Latin American Energy Organization (OLADE); Latin American State Reciprocal Petroleum Assistance (ARPEL); Latin American Economic System (SELA); Andres Bello Agreement.

Example from the U.S. State Department series, Background Notes, which is available for most countries.

Country Consumer Market Research

The Center for International Research works with public and private export marketing specialists who provide services to U.S. businesses. The Center helps U.S. businesses identify markets overseas by providing the following information: consumer preferences and purchases in foreign market; consumer behavior in different categories of income, age, sex, household status, or urban-rural place of residence; number and type of consumers in a foreign market; probable future number and type of consumers in a foreign market; competition from foreign production, imports, and exports; and probable amount of growth on contraction of future imports.

Cost
Varies based on the specific project.

Contact
Richard A. Engels
Senior Demographic Advisor
Center for International Research
U.S. Bureau of the Census
U.S. Department of Commerce
Washington, DC 20233
(301) 763-4713

Country Agricultural Marketing Profiles

Country Marketing Profiles are a series of International Marketing Profile (IMP) reports that are published by the Agricultural Information and Marketing Services (AIMS) within the Department of Agriculture's Foreign and Agricultural Service (FAS). Total agricultural trade activity is outlined for selected foreign countries. Statistical and financial information describes agricultural marketing possibilities and constraints in particular countries. Summaries of trade in specific processed and unprocessed products are available in the profile. To discover foreign competition, tables describe total agricultural imports of the country, as well as information about the relative performance of the U.S. and its competitors. Custom marketing profiles can also be produced.

Cost
$50.00 per profile.

Contact
Philip Letarte
AIMS Coordinator
U.S. Department of Agriculture
Foreign Agricultural Service
Room 4649-S
Washington, DC 20250-1000
(202) 447-7103

Overseas Business Reports

The Commerce Department's *Overseas Business Reports* series provides basic background data for business people who are evaluating export markets or considering entering new areas. The series discusses pertinent marketing factors in individual countries, presents economic and commercial profiles of countries and regions, issues semi-annual outlooks for U.S. trade with countries and geographical regions, and publishes selected statistical reports on the direction, volume, and nature of U.S. foreign trade.

Cost
Annual subscription $14 in U.S.; $17.50 foreign. Single copies vary in price. Order no.: S/N 803-007-00000-4.

Contact
Superintendent of Documents
U.S. Government Printing Office
Washington, DC 20402
(202) 783-3238

Business Risk Assessment

The State Department's Office of Business and Export Affairs provides information on which to base business risk assessments. The Office develops and reviews commercial action programs and strategies for 76 countries in which the Department of State has primary responsibility for business support.

Contact

for export information:

Office of Business and Export Affairs
U.S. Department of State
Room 3638
Washington, DC 20520
(202) 647-5817

for investment information:

Sharon Villarosa
Office of Investment Affairs
U.S. Department of State
Room 2533A
Washington, DC 20520
(202) 647-1448

Country Seminars

The Commerce Department's district offices frequently sponsor seminars on conducting business in specific countries.

Contact
Linda Bell
Trade Specialist
U.S. and Foreign Commercial Service, ITA
U.S. Department of Commerce
Room 3810
Washington, DC 20230
(202) 377-0727

or nearest Commerce district office (see appendix)

Foreign Press Summary Information

The Foreign Broadcast Information Service (FBIS), part of the Central Intelligence Agency, monitors foreign broadcasts, news agency transmissions, newspapers, periodicals, and government statements, publishing translations of these materials in hard copy issued daily and in microfiche issued weekly. FBIS Daily Reports are published under eight geographical titles: Asia and the Pacific; China; Eastern Europe; Latin America; Middle East and Africa; South Asia; Soviet Union; and Western Europe.

Cost

Annual price for hard copy: $290 for first title, $380 for two; $450 for three; $540 for four; $625 for five; $715 for six; $800 for seven; $890 for all eight.

Annual price for microfiche: $125 for first title; $155 for two; $185 for three; $230 for four; $285 for five; $340 for six; $395 for seven; $450 for all eight.

Contact
Subscriptions
National Technical Information Service
5285 Port Royal Road
Springfield, VA 22161
(703) 487-4630

Caribbean Basin Business Information

Caribbean Basin Business Information Center

The Department of Commerce's Caribbean Basin Business Information Center (CBI Center) provides information and assistance to companies seeking to take advantage of the Caribbean Basin Initiative by investing in, or buying products from, the 22 qualifying Caribbean island and Central American countries. The CBI Center advises companies on how they may benefit from the CBI, provides information on U.S. Government support services for CBI trade and investment, organizes product exhibits and business development missions, and assists with locating potential suppliers or joint venture partners in the region.

Contact
CBI Center
Room H-3020
U.S. Department of Commerce
Washington, DC 20230
(202) 377-0703

Information on the trade and investment climate in specific Caribbean Basin countries is available from the country desk officers of the Commerce Department's Caribbean Basin Division (see appendix).

CBI Business Bulletin

The Caribbean Basin Business Information Center publishes the *CBI Business Bulletin*, a monthly newsletter containing information on specific Caribbean Basin trade and investment opportunities as reported by American Embassy commercial officers and private-sector multiplier groups in the region.

Cost
Free.

Contact
Caribbean Basin Business Information Center
U.S. Department of Commerce
Room H-3020
Washington, DC 20230
(202) 377-0703

Caribbean Basin Initiative Guidebook

The *Caribbean Basin Initiative Guidebook* provides information on the CBI, support services for business, and the business environment in each CBI participating country.

Cost

$1.75 in U.S.; $2.20 foreign. Order no.: S/N 003-009-00492-6.

Contact

Superintendent of Documents
U.S. Government Printing Office
Washington, DC 20402
(202) 783-3238

Caribbean Agribusiness Information

A special program of the Department of Agriculture promotes private-sector agribusiness investment in the countries of the Caribbean and Central America. The Agribusiness Investment Information Center assists potential investors seeking technical agricultural expertise and data on the Caribbean Basin. The Center provides information on plant and health inspection requirements, quality standards, and other country regulations. The staff also collects and distributes information on Caribbean investment opportunities.

The Agribusiness Promotion Council, a U.S. private-sector advisory committee, advises the Secretary of Agriculture and the Department on accelerating agricultural development through private-sector investment and marketing activities. The Council's committees focus on transportation and infrastructure, production, processing and marketing, agribusiness investment and trade facilitation, and Caribbean government policies and business climate. The emphasis is on small- and medium-sized enterprises. The range of activities includes business opportunity missions, workshops and seminars, management training, and U.S. distribution outlets.

Contact

Agribusiness Information Center
Private Sector Relations
Office of International Cooperation and Development
U.S. Department of Agriculture
Washington, DC 20250-4300
(202) 653-7889

Egypt Sector Surveys

The Egyptian government, with support from the Agency for International Development, has prepared sector surveys covering 10 industrial areas of special interest to Egypt, as well as to potential American investors. The Sector Surveys include:

Food Crop Production and Processing; Meat, Poultry, and Fish Production and Processing; Health Care Products and Equipment; Construction Materials, Components, and Systems; Nonelectrical Machinery; Integrated Agribusiness; Nonfood Chemical Process Industries; Automotive Components; Electrical and Electronic Machinery; and Maintenance and Repair Facilities.

Cost
Free.

Contact
Project Director
Private Sector Feasibility Study Program
General Authority for Investment and Free Zones
8 Adly Street
P.O. Box 1007
Cairo, Arab Republic of Egypt
Phone: 906796; 906804
Telex: 92235 INVEST UN

or:

Ayman Abdelghaffar, Economic and Commercial Counselor
Embassy of the Arab Republic of Egypt
2232 Massachusetts Avenue, NW
Washington, DC 20008
(202) 265-9111
Telex: 64251 COMRAU WSH

CHAPTER THREE

TARGETING OPPORTUNITIES

After determining an area or industry of interest for an overseas enterprise, the next step is to identify specific business opportunities. A number of agency programs provide trade and investment leads. Many of these programs are based on information and analyses transmitted to offices in Washington by U.S. embassies, foreign governments, and consulates overseas. This chapter reviews over three dozen services and programs for targeting overseas opportunities in four broad categories:

Publications. Magazines and bulletins providing specific trade leads on potential markets and new products.

Systems. Information systems containing data on potential business leads, including computer "match" and response programs.

Customized Services. Services that locate agents or distributors, provide background information on foreign trading companies and businesses, or identify opportunities in specific countries.

Special Programs for Small Business. Management assistance programs to help small businesses make a preliminary assessment of their export potential.

PUBLICATIONS

Business America

The Commerce Department's *Business America* is a biweekly magazine designed to help U.S. exporters penetrate overseas markets by providing timely information on opportunities for trade and methods of doing business in foreign countries. A typical issue includes an analytical piece on U.S. trade policy, a "how to" article for new exporters, a review of the nation's economic trends, and news of Congressional and government actions affecting trade. It also includes trade news generated by the Commerce Department, other U.S. government agencies, and foreign governments; trade and investment opportunities abroad; and a calendar of upcoming catalog shows, exhibitions, seminars, and international trade fairs.

Cost
Annual subscription $57 in U.S.; $71.25 foreign. Single copies $2.50 in U.S.; $3.15 foreign. Order no.: S/N 703-011-00000-4.

Contact
Superintendent of Documents
U.S. Government Printing Office
Washington, DC 20402
(202) 783-3238

Commerce Business Daily

The U.S. Department of Commerce publicizes foreign trade leads, as well as commodity needs of foreign governments in the *Commerce Business Daily*. Contact names and phone numbers are provided for the dozen or more opportunities listed daily.

Cost
Annual subscription $243 (first-class postage), $173 (second-class postage) in U.S. Six month subscription $122 (first-class postage), $87 (second-class postage). Single copies are not sold. Order no.: S/N 703-013-00000-7.

Contact
Superintendent of Documents
U.S. Government Printing Office
Washington, DC 20402
(202) 783-3238

Agriculture Export Briefs

Export Briefs is a weekly bulletin which includes all trade leads processed by the Foreign Agricultural Service of the Department of Agriculture each week. Information is provided concerning product specifications, delivery deadlines, bid requirements, contact points and mailing addresses, upcoming trade shows, foreign trade developments, and changes and updates in trade policy.

Cost
Annual subscription $75.00. Subscriptions are available for a maximum of three years.

Contact
Philip Letarte
AIMS Coordinator
Foreign Agricultural Service
U.S. Department of Agriculture
Room 4649-S
Washington, DC 20250-1000
(202) 447-7103

New Product Publicity

The Commerce Department's New Product Information Service (NPIS) provides worldwide publicity for new U.S. products available for immediate export. This service enables foreign firms to identify and contact U.S. exporters of specific products, thereby giving the U.S. company a direct indication of market interest and often generating sales, agent contacts, and other benefits.

NPIS information is distributed in two ways. The monthly *Commercial News USA* contains short, promotional descriptions of some 100 to 150 new products, together with the names and addresses of the exporters and black and white product photographs. This magazine is distributed to 80,000 overseas readers by the 240 U.S. embassies and consulates. *Commercial News* is also distributed to Chambers of Commerce abroad, and Commerce Department district offices. Product data in *Commercial News USA* ultimately reach approximately 200,000 business and government leaders worldwide. Information on selected NPIS products is also broadcast overseas by the U.S. Information Agency's "Voice of America" radio programs.

To qualify for promotion as new products in *Commercial News USA*, items must be genuinely new and marketed in the U.S. for no

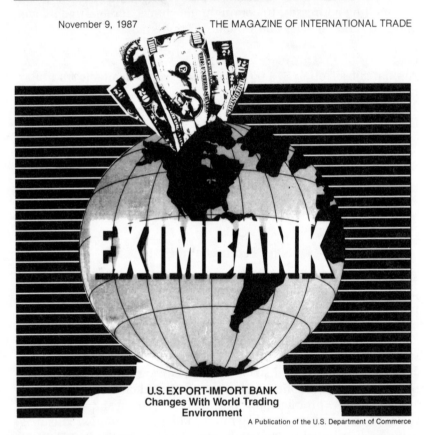

BUSINESS AMERICA

November 9, 1987   THE MAGAZINE OF INTERNATIONAL TRADE

EXIMBANK

U.S. EXPORT-IMPORT BANK
Changes With World Trading
Environment

A Publication of the U.S. Department of Commerce

Cover (above) and calendar of events from Business America, a bi-weekly magazine published by the Department of Commerce for U.S. exporters and others interested in trade and investment opportunities abroad.

42

Calendar for World Traders

Nov. 11—Cleveland—The Greater Cleveland Growth Association is sponsoring a workshop on "International Product Liability." For information, call (216) 621-3300, ext. 324.

Nov. 12—New York—The National Foreign Trade Council Foundation will present "Doing Business with Canada Under the U.S.-Canada Free Trade Agreement" at its 72nd National Foreign Trade Convention, to be held at the Grand Hyatt. For information on the one-day conference, call Barbara Summins at (212) 867-5630.

Nov. 12—Los Angeles—The California Council for International Trade International Taxation Committee will present a program reviewing the current regulations governing the international tax provisions contained in the 1986 Tax Reform Act at the World Trade and Stock Exchange Club. For details, call (213) 617-2248 or (415) 452-0770.

Nov. 12-13—Columbus, Ohio—The Containerization and Intermodal Institute, along with the Maritime Administration of the U.S. Department of Transportation and the Office of Transportation of the U.S. Department of Agriculture, are sponsoring a seminar on "Moving the Midwest to the International Market" at the Hyatt Regency Hotel. For details, call (201) 226-0160.

Nov. 16—New York—The World Trade Institute will hold a one-day workshop on "Drawback Update" at the World Trade Center. For information, call Ken Chai at (212) 466-3170.

Nov. 17—Cedar Rapids, Iowa—The Des Moines District Office of the U.S. Department of Commerce is sponsoring a seminar on "Doing Business with Canada: U.S.-Canada Free Trade Agreement" at the Sheraton Inn. The same seminar will be held in Des Moines on Nov. 18. For information on both seminars, call (515) 284-4222.

Nov. 19—Columbia, S.C.—The Columbia District Office of the U.S. Department of Commerce is sponsoring a technical videoconference on the new Harmonized Commodity Description and Coding System emphasizing the Schedule B classifications for commodities that are exported. The program can be viewed simultaneously at sites in Columbia, Charleston, and Greenville. For details, call the District Office at (803) 765-5345.

Nov. 19—Washington, D.C.—The National Center for Export—Import Studies will present a luncheon address by the Brazilian Ambassador to the U.S., Marcilio Marques Moreira, on "Debt, Trade, and Investment" at the Madison Hotel. For information, call James Spiegelman at (202) 625-8503.

Nov. 19-20—New York—The Practising Law Institute will hold a seminar on "Litigating Copyright, Trademark, and Unfair Competition Cases" at the Peat Marwick Main and Co. Executive Education Center. For details, call (212) 765-5700, ext. 271.

Nov. 30-Dec. 1—New York—The World Trade Institute will hold a two-day course on "Customs Law Issues for Importers of Apparel and Textiles" at the World Trade Center. For details, call Ken Chai at (212) 466-3170.

Nov. 30-Dec. 1—New York—The FSC/DISC Tax Club is holding a two-day seminar on "Export Tax Incentive Programs and the Latest Intercompany Pricing Rules and Regulations." For information, call (212) 838-9292.

Dec. 3-4—New York—The World Trade Institute will sponsor a two-day course on "The 807 Alternative: A Workshop for Apparel and Textile Importers" at the World Trade Center. For information, call Ken Chai at (212) 466-3170.

COMMERCE

A daily list of U.S. Government procurement invitations, contract awards, subcontracting leads, sales of surplus property and foreign business opportunities

BUSINESS DAILY

U.S. GOVERNMENT PROCUREMENTS

Services

A Experimental, Developmental, Test and Research Work (research includes both basic and applied research)

Naval Air Development Center, Warminster, PA 18974-5000
A – LOW INFRARED (IR) REFLECTIVE COATINGS AND FILMS FOR AEROSPACE VEHICLES

BUSINESS NEWS
FEDERAL TRADE EXPO

A Federal Trade Expo will be held in Yuma, Arizona on February 3 and 4, 1988, in conjunction with the Southwest SADBU Council February Conference. This two day Conference and Trade Expo is designed for small businesses, prime contractors, and government employees who interface with small business programs. Yuma Economic Development Corporation is hosting the event to provide an opportunity for small businesses to meet with government and prime contractor representatives. For further information contact 602/783-0193.

SINGLE WEEKLY LISTING OF ALL THE NUMBERED NOTES

The Numbered Notes will be published only on the first working day of each week. As in today's issue, all the active "Numbered Notes" are contained on the last three pages. These pages should be retained for reference during the current week.

Defense Nuclear Agency, 6801 Telegraph Rd., Alex., VA 22310-3398

AMSMC-PCW-D(D), Picatinny Arsenal, NJ 07806-5000
A – DEVELOPMENT OF PROTOTYPE .50 CALIBER ARMOR PIERCING FIN STABILIZED DISCARDING SABOT (APFSDS) CARTRIDGE.

Content

Natl Library of Medicine, Office of Acquisitions Management, 8600 Rockville Pike, Bldg 38A, Rm 1N17, Bethesda MD 20894
A – AUTOMATED ANALYSIS OF BIOMEDICAL TEXT RFP NLM 88-107/MVA

Cover page from sample issue of Commerce Business Daily, *a listing of foreign business opportunities and trade leads, as well as U.S. government contract invitations and awards.*

more than three years. New products and services are promoted in 31 broad industry categories, such as air and water pollution control, chemical and petrochemical, consumer goods, energy, general industrial machinery, healthcare, metalworking, safety and security, and sports and recreation. Trade and technical literature is also eligible for listing.

Cost

$150 per product listing.

Contact

Commercial News USA
Office of Marketing Programs/ITA
U.S. Department of Commerce
Room 2106
Washington, DC 20230
(202) 377-4919

or nearest Commerce Department district office (see appendix)

International Market Search

The Commerce Department also selects new industries each year for promotion through the International Market Search program. This program provides worldwide publicity for U.S. products and technology for each industry. Through publication in *Commercial News USA* magazine, information on these products ultimately reaches approximately 200,000 business and government leaders worldwide.

To qualify for this service, products must conform to the definition of the industry being highlighted, must be currently exported to no more than 15 countries on a regular basis, and must meet other requirements.

Cost

$150 per product listing.

Contact

Commercial News USA
Office of Marketing Programs/ITA
U.S. Department of Commerce
Room 2106
Washington, DC 20230
(202) 377-4918

or nearest Commerce Department district office (see appendix)

U.S. products for export
Produits à exporter
Productos para exportación

Premises protection	3	**Police equipment**	14
Protection des locaux		Equipement policier	
Protección de premisas		Equipo policiaco	
Audio and optical surveillance	9	**Personal protection and rescue**	15
Surveillance acoustique et optique		Protection personnelle et sauvetage	
Vigilancia acústica y óptica		Protección personal y rescate	
Commodity protection	11	**Identification**	20
Protection des biens		Identification	
Protección de bienes		Identificación	
Fire protection	12	**Communication**	20
Sécurité contre l'incendie		Communication	
Protección contra incendio		Comunicación	

N signifies a new product: one that has been on the U.S. market two years or less. Look for the "*N*" after the headline for the product description.

N indique un nouveau produit qui ne se vend sur le marché des E.-U. que depuis deux ans ou moins. On trouve cette désignation après le titre de chaque description du produit.

N significa un producto nuevo que se ha vendido en el mercado estadounidense por dos años o menos. La "*N*" se encuentra después del título que describe el producto.

The U.S. Department of Commerce has accepted the following product information for international promotion. The firms that supply the product data published in *Commercial News USA* attest that their products are marketed as U.S. manufactures available for immediate export. While this information is believed to be reliable, the U.S. government and its representatives assume no responsibility for the accuracy of the product descriptions.

Le ministère du Commerce des E.-U. a accepté les informations ci-dessous concernant divers produits en vue de les faire connaître sur le marché international. Les sociétés fournissant les données attestent que leurs produits sont commercialisés en tant que productions américaines immédiatement disponibles à l'exportation. Bien que considérant ces informations dignes de foi, le gouvernement des E.-U. et ses représentants n'assument aucune responsabilité quant à l'exactitude des descriptions de produits.

El Departamento de Comercio de los E.E.U.U. distribuye esta revista en todo el mundo como un servicio a exportadores estadounidenses. Al suministrar las descripciones de los productos, las firmas atestan que el contenido de los mismos es de origen estadounidense, que la información es correcta, y que los productos están disponibles para ser exportados. El gobierno de los E.E.U.U. y sus representantes no asumen responsabilidad por errores en las descripciones.

SECURITY SYSTEM COVERS 32 ZONES (*N*) -- The "Vector 2000 Digital Point Annunciation Alarm Control System" is a control/communicator that identifies 32 protection points for easy operation and dealer service. It uses a two-wire multiplex polling loop for two-way communication between the annunciation points and the microcomputer-based control panel. This loop enables each annunciated point to be interrogated by the control and to respond. The complete system operates through 14 remote point modules that have two identification points each, its own passive infrared detector, and its own base for smoke detectors. Distributors are sought for the $380 system. WRITE: Daniel M. Picchi, Intl. Sales Mgr., ADEMCO, Dept. CN, 165 Eileen Way, Syosset, New York 11791 U.S.A. Telex: 685-2062. Target: Western Europe; Mexico, Central America, Caribbean; North Africa, Near East, South Asia.

≈ CN ≈

HEAT DETECTOR PROTECTS HAZARDOUS AREAS -- The explosion- and moisture-proof "Chemtronics Heat Detector" prevents fires in hazardous environments such as aircraft

Premises protection

VERSATILE ELECTRONIC GAS DETECTOR (*N*) -- This firm's newly developed "Gas Alert" is an electronic sensoring device designed for use wherever there may be potentially hazardous or toxic gases. The unit can detect propane, butane, natural gas (methane), gasoline, alcohol, and carbon monoxide at low levels of concentration, which allows time for action to be taken before disaster hits. Available in several models for use in 12-VDC applications such as boats and recreational vehicles, this safety device also comes in 110/220 VAC versions for use in homes, hotels, factories, and restaurants. This versatile sensor costs from $40 to $50, and the company welcomes distributor inquiries. WRITE: Joseph A. Hannan, Vice Pres., Business Development, Norton-Goodwin Associates, Inc., Dept. CN, 244 S. Military Trail, Deerfield Beach, Florida 33442 U.S.A. Telex: 15-9322.

≈ CN ≈

Page from the new product information service section of Commercial News USA, a monthly publication that describes new U.S. products as a means of fostering exports. The publication is distributed to all U.S. embassy and consulate libraries around the world.

46

Business Opportunities Service

The World Bank's International Business Opportunities Service provides advance information on World Bank project funding and potential contracts in the manufacturing, civil works, and consulting sectors. Through international competitive bidding, U.S. firms are eligible to receive overseas contracts for exporting goods and services. Responsibility for procurement rests with the borrowing country.

The primary source of project-specific information on World Bank financing under consideration and on potential procurement opportunities is the *International Business Opportunities Service (IBOS)*, a weekly publication.

Cost
$250 per year.

Contact
The World Bank's International Business
Opportunities Service
The John Hopkins University Press
P.O. Box 11101
Baltimore, MD 21211-0101
(301) 338-6988

Project Status Reports

The *Monthly Operational Summary* reports on the status of every project under consideration for financing by the World Bank, from the earliest stages in the project cycle through approval. The MOS lists the country in which the project is located, the administering government agency or ministry, and the amount of bank lending expected. This information is included in the *International Business Opportunities Service* listed previously.

Cost
$95 per year.

Contact
The Monthly Operational Summary
The Johns Hopkins University Press
P.O. Box 11101
Baltimore, MD 21211-0101
(301) 338-6988

Development Business

Development Business, a publication of the United Nations, provides procurement information on projects financed by the World Bank, regional development banks, and other international organizations.

Cost

$295 per year.

Contact

Development Business
The World Bank
N-2075
1818 H Street, NW
Washington, DC 20433
(202) 473-2939

A Basic Guide to Exporting

This Department of Commerce guidebook provides the information that U.S. exporters need to facilitate their sales abroad. It describes what decisions have to be made, what knowledge is needed to make them, and where to get the necessary information. Further, the book links readers to many helpful resource people who can supply expert information and advice, often at no cost.

A Basic Guide to Exporting offers detailed information about developing an export strategy, finding economical market research, pricing for profits, shipping overseas, export documentation, traveling abroad, answering overseas inquiries, making an overseas sales contact, using an export management company, antitrust, copyrights, trade secrets, technology licensing, getting paid for overseas sales, joint ventures, patents, licensing exports, financing overseas sales, foreign sales corporations and government assistance to exporters.

Cost

$8.50 per copy. Order no.: S/N 003-009-00487-0.

Contact

Superintendent of Documents
U.S. Government Printing Office
Washington, DC 20402
(202) 783-3238

Eximbank Guide

The Eximbank/FCIA Users' Guide provides basic information concerning Eximbank and FCIA programs. The guide includes sample documents and case studies.

Cost
$50.

Contact
Marketing and Program Development
Export-Import Bank
811 Vermont Avenue, NW
Washington, DC 20571
(202) 566-8873

The Export Trading Company Guidebook

A guidebook published by the Department of Commerce, *The Export Trading Company Guidebook* provides essential information on the functions and advantages of establishing or using an Export Trading Company. Export trading companies assume risks associated with international trade by taking title to goods domestically and handling subsequent export operations for the small business owner.

Cost
$8.00 per copy. Order no.: S/N 003-009-00523-0.

Contact
Superintendent of Documents
U.S. Government Printing Office
Washington, DC 20402
(202) 783-3238

Partners in Export Trade

The Department of Commerce has released this practical guide for promoting contact between producers of exportable goods and services, and firms offering export trade services. The directory consists of over 4500 U.S. based companies, their key contacts, products, and services, arranged alphabetically by state. It also contains a listing of all firms under the category of product or service which the firms manufacture or provide.

Cost

$11. Order no.: S/N 003-009-00512-4.

Contact

Superintendent of Documents
U.S. Government Printing Office
Washington, DC 20402
(202) 783-3238

International Countertrade: A Guide for Managers and Executives

This handbook on countertrade covers various aspects of counter-trade practices, citing examples from a number of countries in Latin America, Africa, the Middle East, and Asia. The current countertrade environment, forms of countertrade, and regulations affecting U.S. companies are among the topics discussed.

Cost

$3.75. Order no.: S/N 003-009-00435-7.

Contact

Superintendent of Documents
U.S. Government Printing Office
Washington, DC 20402
(202) 783-3238

SYSTEMS

Commercial Information System

The new Commercial Information Management System (CIMS) links the information resources of the Commerce Department's worldwide network of trade specialists to provide the U.S. business community with timely, accurate and in-depth marketing data. Using SIC codes and/or key words, a trade specialist can create an information package for the industry or product and country specified. Customized retrievals are available in printed or electronic format.

Cost
Varies.

Contact
Commercial Information Management System
Office of Trade Information Services
U.S. Department of Commerce
Room 1324
Washington, DC 20230
(202) 377-4203

or nearest Commerce Department district office (see appendix)

Trade Opportunities Information

The Commerce Department's Trade Opportunities Program (TOP) provides timely sales leads from overseas firms seeking to buy or represent U.S. products and services. U.S. commercial officers worldwide gather leads through local channels. Lead details, such as specifications, quantities, end-use, delivery and bid deadlines are delivered daily to Washington, and then made available electronically within 24 hours directly to the U.S. business community in both printed and electronic form through private sector nationwide distributors.

Cost
Varies.

Contact
Trade Opportunities Program
Office of Trade Information Services
U.S. Department of Commerce
Room 1324
Washington, DC 20230
(202) 377-4203

or nearest Commerce Department district office (see appendix)

Multilateral Contract Information

The World Bank's DACON Information Center provides a computerized data bank that lists information concerning the qualifications and past experience of consulting firms who have participated in multilateral bank financed projects.

Cost
Free.

Contact
DACON Information Center
The World Bank
1818 H Street, NW
Washington, DC 20433
(202) 477-4763

International Major Project Contracts Information

The Commerce Department's Office of International Major Projects helps U.S. firms compete for major planning, engineering, and construction contracts on large foreign construction projects, including equipment and "turn-key" installations. The Office identifies foreign capital projects with export potential of $5 million and over and distributes this information to engineering and construction firms and equipment manufacturers. It assists U.S. firms on a case-by-case basis in competing for these projects and coordinates support when needed from other areas of the Commerce Department and other federal agencies.

A monthly listing of new major overseas engineering and construction projects requiring procurement of products and services of more than $5 million is available to firms and associations interested in obtaining early, limited information on overseas projects.

```
9220762EVHOT

1631328 A 1-08-01-015033 FTS SVC 6513232
RATUZYUW RUFHFTA9350 3281420-UUUU--RUEVHOT.
ZNR UUUUU ZZH                                          PRIORITY
R 241419Z NOV 87
FM AMCONSUL FRANKFURT
TO RUEHDC/USDOC WASHDC
RUWLSRO/USDOCDISTDIR SAN DIEGO CA
RUEVHPC/USDOCDISTDIR HARTFORD CT
RHHMGSC/USDOCDISTDIR HONOLULU HI
RUCHOFZ/USDOCDISTDIR CHICAGO IL
RUEVHOT/USDOCDISTDIR BALTIMORE MD
INFO RUFHOL/AMEMBASSY BONN 5524
RUEHBS/AMEMBASSY BRUSSELS 6073
RUFHMU/AMCONSUL MUNICH 8587
BT
UNCLAS FRANKFURT 19350

POSTS FOR FCS

E.O. 12356:N/A
TAGS: BTIO, GE
SUBJECT:  HOT TOP--TRADE OPPORTUNITY

1.  428/05/P0015
2.  112487
3.  THOMAS L. BOAM
4.  428
5.  ID
6A.  WRITE TO:
6B.  HANS VAN GOGH, MGR.
6C.  MARZIK GMBH
POSTFACH 60
D-8759 HOESBACH
7.  TELEPHONE:  6024-4405
8.  TELEX:  N.A.
9.  101 111 300
10A.  3651XXX-0000 COMPLETE LINE OF HI-FI COMPONENTS
10B.  366221X-0000 BROADCAST AND STUDIO ELECTRONIC
EQUIPMENT
10C.  366223X-0000 TV EQUIPMENT
11.  COMPANY ESTABLISHED IN 1951, DISTRIBUTOR OF
COMMUNICATIONS AND RADIO EQUIPMENT, DATA TRANSMISSION
EQUIPMENT.  4 EMPLOYEES AND 12 SALES AGENTS, ANNUAL
BUSINESS VOLUME OVER DM 3 MILLION.
DRAFTER:  2124 H/HCLABUSCH    RATTRAY
BT
#9350
```

Example of a notice giving the name of a potential foreign company "match" for an American company subscribing to the Commerce Department's Trade Opportunities Program. U.S. firms can receive active trade leads from overseas companies in their product categories.

Cost
Free.

Contact
Wally Haraguchi
Office of Major Projects
U.S. Department of Commerce
Room 2015B
Washington, DC 20230
(202) 377-4877

or nearest Commerce Department district office (see appendix)

KENTRON INTERNATIONAL

For many American businesses, it is important to learn early of bidding opportunities overseas and then to obtain the necessary information to effectively compete for sales. The Commerce Department's Office of Major Projects has assisted scores of small and medium-sized U.S. firms in gaining such information. Take the case of Kentron International of Dallas.

The Office of Major Projects learned that a contract worth $30 million would be let to upgrade the Pakistan Railway's communication system. The Office alerted a variety of U.S. firms to the upcoming tender. When Kentron notified the Commerce Department office of its interest in the contract, Kentron was provided with a World Bank loan appraisal report that outlined the project's scope.

Over the next two years, the Office of Major Projects continued to work with Kentron, coordinating action with the U.S. Embassy in Islamabad on visits by Pakistani officials to the United States, and on using the Embassy's resources to verify information received by Kentron on the project's status. Ultimately, Kentron was awarded a contract valued at approximately $50 million.

Procurement Cable System

The Commerce Department's Office of International Major Projects provides up-to-date information and contacts regarding specific overseas projects through its procurement cable system. The information is obtained from posts abroad and made available at U.S. district offices.

Cost
Free.

Contact
nearest Commerce Department district office (see appendix)

Export Opportunities

Foreign government requirements for U.S. commodities are advertised in two bulletins published by the U.S. Agency for International Development's (AID) Office of Small and Disadvantaged Business Utilization (ODSBU). *AID—Financial Export Opportunities* and *AID Procurement Information* are available to any U.S. company on the AID mailing list.

Cost
Free.

Contact
Vicki Jones
Program Operations Assistant
Office of Business Relations
U.S. Agency for International Development
OSDBU/MRC, Room 1400A, SA-14
Washington, DC 20523
(202) 875-1551

Investment Opportunities Search

The Overseas Private Investment Corporation (OPIC) offers an investment information network, called the Opportunity Bank, which enables firms considering investment in the developing world to identify appropriate joint venture opportunities. A U.S. firm can submit its profile, listing the type of investment sought, intended product lines, and countries or regions of interest. This information is then matched with corresponding joint venture opportunities submitted by foreign businesses and governments. The firm receives a summary of matching projects, from which it may order detailed profiles of the specific projects in which it is interested. The data base contains information on more than 1,800 U.S. companies that are considering overseas business, and more than 2,400 overseas projects for which U.S. business participation is being sought.

Cost
Registration free. $50 for up to ten project profiles.

The *Catalog of Investment Opportunities in Developing Countries*, published annually, lists more than 2,000 joint venture opportunities.

Cost
$5.00.

Contact
Dana Stahl
Opportunity Bank
Overseas Private Investment Corporation
1615 M Street, NW
Washington, DC 20527

Project Profiles

The Inter-American Development Bank (IDB) provides current information concerning the status of IDB-sponsored procurement projects. The profile identifies the project and the executing agency, as well as a brief project description, and the goods and services required.

Cost
Free.

Contact
Joseph Hinshaw
External Relations Office
Inter-American Development Bank
1300 New York Avenue, NW
Washington, DC 20577
(202) 623-1369

Overseas
Private
Investment
Corporation

1615 M Street, N.W.
Washington, D.C. 20527
(202) 457-7200
Telex: 440227 OPIC UI

OPIC OPPORTUNITY BANK INVESTMENT PROJECT PROFILE

1. Investment Project in DOMINICAN REPUBLIC   Ref #: B 54

2. Project Name: Agro-Industrial Project   Date: 05/28/87

3. Project Description:
Project sponsor seeks a U.S. partner to expand the processing of pineapple, coconut, grated coconut, lemon juice, as well as caladium and sapodilla. National government approval has been granted. A feasibility study is available.

4. Project is an expansion of an existing project
5. Primary markets are anticipated to be   Export.
6. Approval granted by these govt. bodies: National
7. Project info. available: Feasibility Study Completed   05/80

8. Resources to be provided by Project Sponsor:
    Land   Capital

9. Resources desired from U.S. Partner(s):
    Equity Investment   Contract Services

10. Project Costs (U.S.$):   Local Currency requirement: $1,000,000
                    Foreign Exchange requirement:$1,000,000

11. Desired Ownership Structure: Host-Country Private: 0-25%
                          Host-Country Government: 0-25%
                          U.S. Private Partner: 76-100%

----

12. Project Sponsor Information

      Contact Name: Ramon O. Valdez
      Company Name: Corporacion Oriental
         Address: Roberto Pastoriza #158
            City: Santo Domingo   Country: DOMINICAN REPUBLIC
        Telephone:(809) 565-3845   Telex: PESCA 3460728

13. Company Financials: Company annual sales: $1 to $10 million.
                     Total No. of Employees: 300 to 500
                     Year Company established: 1980

14. Financial Reference: Local Bank: Metropolitano Bank
                  Address: Lope de Vega, Santo Domingo
                  Int'l Bank: City Bank
                  Address: Jon F. Kennedy, Santo Domingo

----

15. Source   EXPORTADORA ORIENTAL
    of Project: RAUL VILLA

                ROBERTO PASTORIZA #158
                SANTO DOMINGO, DOMINICAN REP.

Type of profile information on a foreign investment project seeking American business participation that is provided upon request by the Opportunity Bank of OPIC.

Agricultural Trade Leads

The Agricultural Information and Marketing Services (AIMS), within the Department of Agriculture's Foreign Agricultural Service (FAS), provides continual access to timely sales leads from overseas firms through its Trade Lead Service. FAS offices gather trade leads that are located and developed by FAS agricultural counselors, attachés, and trade officers around the world. Information is provided concerning product specifications, delivery deadlines, bid requirements, contact points, and mailing addresses. Trade leads can be received in the following ways:

Commercial electronic dissemination trade leads are processed daily and are available the same day to U.S. exporters.

Cost

Though AIMS does not charge for this service, fees are assessed by the commercial firms operating the networks.

Computerized direct mail trade leads are mailed daily to AIMS clients in the U.S. who have subscribed to the direct mail service.

Cost

Annual subscription costs for individual commodities is generally $25.00, but are higher for some commodities based on usage. Subscriptions are available for a maximum of three years.

Contact

Philip Letarte
AIMS Coordinator
U.S. Department of Agriculture
Foreign Agricultural Service
Room 4649S
Washington, DC 20250
(202) 447-7103

Seafood Export Opportunities

The National Marine Fisheries Service (NMFS), in conjunction with the Department of Commerce's United States and Foreign Commercial Service (US&FCS), assist the fishing industry through seafood export promotion activities.

A full-time fisheries trade coordinator, assigned to the US&FCS, develops and implements seafood export programs. The trade co-

******** CATEGORY: GRAINS

Concerning BARLEY
Issued From Iraq   12/08   SIC Number: 01131010
HOPS EXTRACT (IRAQ). QUANTITY: 6 TONS. QUALITY: ACCORDING TO THE FOLLOWING
                            U.S.D.A. Ref Num: 3841-871207-505A0156
SPECIFICATIONS: VARIETY, NORTHERN BREWERS GOLD AND ALPHA ACID CONTENT 80.
USAGE: FOR BEER PRODUCTION. DELIVERY: NEGOTIABLE. QUOTE: FOB, C&F AQABA,
C&F BAGHDAD AND C&F TURKISH PORTS. PACKING: IN TINS OF 2.4 KGS EACH AND
PACKED IN STRONG CARTON BOXES. PAYMENT: DEFERRED PAYMENT FOR AT LEAST TWO
YEARS. ANALYSIS LIST SHOULD ACCOMPANY THE OFFER. BANK REF: RAFIDAIN BANK.
CONTACT: SAHBA'A AL-ANI - COMM. MGR, NATIONAL FOOD INDUSTRIES, P.O. BOX 29021,
ZA'AFARANIYA, BAGHDAD, IRAQ. TELEX: 214214 AND 213714 NFI IK. PHONE:
773-0311-3. (WK 49/TOFAS 0156)

******** CATEGORY: SEEDSANDHORT

Concerning HORTICULTURAL SPECIALTIES   12/08   SIC Number: 01920000
Issued From Greece   U.S.D.A. Ref Num: 3839-871207-484B0167
SEEDLING (GREECE). FIRM IS INTERESTED IN IMPORTING WALNUT TREE SEEDLINSS FOR
PLANTING PREFERABLY DWARF VARIETIES. BANK REF: NATIONAL BANK OF GREECE AND
AGRICULTURAL BANK, ALMYROS BRANCHES. CONTACT: MR. CHRISTOPHER PAVLIDIS,
AGEBEE S.A., ALMYROS MAGNISIAS, GR-371 00, GREECE. PHONE: (0422) 21-885 OR
22-800. TELEX: 255282 OR 255216. (WK 49/TOFAS 0167)

******** CATEGORY: FRUITANDNUTS

Concerning APPLES
Issued From Colombia   12/08   SIC Number: 01222010
APPLES (COLOMBIA). EXPERIENCED FRUIT IMPORTER WANTS ASAP FOB US PORT
                             U.S.D.A. Ref Num: 3155-871207-301B0224
QUOTATIONS FOR APPLES, TYPE A, RED AND GREEN. WOULD IMPORT ABOUT 10,000 20
KILO BOXES. PHYTOSANITARY CERTIFICATE MUST BE SECURED BY THE EXPORTER. BANK
REF: MAY BE OBTAINED FROM BANCO SUDAMERIS-PRINCIPAL BRANCH IN CARTAGENA.
CONTACT: MR. FADER VILLAMIZAR, FRUCAR, APDO. 2080, CARTAGENA, COLOMBIA.
PHONE: 45-282. (WK 49/TOFAS 0224)

******** CATEGORY: CATTLE

Concerning DAIRY CATTLE
Issued From Venezuela   12/08   SIC Number: 01393000
HOLSTEIN CATTLE (VENEZUELA). QUANTITY: 200 HEAD. QUALITY: REGISTERED,
                             U.S.D.A. Ref Num: 3838-871207-307T0113
PREGNANT. OTHER REQUIREMENTS: SANITARY CERTIFICATE. QUOTE: FOB & CIF.
CONTACT: MR. RICARDO VEGAS BRICENO, VHB VENEZOLANA DE BROKERS, AV. FRANCISCO
DE MIRANDA, CENTRO PERU, PISO 6, OFIC. 106, CHACAO, CARACAS, VENEZUELA.
TELEX: 32124 FAREN VC. PHONE: (2) 32.57.35 OR 32.93.08. (WK 49/TOFAS 0113)

******** CATEGORY: LIVESTOCK

Concerning SHEEP, LAMBS, AND GOATS   12/08   SIC Number: 01391014
Issued From Venezuela   U.S.D.A. Ref Num: 3845-871207-307T0114
DAIRY GOATS (VENEZUELA). QUANTITY: 20 HEADS, 2 MALES AND 18 FEMALES.
QUALITY: PURE, SAAMEN OR TOGGENBURG. PACKAGING: AIRPLANE. QUOTE: CIF
MAIQUETIA. OTHER REQ: SANITARY CERTIFICATE FROM COUNTRY OF ORIGIN. BANK
REF: BANCO METROPOLITANO, FINAL BOULEVARD EL CAFETAL, CARACAS, VENEZUELA.
CONTACT: MR. BERNARDO LUPI E., AV. CIRCUNVALACION DEL SOL, EDIF. EL JARDIN,
#31, SANTA PAULA, CARACAS, VENEZUELA. PHONE: (2)987-5382. (WK 49/TOFAS 0114)

Sample printout of foreign trade leads provided by the FAS for various commodities.

ordinator develops markets for fish and fishing products through market research on seafood and participation in international trade shows, missions and other trade events. In addition, listings of trade, government and other organizations that have an interest in international trade in U.S. fish and fishing equipment are made available.

The US&FCS U.S. district offices plan promotion events and fish and fishery products seminars.

The US&FCS overseas posts develop trade promotion activities which are related to U.S. fish and fisheries products and fishing equipment. These include recruiting foreign buyers to attend U.S. trade events and assisting with fisheries trade and investment policy analysis and implementation.

Contact

Tapan Banerjee, Manager
Fisheries Trade Promotion
U.S. Department of Commerce
United States and Foreign Commercial Service
Washington, DC 20230
(202) 377-3922

CUSTOMIZED SERVICES

World Traders Information

The World Traders Data Reports service of the Department of Commerce provides U.S. companies with information on foreign companies with which they might be interested in doing business. Reports contain information on foreign companies such as the type of organization, year established, relative size, number of employees, general reputation, territory covered, language preferred, product lines handled, principal owners, and financial and trade references. Each report also contains a general comment on the foreign firm's reliability by the U.S. Commercial Officer who conducted the investigation.

Reports are prepared upon request by a U.S. company, which must submit the complete name and address of the foreign firm. Reports are not available on firms located in the United States, Puerto Rico, U.S. Trust Territories, the Soviet Union or Soviet bloc countries, or in countries where credit reports are available only from private sources.

Cost
$75 per search.

Contact
nearest Commerce Department district office (see appendix)

Exporter Assistance

The Office of Export Trading Company Affairs (OETCA) has the lead role in implementing the provisions of the Export Trading Company Act of 1982. The OETCA promotes the formation of export trading companies, provides a referral service that facilitates contact between U.S. goods and services producers and firms offering export trade services, and administers the Act's antitrust certification program.

Contact
Office of Export Trading Company Affairs
Room H5618
U.S. Department of Commerce
Washington, DC 20230
(202) 377-5131

SAMPLE WTDR/FTI TELEGRAPHIC REPORT

RR RUEHDC
DE RUEHBS #0303 2061035
ZNR UUUUU ZZH
R 251034Z JUL 85
FM AMEMBASSY BRUSSELS
TO RUCHLAC/USDOCDISDIR MILWAUKEE WI
INFO RUEHDC/USDOC WASHDC
BT
UNCLAS BRUSSELS 10303
E.O. 12356: NA
TAGS: BBSR, BE
SUBJECT: WTDR/FTI APRE S.P.R.L.
REFS: MILWAUKEE 0313 and 0331, REQUESTED BY:
CLACK CORP., P.O. BOX 500, WINDSOR
THE FOLLOWING REPORT IS BASED UPON INFORMATION OBTAINED FROM LOCAL CREDIT AND BANKING
SOURCES SINCE FIRM FAILED TO RESPOND TO EMBASSY'S INQUIRIES.

1. BELGIUM
2. OFFICE USE: 423 3. OFFICE USE: 0173600 4. OFFICE USE: 01
5. APRE S.P.R.L.
6. RUE GUILLAUME STOCO, 34
7. 1050 BRUSSELS
8. CONTACT: BERNARD SEMET
9. TITLE: MANAGER
10. PHONE: 02/6492018   11. TELEX: 62541
12. CABLE: APREAU
13. ESTABL: 1952   14. EMPL: 14   15. SIZE: MEDIUM
16. REPUTATION: Y-GOOD   17. RPT. DATE: 07/85
18. NA   19. NA   20. NA   21. NA   22. 41
23A. 35890/04   MFR. & EXP. OF ANTI-LIMESTONE (CHALK) DEPOSIT APPARATUS
23B. 35892/2345   AGT. DIS. EXP. & IMP. OF WATER SOFTENERS, PURIFICATION EQUIPMENT AND CLEANING APPARATUS FOR
WATER TREATING EQUIPMENT
23C. 28995/2345   AGT. DIS. EXP. & IMP. OF WATER TREATING COMPOUNDS
23D. 35692/2345   AGT. DIS. EXP. & IMP. OF WATER FILTERING EQUIPMENT
24. FOREIGN SALES: FRANCE 35%, SPAIN 28%, GERMANY 15%, AND USA 10% (BY VALUE).
25. FINANCIAL REFS: SOCIETE GENERALE DE BANQUE, MONTAGNE DU PARC, 3, 1000 BRUSSELS AND KREDIETBANK, RUE
D'ARENBERG, 7, 1000 BRUSSELS.
26. TRADE REFS: JOHNSON MACHINERY, INC., 862 S. LOS ANGELES ST., LOS ANGELES, CA. 96102; TEDENSON CO., INC., 125
SOUTH STREET BOSTON, MA. 02111.
27. FOREIGN FIRMS REPRESENTED: AGENCY REP. OF ACQUAMATIC INC., 2412 GRANT AVE., ROCKFORD, IL., WATER SOFTENERS;
CLACK CORP., P.O. BOX 500, DURAFORM LANE, WINDSOR, WI., WATER TREATMENT MATERIALS; MATT-SON INC., 1541
BURGUNDY PARKWAY, STREAMWOOD, IL., SAME; BENCKISTER GMBH, LUDWIGSHAFEN, GERMANY, "MIKROPHOS" CONDITION-
ERS; ATLAS FILTRI, PADOVA, ITALY, FILTERS.
28. POST EVALUATION: THIS PARTNERSHIP ACTS AS AGENT-DISTRIBUTOR, IMPORTER AND EXPORTER OF WATER SOFTENERS,
FILTERING AND PURIFICATION EQUIPMENT INCLUDING WATER TREATING COMPOUNDS. THE FIRM ALSO MANUFACTURES
ANTI-LIMESTONE (CHALK) DEPOSIT APPARATUS AND WATER SOFTENERS SOLD UNDER THE "AMPHORA" TRADEMARK. FIRM
IMPORTS FROM THE U.S., GERMANY AND ITALY. THE FOLLOWING FIGURES ARE TAKEN FROM THE FIRM'S LATEST PUBLISHED
BALANCE SHEET WHICH REFLECTS THE FINANCIAL SITUATION IN 1983, (1.00 DOL. EQUALS 57 BELGIAN FRANCS) AUTHORIZED
CAPTIAL: 87,719 DOL.; NET WORTH: 92,099 DOLS. LOCAL SOURCES REPORT THAT THIS FIRM HAS A GOOD BUSINESS
REPUTATION AND PAYMENTS ARE MADE NORMALLY. EMBASSY CONSIDERS APRE S.P.R.L. A SUITABLE CONTACT FOR U.S.
FIRMS.
29. PREP: YVETTE PAUWELS   APPR: HENDRIK N. SMIT
SWAEBE
BT
#0303

Example of the information provided by the World Traders Data Reports Service of the Commerce Department. U.S. firms can, upon request, receive information on foreign companies with which they are interested in doing business.

Contact Facilitation Service

The Commerce Department has established a clearinghouse for U.S. suppliers, banks, service organizations and export trading companies. This service will help U.S. producers identify and contact newly formed export trading companies. Similarly, export trading companies may want to utilize this program to identify possible clients for their services.

Cost
Free.

Contact
Office of Export Trading Company Affairs
Room H5618
U.S. Department of Commerce
Washington, DC 20230
(202) 377-5131

MACHINE TOOL BUILDERS' ASSOCIATION

Many U.S. firms are reluctant to join together to compete for large projects overseas because of U.S. antitrust laws. Today, the U.S. Department of Commerce's Office of Export Trading Company Affairs has a solution. Since 1983, this office has issued certificates of review to companies and organizations who request protection from antitrust laws when pursuing business overseas.

The National Machine Tool Builders' Association (NMTBA) was issued a certificate that provides antitrust protection for cooperative export activities such as joint bidding and selling. NMTBA members may pool their talents and resources and share export information to capture foreign sales and generate new trading opportunities. NMTBA and its 268 member firms are immune from state and federal antitrust prosecution for activities specified in the certificate. It is the first certificate to extend this protection to more than 200 firms belonging to the same association.

Agent/Distributor Information

The Agent/Distributor Service, administered by the Department of Commerce, helps U.S. companies find interested and qualified overseas agents or distributors for their products or services. On request, U.S. foreign commercial specialists will seek a foreign representative specifically for a U.S. company's product line. The report sent to the requesting company provides information on up to six qualified representatives with interest in the U.S. company's proposal, including the name and address of the foreign firm, name and title of contact person, telephone number, cable address and telex number, and brief comments about the firm or its stated interest in the proposal. A search usually requires 30 days.

Cost
$90 per search.

Contact
nearest Commerce Department district office (see appendix)

Comparison Shopping

This is a custom-tailored service which provides firms with key marketing and foreign representation information about their specific products. U.S. and Foreign Commercial staff conduct on-the-spot interviews to determine nine key marketing facts about the product, such as sales potential in the market, comparable products, distribution channels, going price, competitive factors, and qualified purchasers.

Cost
$500 per country per product.

Contact
nearest Commerce Department district office (see appendix)

Agricultural Information and Marketing Services

The Agricultural Information and Marketing Services (AIMS) within the Department of Agriculture's Foreign and Agricultural Service (FAS) is a central conduit for foreign market information. AIMS assists agricultural exporters in finding foreign market opportunities and promoting their products overseas in the following ways:

Product Publicity

FAS publishes a monthly newsletter, *Contacts for U.S. Agricultural Products*, which assists American firms by introducing their food and agricultural products to foreign markets. Brief 100-word descriptions of products submitted by U.S. firms are published in the newsletter on a first-come, first-served basis.

Contacts is sent to FAS agricultural counselors, attachés, and trade officers for distribution to prospective foreign buyers. It is translated into Japanese, Spanish, French, Italian, and Greek and mailed to thousands of buyers worldwide.

Cost
Free.

Foreign Importer Listings

The Foreign Importer Listings is a database designed to match a U.S. firm's product or country interests with prospective foreign buyers. This match will generate listings providing contacts in all foreign countries for a single product, or with all importers of all agricultural products in a single country.

Cost
$15 per list.

Buyer Alert Program

Every Monday, AIMS electronically transmits sales announcements of featured products to interested overseas buyers. Each announcement features a short description of the product, timely price information, and U.S. supplier contact information.

These announcements are disseminated to prospective importers in the leading value-added export markets for U.S. products.

Cost
Free.

Contact
Philip Letarte
AIMS Coordinator
U.S. Department of Agriculture
Foreign Agricultural Service
Room 4649-S
Washington, DC 20250-1000
(202) 447-7103

9220762EVHOT

1234346 A 1-26-01-010812 FTS SVC 6513232
RTTUZYUW RUEHDNA5641 3460331-UUUU--RUEVHOT.
ZNR UUUUU ZZH
R 120329Z DEC 86
FM AMCONSUL SYDNEY
TO RUEVHOT/USDOCDISTDIR BALTIMORE MD
INFO RUEHDC/USDOC WASHDC
RUEHBCB/AMCONSUL BRISBANE 1333
RUEHBN/AMCONSUL MELBOURNE 6747
BT
UNCLAS SECTION 01 OF 02 SYDNEY 05641

USDOC FOR 3310/USFCS/EPS/OIPDD

E.O. 12356: N/A
TAGS: BEXP, AS
SUBJ: ADS -

REFS: (A) SYDNEY 05442; (B) MELBOURNE 02622

POST HAS CONTACTED INDIVIDUALLY ELEVEN POTENTIAL
AGENTS/DISTRIBUTORS OF INDUSTRIAL TRAINING AIDS.
THE FOLLOWING COMPANIES HAVE EXPRESSED INTEREST.
LITERATURE HAS BEEN SENT.

1. LEARNING SYSTEMS INTERNATIONAL PTY. LTD.
P.O. BOX 289 (214 CROWN STREET)
DARLINGHURST, NSW 2010, AUSTRALIA
CONTACT: MR. RON ALLEN, MANAGING DIRECTOR
PHONE: 02/331.7333
COMMENT: FIRM IMPORTS AND MARKETS RANGE OF HUMAN
RESOURCES AND DEVELOPMENT TRAINING PROGRAMS.
INDUSTRIAL/SAFETY AIDS COULD WELL COMPLEMENT EXISTING
PRODUCTS AND SERVICES. BRANCH OFFICES ARE MAINTAINED
IN VICTORIA, QUEENSLAND, AND WESTERN AUSTRALIA.

2. ASI ADVANCED SYSTEMS AUSTRALASIA PTY. LTD.
P.O. BOX 365 (71 EPPING ROAD)
NORTH RYDE, NSW 2113, AUSTRALIA
CONTACT: MR. ARI BAALBERGEN, DIRECTOR
PHONE: 02/887.3988
TELEX: AA71909
COMMENT: IMPORTERS AND DISTRIBUTORS OF VIDEO
EDUCATIONAL COURSES AND MICRO TRAINING COURSES. PROGRAMS
INCLUDE COMPLETE RANGE OF DATA PROCESSING MANU-
FACTURING, MANAGEMENT AND SUPERVISORY AND SALES TRAINING.
INTERESTED IN PRODUCT EXPANSION TO INCLUDE INDUSTRIAL
TRAINING. BRANCH OFFICE IS LOCATED IN VICTORIA.

3. FOCAL COMMUNICATIONS PTY. LTD.
123 CLARENCE STREET
SYDNEY, NSW 2000, AUSTRALIA
CONTACT: MR. KERRY WONKA, GENERAL MANAGER
PHONE: 02/290.1499
TELEX: 177123
COMMENT: IMPORTER AND DISTRIBUTOR OF TRAINING PROGRAMS.
SPECIALIZING IN INDUSTRIAL AND SAFETY AIDS. FIRM HAS
ESTABLISHED INDUSTRY CONTACTS. GOOD INTEREST EXPRESSED.

4. FSE SCIENTIFIC
P.O. BOX 501
CONCORD, NSW 2137, AUSTRALIA
(74 BURWOOD ROAD
BURWOOD, NSW 2137, AUSTRALIA)
CONTACT: MR. GUNTHER HASSMANN, PRODUCT GROUP MANAGER
PHONE: 02/745.3377
TELEX: AA71861
COMMENT: DIVISION OF WELL ESTABLISHED BRITISH GROUP--
FISONS PLC. UK. IMPORTER AND DISTRIBUTOR OF SCIENTIFIC,
HEALTH CARE, INDUSTRIAL INSTRUMENTS AND PRODUCTS, AS
WELL AS EDUCATIONAL AIDS AND APPARATUS. SALES AND
SERVICE IN ALL AUSTRALIAN STATES. FIRM HOLDS SEVERAL
INTERNATIONAL AGENCIES, INCLUDING U.S. AGREEMENTS.

POST COMMENT: WE CONCUR WITH FCS/MELBOURNE COMMENTS
(REF. B). A MARKET FOR INDUSTRIAL TRAINING PROGRAMS
HAS BEEN IDENTIFIED, AND A NEED ESTABLISHED FOR QUALITY
MATERIALS, ESPECIALLY THOSE THAT ARE TECHNOLOGICALLY
PROGRESSIVE. 5$3,58!68,$ 049!389,-))6 785-?)3
-,$ 3!!3!58!3 $854877594. HOWEVER, HAS PROVED DIFFICULT
APPROACHES HAVE BEEN MADE TO VARIOUS TYPES OF COMPANIES,
INCLUDING INDUSTRIAL PRODUCT DISTRIBUTORS/MANUFACTURERS,
MARKETERS OF TRAINING PROGRAMS AND VIDEO SPECIALISTS.
IT WOULD SEEM THE FIRMS ENGAGED IN DISTRIBUTING GENERAL
EDUCATIONAL PROGRAMS ARE MOST MOTIVATED AND SALES
ORIENTED. ONLY A FEW, HOWEVER, SEEM TO BE SPECIFICALLY
QUALIFIED TO HANDLE INDUSTRIAL MATERIALS.

PROVIDED PROGRAM SUITABILITY FOR AN AUSTRALIAN AUDIENCE
HAS BEEN ESTABLISHED IN EACH INDUSTRY SECTOR, POST
BELIEVES AN INCREASING MARKET SHARE SHOULD EMERGE.

A FOLLOW-UP VISIT WOULD SEEM HIGHLY DESIRABLE WHERE
ACTUAL PRODUCT PRESENTATIONS CAN BE MADE. POST
WOULD BE PLEASED TO ASSIST IN ANY FOLLOW-UPS DESIRED
PRIOR TO A SCHEDULED VISIT. WE WOULD ALSO WELCOME ANY
SUGGESTIONS NUS MAY WISH TO MAKE IN PURSUING
ADDITIONAL TRADE LEADS. (FCSN/CMZSIROSSY)
DORRANCE
BT
#5641

Sample report from the Agent/Distributor Service, which can provide
an American firm with information on a potential foreign representative for a certain product or service.

UNITED STATES DEPARTMENT OF COMMERCE
INTERNATIONAL TRADE ADMINISTRATION

INFORMATION SERVICES ORDER

PART 1—COMPANY DATA AND PRODUCT INFORMATION

COMPANY DATA	Date 10/2/86

Company Name

Street Address 910 Clopper Road

City Gaithersburg	State Maryland	ZIP 20878

Key Contact (1) William F. Cummings
Consultant - Training Programs   Telephone Number (301) 258-2500

(2) Key Contact Sinnammal Souppaya
Associate Marketing Engineer/International Operations

Cable Address   Telex No 710-828-0540 NUSWASH

TYPE OF SERVICE ORDERED

		Amount			Amount
WTDR	☐		EML/CIRS	☐	
ADS	☒	90.00	MARKET RESEARCH	☐	
TOP NOTICE	☐		COMMERCIAL NEWSLETTER	☐	
TOP BULLETIN	☐		OTHER	☐	

PRODUCT INFORMATION (See instructions)

NUS Training Corporation provides video-based training programs to utility and industrial clients around the world. The company offers an extensive line of comprehensive programs designed to meet the needs of a wide range of clients. Some of these programs include: Electrical Maintenance; General and Mechanical Maintenance; Instrumentation and Control; Pulp and Paper, Chemical, and Refinery Operations; Power Principles; Transmission and Distribution; Coal Handling; Nuclear Energy Training; Fundamentals of Digital Electronics

TOTAL ORDER: $_____ ☐ Check/money order enclosed
☐ Visa ☐ MC Acct. No. _____ Exp. _____

Signature _____

MAIL TO:

DOC USE ONLY

US/FCS Code: _____ _____

Sequence No. ____ ____ ____ ____ ____-____

Paym't rec'd at D.O.: ☐Y ☐N

Amount: $ _____

Date filled: _____

Eximbank Briefing Series

Eximbank offers briefings to businesses which outline various financing programs of the Export-Import Bank. These meetings are designed to familiarize the participants with Eximbank's facilities and methods of operation.

Eximbank offers a one-day program primarily directed toward the U.S. exporter. Emphasis is placed on the use of Eximbank programs by manufacturers and service entities. In addition, each month Eximbank offers both a two-day and four-day program primarily directed toward the commercial banking community.

Cost
Free.

Contact
Marketing and Program Development
Export-Import Bank of the U.S.
811 Vermont Avenue, NW
Washington, DC 20571
(202) 566-8873

FCIA Orientation Seminars

The Foreign Credit Insurance Association (FCIA), Eximbank's export credit insurance agent, also provides periodic seminars.

Cost
$65 per seminar.

Contact
Foreign Credit Insurance Association
Office of Corporate Marketing
40 Rector Street, 16th Floor
New York, NY 10006
(212) 227-7020

World Bank Seminars

The World Bank holds Monthly Business Briefings to provide information concerning export opportunities arising from Bank-supported projects. The briefing is available to firms of all sizes interested in expanding or developing international business opportunities in manufacturing, civil works, and consulting.

Cost

Free. Registration is required at least two weeks prior to briefing date and accepted on a first-come first-served basis.

Contact

Carol D. Stitt
Business Relations Advisor
The World Bank
Office of External Relations
1818 H Street, NW
Washington, DC 20433
(202) 477-5322

Business Assistance Service

The Commerce Department's Business Assistance Service (BAS), established within the Office of Business Liaison, provides information and guidance on programs throughout the federal government. BAS focuses on providing information concerning government procurement, exporting, marketing, statistical sources, and regulatory matters.

Contact

Business Assistance Service
Office of Business Liaison
U.S. Department of Commerce
Room 5898C
Washington, DC 20230
(202) 377-3176

Business Consultation

Minority entrepreneurs can receive advice and assistance in entering the international marketplace from the Commerce Department's Minority Business Development Agency. The Agency has created a nationwide network of Minority Export Development Consultant organizations to help minority firms develop export marketing plans, identify potential markets and trade leads, and complete international transactions. In addition, the Agency's six regional offices can provide guidance on other minority assistance programs and refer minority firms to a locally funded Minority Business Development Center in their area for further specialized help at a nominal fee. The Minority Business Development Agency has six regional offices:

For Your Information

THE OFFICE OF PUBLIC AFFAIRS
TELEPHONE (202) 566-8990

BRIEFING PROGRAM FOR EXPORTERS - ONE DAY

Eximbank offers briefings for those wishing to learn more about the various financing programs of the Export-Import Bank. These meetings are designed to familiarize the participants with Eximbank's facilities and methods of operation.

Each month Eximbank offers a one-day program primarily directed towards the U.S. exporter. Emphasis is placed on the use of Eximbank programs by manufacturers and service entities. In addition, each month Eximbank offers both a two-day and four-day program primarily directed toward the commercial banking community. Schedules of these briefings are available on request.

Briefings are built around a series of presentations by Eximbank Officers starting at 9:15 a.m. The briefings, other than the Annual Conference, are free of charge. A sample agenda for the one-day briefing is on the reverse side.

Anyone interested in participating in the ONE-DAY EXPORTERS BRIEFING is invited to contact the Office of Public Affairs. Since space is limited, please contact the Bank as early as possible prior to the date you wish to attend.

1988 ONE-DAY BRIEFING SCHEDULE FOR EXPORTERS

January 13	July 20
February 10	September 14
March 29	October 19
April 13 (Annual Conference)	November 16
May 18	December 16
June 15	

The Foreign Credit Insurance Association, Eximbank's Export Credit insurance agent, also provides periodic briefings. To obtain additional information, please contact:
Foreign Credit Insurance Association
Office of Corporate Marketing
40 Rector Street 16th Floor
New York, New York 10006
212-227-7834 or 227-7149

The World Bank offers a Business Orientation Program on their activities one day each month generally following Eximbank's Briefing Program for Exporters. For a schedule and information on the World Bank's briefings, please contact:
The World Bank
Office of External Relations
1818 H Street, N.W.
Washington, D.C. 20433

EXPORT-IMPORT BANK OF THE UNITED STATES
811 VERMONT AVENUE, NW
WASHINGTON, DC 20571

Sample description of Eximbank seminar briefings held monthly.

SAMPLE BRIEFING SCHEDULE

9:15 a.m.	Welcome and Introduction to Eximbank	Public Affairs Officer Office of Public Affairs

INSURANCE AND BANKING

10:00 a.m.	Working Capital Guarantee Program	Loan Officer U.S. Division
10:30 a.m.	Break	
10:45 a.m.	Export Credit Insurance (Foreign Credit Insurance Association)	Loan Officer Insurance Division
11:30 a.m.	Credit Information ·	Specialist Computer Applications Section
12:00 p.m.	Lunch Break	

INTERNATIONAL LENDING

1:30 p.m.	Loans and Guarantees Direct Loans Intermediary Loans Guarantees	Loan Officer Area Division
2:30 p.m.	Break	
2:45 p.m.	Country Risk Assessment	Economist Country Risk Analysis
3:30 p.m.	Legal Issues	Attorney Office of the General Counsel
4:00 p.m.	Concluding Remarks	Director/Senior Exim Official
4:15 p.m.	Adjourn	

71

Contact

Atlanta Region

Carlton Eccles
Regional Director
Minority Business Development
  Agency
U.S. Department of Commerce
1371 Peachtree Street, NE
Suite 505
Atlanta, GA 30309
(404) 881-4091

Chicago Region

David Vega
Regional Director
Minority Business Development
  Agency
U.S. Department of Commerce
55 E. Monroe Street, Suite 1440
Chicago, IL 60603
(312) 353-0182

San Francisco Region

Xavier Mena
Regional Director
Minority Business Development
  Agency
U.S. Department of Commerce
221 Main Street
Room 1280
San Francisco, CA 94102
(415) 974-9597

Dallas Region

Melba Cabrera
Regional Director
Minority Business Development
  Agency
U.S. Department of Commerce
1100 Commerce Street
Room 7B19
Dallas, TX 75242
(214) 767-8001

New York

Georgina Sanchez
Regional Director
Minority Business Development
  Agency
U.S. Department of Commerce
Federal Office Building
26 Federal Plaza, Room 37-20
New York, NY 10278
(212) 264-3262

Washington, DC Region

Willie J. Williams
Regional Director
Minority Business Development
  Agency
U.S. Department of Commerce
Room 6711
14th and Constitution Avenue, NW
Washington, DC 20230
(202) 377-8275

Eastern Caribbean Investment Promotion Service

Eastern Caribbean Investment Promotion Service (ECIPS), in conjunction with the Organization of Eastern Caribbean States and the U.S. Agency for International Development, assists companies who are considering offshore operations in the English speaking Caribbean countries of Antigua and Barbuda, Dominica, Grenada, Montserrat, St. Kitts/Nevis, St. Lucia, and St. Vincent and the Grenadines.

ECIPS provides counseling and advice to assist companies in determining whether an offshore manufacturing or assembly operation may be beneficial to their business.

Contact

Allen Chastanet
Investment Promotion Officer
Eastern Caribbean Investment Promotion Service
1730 M Street, NW
Suite 901N
Washington, DC 20036
(202) 659-8689

High Impact Agricultural Marketing and Production Project

The High Impact Agricultural Marketing and Production Project (HIAMP) is funded by the Agency for International Development and is designed to foster economic development in the Eastern Caribbean region through encouraging private sector enterprises to invest in non-traditional, export-oriented, agricultural and agribusiness ventures.

Contact

Michael Julien   or   Kim Finan, Chief
Project Director   Project Design Office
HIAMP Project   USAID Barbados
P.O. Box 1271   FPO Miami 34054
Bridgetown, Barbados   (809) 436-4950
(809) 436-9916

or the following individual island advisors:

Island	Advisor	Telephone
Grenada	Henry Harmon	(809) 444-4102
St. Vincent and		
the Grenadines	Joe Tokar	(809) 457-2649
St. Lucia	Bill Kedrock	(809) 452-7596
Dominica	Ahmed Zedahalka	(809) 448-3660
St. Kitts and		
Nievis	Ed Reinauer	(809) 465-2040

AID: COUNTRY MARKET INFORMATION

The Agency for International Development (AID) contracted with a New York publisher to prepare a study of the investment climate in five developing nations. The countries—Zimbabwe, Jamaica, Haiti, the Ivory Coast, and Sri Lanka—were selected because of low per capita income and their importance to the United States. Sri Lanka, for example, receives about $45 million in bilateral aid from the development agency each year. But AID also sees a need to strengthen Sri Lanka's economy through private U.S. investment. The $72,000 AID-sponsored study is designed to augment investment knowledge about the political and labor climate, taxes, incentives, and import tariffs in these countries.

Thailand, Indonesia, and Sri Lanka Investment Opportunities

The Agency for International Development has awarded contracts to several U.S. consulting firms to provide information and assistance to U.S. companies interested in exploring business opportunities in Thailand, Indonesia, and Sri Lanka. Information on specific project opportunities, potential local joint-venture partners, and investment incentives and policies are among the services offered.

Cost
Free.

Contact
Agency for International Development
Bureau for Asia/Near East
22nd & C Streets, NW
Washington, DC 20523

For Thailand: Karl Schwartz   (202) 647-9240
For Indonesia: Helen Kaufman   (202) 647-9136
For Sri Lanka: David Garms   (202) 647-4516

SPECIAL PROGRAMS FOR SMALL BUSINESS

Advice on Overseas Contracts

The Office of Small and Disadvantaged Business Utilization in the Agency for International Development (AID) is the principal distribution point for information on AID programs. The Office provides information to U.S. suppliers, particularly small, independent enterprises, regarding purchases to be financed with AID funds.

The Office maintains an Automated Consultant Registry Information System (ACRIS) of approximately 5000 firms and consultants interested in providing professional and technical services under AID programs.

U.S. small businesses can obtain special counseling and related services in order to furnish equipment, materials, and services to AID-financed projects.

Cost
Free.

Contact
Office of Small and Disadvantaged Business Utilization
Agency for International Development
OSDBU/MRC
Washington, DC 20523
(703) 875-1551

SOLIO RANCH, LTD.

A Colorado mining engineer revolutionized the cattle industry in Kenya with a ranch insured by a U.S. government agency. Courtland Parfet established the Solio Ranch, Ltd. near Mt. Kenya. There he built a modern breeding operation in which he cross-bred a native breed of cattle with French Charolais bulls. The ranch now has approximately 20,000 head of top-grade cattle and is one of the largest suppliers of beef in Kenya. What's more, Kenyan beef is now exported to Switzerland and other countries. The Solio Ranch enterprise employs more than 200 Kenyans and is an important exporter for the country.

Initial Trade Consultation

Under an agreement signed between the SBA and the Federal Bar Association, qualified attorneys from the International Law Council of the FBA will provide free initial consultations to small companies in an effort to answer some of their basic legal questions concerning international trade and investment. Interested small businesses will be referred by local SBA offices to nearby attorneys through program coordinators of the FBA local chapters around the country.

Cost
Free.

Contact
nearest Small Business Administration district office (see appendix)

Export Marketing Assistance

The Department of Commerce and the Small Business Administration formalized a cooperative program designed to assist high potential small business exporters to enter or expand international markets. The joint program offers seminars and workshops, trade promotion events, trade missions, trade information and statistics, training programs, and coordination of export assistance.

Contact
nearest Commerce Department or Small Business Administration district office (see appendix)

Consulting Opportunities

The Agency for International Development (AID) provides loans and grants to finance technical and professional services that support project activities related to agriculture, rural development, nutrition, health, population planning, education, human resources, and housing. At times, AID acts on behalf of the foreign country and serves as the prime contractor for the procurement of technical experts. In such cases, AID frequently restricts competition for technical services through small business set-asides and the Small Business Administration's 8(a) Program.

Contact
Office of Small and Disadvantaged Business Utilization
Agency for International Development
OSDBU/MRC
Washington, DC 20523
(703) 875-1551

CHAPTER FOUR

THE FIRST TRIP

After identifying trade leads and opportunities in individual countries, most firms want to determine the general climate for doing business or investing in these countries. Several services are available to help American businesses plan and pay for a first trip, as well as provide a temporary base of operations for business people visiting the country. This chapter is organized in three subsections:

Pretrip Preparation. Obtaining business counseling and commercial information from regional desk officers, country and commodity specialists, and foreign government officials.

Planning the Trip. Coordinating and planning the trip to take advantage of investment missions, trade fairs, shows, exhibits, and other special programs.

People to See. Listing of people to see during a first trip, including overseas commercial officers in the U.S. embassies; provision of temporary base of operations.

PRETRIP PREPARATION

Country Officers

Several U.S. Government agencies have country desk officers located in Washington. These officers provide general and specific country information to U.S. businesses involved in overseas business activities:

Department of Commerce

The Department of Commerce offers professional business counseling and commercial information on a geographical basis for major overseas markets. Country specialists provide the following services:

Statistical data on production, exports and imports, market share, and third-country competition.

Analyses of industrial sector reports and growth projections.

Counseling on foreign country laws, regulations and practices affecting international trade and investment.

Listings of overseas market research firms that assist companies in preparing marketing strategies.

Advice on selecting agents or distributors.

Contacts with U.S. and Foreign Commercial Service officers at U.S. embassies and consulates and with U.S. companies successfully operating in the country.

Department of Commerce District Offices

The Department of Commerce's 48 district offices and 19 branch offices throughout the United States are staffed by trade specialists who provide trade-related information, business advice, and counseling. Each district office maintains an extensive business library containing the Department's latest reports and statistical data. District offices are linked by direct telex communication to the commercial sections of U.S. embassies around the world, enabling U.S. companies to obtain specific market information, assistance with export-related problems, or help in planning a business trip itinerary.

Customized commercial information packages are available through the Commercial Information Management System (CIMS) to client firms. All offices of ITA, selected international trade agencies, state governments and other users can access this information and disseminate it to U.S. business.

Trade specialists in the U.S. district offices can provide individual counseling and information on trade and investment opportunities abroad, foreign markets for U.S. products and services, financing and insurance, tax advantages of exporting, international trade exhibitions, export documentation requirements, and export licensing and import requirements. To encourage U.S. businesses to enter the international marketplace, trade specialists draw on the Commerce Department's many export marketing aids and services, including assistance in promoting U.S. products in special markets, computerized trade and investment opportunities, locating overseas agents or distributors, promoting U.S. products through Export Development Offices abroad, introducing foreign buyers to U.S. firms, sponsoring export seminars and conferences, organizing trade missions and promoting international trade fairs, and assisting in establishing relationships with, and forming, export trading companies.

The district offices work closely with U.S. business people experienced in all aspects of export trade through the District Export Councils (DECs). Volunteer DEC members counsel prospective exporters on getting started in international trade, co-sponsor export seminars and workshops and the district offices, address business groups on exporting, and promote awareness of the export-assistance programs of the Department of Commerce. A council has been established in every city that has a Department of Commerce district office.

Contact
nearest Commerce Department district office (see appendix)

Federal-State Partnership

Each Department of Commerce district office has signed a partnership agreement with its corresponding state to encourage a greater state role in export promotion and maximize federal resources for export promotion. The objective is to avoid duplication of effort between the Federal and State governments and, working with other multipliers, maximize the delivery of services in the most cost effective manner. Local academic institutions and the private sector have joined with the district offices and State governments to provide a wide variety of export promotion activities, including trade shows, trade missions, matchmakers, state level economic analyses, individually designed export promotion conferences, and loans to finance exports through the State Agenda for Exporting program.

Contact
Gordon Studebaker
Federal-State Coordinator
U.S. and Foreign Commercial Service, Office of Domestic Operations
U.S. Department of Commerce, ITA
Washington, DC 20230
(202) 377-1289

or your nearest Commerce Department district office (see appendix)

Department of State

Country officers at the Department of State can provide information on their assigned country's political, economic, and investment climate.

Contact
see appendix for listing of State Department country officers

Agency for International Development

Country officers at the Agency for International Development (AID) can provide information on development programs in the countries for which they are responsible.

Contact
see appendix for listing of AID country officers

Department of Agriculture

Foreign Agricultural Service (FAS) officers stationed in Washington provide agricultural information on specific blocs of countries:

Contact

Region	Officer	Telephone
European area (Non-EC)	Gordon Nicks	(202) 447-6083
European area (EC)	Dale Douglas	(202) 447-2144
North & South America	Edwin A. Bauer	(202) 447-3221
Caribbean Basin	Franklin D. Lee	(202) 447-3221
East Asia & Pacific Area	Lyle Moe	(202) 447-7053
Near East, South Asia and Africa	Verle Lanier	(202) 447-7053

Analysts in the Department of Agriculture's Economic Research Service provide information on the current agricultural situation and forecast future market trends.

Contact

Section	Leader	Telephone
Developing Economies Countries Branch	Gene Mathia, Chief	(202) 786-1680
Commercial Trade	Rip Landes	(202) 786-1668
Food Aid	Michael Kurtzig	(202) 786-1680
Macroeconomics	Mathew Shane	(202) 786-1668
Centrally Planned Economies Branch	Ken Gray, Chief	(202) 786-1620
U.S.S.R.	Kathryn Zeimetz	(202) 786-1620
China	Francis Tuan	(202) 786-1620
Planned Systems Analysis Section	Ken Gray, Acting	(202) 786-1620
Developed Market Economies Branch	Mark Newman, Acting	(202) 786-1610
Pacific Rim	William Coyle	(202) 786-1610
Western Europe	Mark Newman	(202) 786-1610
Developed Market Economies	Larry Deaton	(202) 786-1610

USDA: China Trade Show

Since the start of the 1980s, the People's Republic of China has become a large and fast-growing market for U.S. leather. Trade shows held in China have helped develop this market. Participating at the International Leather and Equipment Show in Canton, for example, were the Tanner's Council of America and representatives of six U.S. tanning companies. To assist them, the Department of Agriculture's Foreign Agricultural Service gave financial and logistical support through its Washington headquarters and its field officers in China. Through this help, the tanners were able to take along a large assortment of U.S. leather products to show Chinese leather executives, some of whom had come 3000 miles to see the exhibit. This trade show helped ease the American business executives' entry into China's leather market.

Peace Corps

Country officers at the Peace Corps can provide information on host-country contacts familiar with small-scale enterprises.

Contact

Region	Officer	Telephone
Africa		
Cameroon/Gabon/Niger/ Equatorial Guinea/ Sudan	Djodi Deutsch	(202) 254-8397
Malawi/Tanzania/Kenya/	Bill Ferguson	(202) 254-5634
Botswana/Lesotho/ Swaziland	Carrie Moore	(202) 254-6046
Zaire/CAR/Burundi/ Rwanda	Tom Elan	(202) 254-8694
Mali/Chad/Mauritania	Mary Lange	(202) 254-7004
Senegal/Guinea/ The Gambia	R.J. Benn	(202) 254-3185
Ghana/Sierra Leone/ Liberia	Anna West	(202) 254-5644

Togo/Benin/Cape Verde/	Theresa	
Guinea Bissau	Queenan	(202) 254-7036

Inter-American Operations

Paraguay/Ecuador/		
Costa Rica	Jeanne Jensen	(202) 254-6298
Dominican Republic/		
Haiti/Jamaica	Allison Moore	(202) 254-6375
Guatemala/Honduras	Rob Cowan	(202) 254-6320
Belize/Eastern		
Caribbean	Carole Cook	(202) 254-6322

North Africa, Near East and Pacific

Cook Islands/Fiji		
Tuvalu/		
Western Samoa/		
Tonga	Jan McMahan	(202) 254-3227
Philippines	Brooke Finn	(202) 254-3290
Papua New Guinea/		
Thailand/Seychelles	Chuck Howell	(202) 254-3040
Kiribati/Micronesia/		
Solomon Islands	Christopher Rich	(202) 254-3231
Nepal/Sri Lanka	Christine Leggett	(202) 254-3118
Morocco/Tunisia/Yemen	Karen Blythe	(202) 254-3196

Small Business Administration District Offices

The Small Business Administration's district offices are located throughout the United States. Each district office is staffed by a team of experts in the lending, procurement, and assistance areas, who consider loan applications, offer individual management assistance, and coordinate other small business services. District offices are the contact point for small businesses needing information or assistance concerning SBA programs.

Contact
nearest SBA district office (see appendix)

Foreign Diplomats in the United States

The Diplomatic List, compiled by the U.S. Department of State, lists all foreign diplomats residing in the Washington, DC metropolitan area. This list is issued quarterly.

Cost
$7.50 in U.S.; $9.40 foreign. Order no.: S/N 744-004-00000-4.

Employees of Diplomatic Missions, known as the "White List", provides updated information on staff members in foreign missions in and around Washington, DC. The publication is issued quarterly.

Cost
$5.00 in U.S.; $6.25 foreign. Order no.: S/N744-005-00000-1.

Foreign Consular Offices in the United States contains a complete and official listing of the foreign jurisdictions and recognized consular officers.

Cost
$4.50 in U.S.; $5.65 foreign. Order no.: S/N 044-000-02171-4.

Contact
Superintendent of Documents
U.S. Government Printing Office
Washington, DC 20402
(202) 783-3238

PLANNING THE TRIP

International Trade Fairs and Exhibitions

The Department of Commerce sponsors official U.S. participation in selected major international trade fairs and exhibitions to promote the sale of U.S. goods and services overseas. When research reveals promising sales potential in areas where no suitable international trade fairs are planned, the Department sponsors, conducts, and manages its own exhibitions of U.S. products organized along an industry sector.

Participating U.S. firms receive a full range of promotional and display assistance. Companies make a financial contribution to offset the cost of the services provided. In addition to pre-show promotional services, the Department of Commerce provides exhibit space, lounge or meeting rooms for exhibitor-customer conferences, market counseling, design and construction of the exhibit area, advice on shipment of products to the site, unpacking and positioning of displays, and basic utilities and housekeeping services.

The Department of Commerce also certifies private-sector shows to verify that good service to participants will be provided, and that the event is, in fact, a good marketing opportunity for the firm.

In addition, through its Foreign Buyer Program, the Commerce Department encourages foreign buyers to attend selected domestic trade shows, enabling participating U.S. firms to meet with foreign buyers, agents, distributors, potential licensees, or joint venture partners.

Contact

nearest Commerce district office (see appendix) for a complete list of all certified trade shows and Commerce-sponsored trade shows.

For additional information on certified shows:

David Earle, Director
Overseas Trade Fair, Certification Program
Room 2114
U.S. Department of Commerce
Washington, DC 20230
(202) 377-2525

Trade Delegations

The Department of Commerce Matchmaker programs are high-visibility trade delegations organized to introduce U.S. firms to new markets. Agents and distributors in a foreign market are "matched" with the company's products in that market.

Contact
Porter Clary, Account Executive
Office of Export Promotion Service
Room 2119
Department of Commerce
Washington, DC 20230
(202) 377-3119

or nearest Department of Commerce district office (see appendix)

Catalog Shows and Video/Catalog Exhibitions

The Department of Commerce annually schedules 20 to 30 catalog shows and video-catalog exhibitions worldwide. These shows allow U.S. firms to test product interest in foreign markets, develop sales leads, and locate agents or distributors. These exhibitions, held at U.S. embassies and consulates, feature displays of U.S. product catalogs, sales brochures, and other graphic sales aids at American embassy and consulate trade shows.

Exhibitions are supported by the U.S. and Foreign Commercial Service. Participating companies make a contribution to offset the Department's costs.

Contact
Marketing Programs Division
U.S. Department of Commerce
Room 2119
Washington, DC 20230
(202) 377-3973

or nearest Commerce Department district office (see appendix)

Agricultural Shows and Exhibits

National Food and Agriculture Exposition

The National Association of State Departments of Agriculture (NASDA), in cooperation with the Foreign Agricultural Service, sponsors expositions for foreign food buyers.

Contact

F. Farrell Higbee, Director
NASDA National Food and Agriculture Exposition
National Association of State Departments of Agriculture
1616 H Street, NW
Room 710
Washington, DC 20006
(202) 628-1566

Trade Fair Exhibits

The Foreign Agricultural Service (FAS) conducts trade fair exhibits to attract buyers for U.S. agricultural products. These exhibits are an effective means for U.S. companies to introduce and promote their food products overseas. A fee covers exhibit space, facilities, and trade relations services. Exhibitors are responsible for providing the products and full-time representation at their displays.

Hotel-restaurant institutional exhibits are held in several countries each year for all segments of the foreign food service trade. Usually, 25 to 50 U.S. firms exhibit institutional-size packs of products. Professional demonstrators are used. Exhibits run two to three days.

International food shows are held annually in some of the leading foreign markets. Exhibits sponsored by FAS are generally consumer-trade-oriented food and beverage expositions attracting exhibitors and buyers from many foreign countries.

Agent food exhibits are organized and managed by representatives of the Foreign Agricultural Service overseas, in cooperation with foreign agents of U.S. food companies.

Agricultural attaché product displays offer an opportunity to show U.S. food products to key officials in controlled economies where the consumer is unable to influence imports.

Point-of-purchase promotion is utilized in leading foreign markets for drawing consumer attention to U.S. food products. Foreign Agricultural Service representatives contact the chain and/or department stores and foreign agents of U.S. food manufacturers to make arrangements for these promotions.

Livestock shows are held in a number of countries to promote the sale of U.S. breeding stock and feedstuffs.

Sales teams are arranged through the FAS to put U.S. suppliers and foreign buyers together. The FAS selects a market with export potential and invites five or six U.S. firms handling food products to participate in a coordinated sales mission.

Contact
Kerry Reynolds, Director
Export Programs Division
Foreign Agricultural Service
U.S. Department of Agriculture
Room 4506-S
Washington, DC 20250-1000
(202) 382-9221

Trade Missions

The Commerce Department sponsors and supports several types of trade missions to promote the sale of U.S. goods and services abroad and to help establish sales agents and other foreign representatives for U.S. exporters.

Seminar missions are multicountry business trips designed to facilitate the sale of sophisticated products and technology. During a mission, a team of U.S. high-technology industry representatives presents papers of interest to potential foreign buyers, agents, and distributors. Mission members also participate in private appointments arranged by the overseas post.

Specialized trade missions are planned, organized, and led by officers of the Department of Commerce. The mission itinerary may involve three or four stops within a country or region. The Department plans the details, publicizes the event, and arranges appointments for mission members with government officials and potential agents and distributors. Missions usually are limited to representatives of eight U.S. companies. Participants pay their own travel expenses and reimburse the Department for its costs in supporting the mission.

Industry-organized, government-approved trade missions are organized by trade associations, chambers of commerce, state development agencies, and similar groups with the advice and support of the Department of Commerce. The Department assists in planning these missions and in coordinating arrangements and support through its Export Development Offices, the Foreign Commercial Service, and Foreign Service posts.

Contact
nearest Commerce Department district office (see appendix)

Investment Missions

The Overseas Private Investment Corporation annually conducts four to five investment missions per year to introduce U.S. corporate executives to overseas investment opportunities. An investment mission usually visits one country for five days. During the mission, participants meet with host-country officials, U.S. government officials, and private-sector representatives for briefings on the country's investment climate. Mission members hold private business meetings with potential joint-venture partners to discuss specific projects. They may also meet with local bankers, accountants, and lawyers to discuss structuring their investment.

Cost
Participants pay round-trip air travel between their home city and mission country, lodging, meals and administrative costs.

Contact
Edie Stancioff, Investment Missions Manager
Overseas Private Investment Corporation
1615 M Street, NW
Washington, DC 20527
(202) 457-7121

Textile and Apparel Export Development Program

This is a joint industry and Commerce Department program to promote exports of textiles and apparel. The program assists textile and apparel industry participation in overseas trade shows and trade missions, encourages foreign buyers to attend U.S. trade shows, and holds seminars on exporting. In addition, it provides market research in support of the Department of Commerce trade promotion events. The program provides assistance to U.S. textile and apparel exporters in eliminating nontariff trade barriers. It furnishes U.S. businesses with detailed opportunities for direct sales to overseas buyers of textile and apparel products, in private industry as well as government. It also includes useful announcements of foreign companies offering to represent U.S. textile and apparel firms overseas.

Contact
Serenc Molnar, Director
Market Expansion Division
Office of Textiles and Apparel
Room H3100
U.S. Department of Commerce
Washington, DC 20230
(202) 377-2043

```
                      1988-1989
                U.S. Department of Commerce
               Export Promotion Calendar of Events
            Office of Microelectronics and Instrumentation


    Date    Event                                    Country

    4-88    Hannover Trade Fair         (1)    Germany
    5-88    Tropictronics               (3)    Brazil
    6-88    Trade Mission               (3)    China
    6-88    Trade Mission               (3)    Belgium, Netherlands
    9-88    Trade Mission               (3)    India
   10-88    Korea Electronics Show      (3)    Korea
   11-88    Pronic                      (2)    France
   11-88    Electronica                 (1)    Germany
   12-88    SemiPro                     (3)    Korea
    2-89    Internepcon-Semiconductor   (2)    India
    3-89    Trade Mission               (3)    China
    3-89    BIAS                        (3)    Italy


(1)Electronic Components & Test Equipment
(2)Electronics Industry Production & Test Equipment
(3)Includes 1 & 2

For further information contact: Joseph Burke, U.S. Department of
Commerce, (202) 377-2470
```

Example of a schedule of U.S. Department of Commerce sponsored export promotion events for the electronics industry.

COMMERCE: TRADE MISSIONS

For more than 15 years, Gerhardt's, Inc. of Louisiana and Texas has sold engines and turbine accessories to the oil and gas industry abroad. Its international division won a Presidential E award for export success in Latin America, but until the company took part in a trade mission organized by the Commerce Department it was unfamiliar with the oil and gas market in the Gulf States of the Middle East. Bruce Gerhardt, the firm's Houston assistant general manager and trade mission participant, not only had the chance to locate potential sales representatives during the mission to Kuwait, the United Arab Emirates, and Saudi Arabia, but was able to learn about the market potential and the necessary ways to sell in these Gulf countries. As a result of the mission, Gerhardt's International, Inc. expects to sign several new sales representatives. Bruce Gerhardt anticipates that the sales developing from the Middle East will help offset the present lag in the Latin American oil markets.

Travel and Tourism Promotion

In order to increase U.S. exports of goods and services through tourism, the United States Travel and Tourism Administration (USTTA) works to increase foreign demand, remove barriers and encourage small- and medium-size travel exporters. Additionally, USTTA provides accurate and timely statistics and data, forms partnerships with state and local governments, and develops international marketing strategies for the private and public sector.

Contact

Eric Peterson, Deputy Under Secretary
United States Travel and Tourism Administration
U.S. Department of Commerce
Room 1865
Washington, DC 20230
(202) 377-0137

SPONSORED BY

OPIC Overseas Private Investment Corporation

FEBRUARY 20-28, 1987

PHILIPPINES

INVESTMENT MISSION

FEBRUARY 20-28, 1987

Sponsored by the
Overseas Private Investment Corporation

INVESTMENT OPPORTUNITIES

The following are brief descriptions of project proposals submitted to OPIC by Philippine firms seeking U.S. joint ventures. Additional project proposals are expected. Firms interested in participating in the mission, but unable to find suitable projects listed below, should contact OPIC to determine if arrangements can be made to pursue their interests during the mission.

Agribusiness
- Cassava starch and glucose processing
- Oil milling
- Cassava flour
- Food terminal complex
- Palay production
- Fish canning
- Poultry
- Cashew nut production
- Deep sea fishing
- Fruit juice processing
- MSG manufacture
- Food processing
- Cold storage
- Vegetables and flowers

Manufacturing
- Metal forming
- Ceramic tiles
- Round rubber thread
- Rubber hose
- Kitchen appliances
- Coated paper
- Deuterium processing
- Cosmetic marketing
- Activated carbon plant
- Semi-conductor assembly
- Consumer electronics assembly
- Printed circuit board manufacture
- Jewelry

Mining
- Gold mining
- Nickel mining

Construction
- Pre-fab steel housing
- Plywood manufacture
- Cement production

Hotel Services
- Beach club
- Five-star hotel

TENTATIVE MISSION SCHEDULE

Friday, February 20

11:55 a.m.   Depart San Francisco for Manila

Saturday, February 21

9:40 p.m.   Arrive Manila

Sunday, February 22

                  Free Morning
3:30 p.m.   OPIC Briefing

Monday, February 23

9:00 a.m.   Briefing by U.S. Embassy staff
10:30 a.m.   "Doing Business In the Philippines" panel discussion with U.S. businessmen residing in Philippines
2:00 p.m.   "Doing Business In the Philippines" panel discussion with Philippine businessmen
3:30 p.m.   Briefings by Philippine government officials
7:00 p.m.   Ambassador's reception

Tuesday-Thursday, February 24-26

Individual business appointments and trips to project sites.

Friday, February 27

11:00 a.m.   Final meeting with Government of Philippines and U.S. Embassy officials

Saturday, February 28

12:10 p.m.   Depart Manila for San Francisco
10:45 a.m.   Arrive San Francisco

OPIC
Overseas
Private
Investment
Corporation

Portions of a pamphlet describing an investment mission to the Philippines sponsored by OPIC.

93

PEOPLE TO SEE

Overseas Officers

U.S. embassies and most consulates overseas are staffed with commercial, agricultural, development, and political officers to assist U.S. firms in their business activities. Overseas officers promote U.S. trade and investment by assisting U.S. companies in bidding on major contracts and identifying potential joint-venture partners, buyers, and representatives. Officers gather data on country trends affecting trade and investment and analyze industry sector prospects. They also monitor and analyze local laws, regulations, and practices that affect market access and business conditions, including local standards, licensing, import and investment restrictions, subsidies, taxes, patents and trademarks, and investment codes.

Contact
U.S. embassies overseas (see appendix)

USDA: MARKET STUDIES

Malaysia lowered the customs duty for fresh fruits by 50 percent and to 45 percent for fresh oranges shipped directly to Malaysia rather than through Singapore.

Sunkist Growers, Inc. of California, seizing the opportunity to promote U.S. products in this market, conducted a survey to explore the structure and distribution system for perishables in Malaysia's three largest markets. The Sunkist survey team, with the help of the Foreign Agricultural Service's Horticulture and Tropical Products Division, interviewed local importers, wholesalers, and retailers to determine produce distribution in that market.

Ultimately, Malaysia bought approximately $2 million of Sunkist fresh valencia and navel oranges. Two years earlier, the California grower's cooperative had sales of a little over $200,000 in the Malaysian market.

Agricultural Trade Offices

Agricultural trade offices, located in established overseas markets, offer assistance to U.S. companies interested in selling and investing overseas. The agricultural trade officer at each office can help establish government and business contacts, provide leads on potential buyers and joint-venture investors, and assist in setting up product displays. Overseas cooperators with U.S. trade associations also provide assistance at some trade offices. Offices are fully equipped to provide a full range of support services and to accommodate small product displays for visiting exporters. Visiting executives are expected to pay long distance telephone and other similar charges they incur at the trade office.

Contact
> Wayne W. Sharp
> Assistant Administrator for Foreign Agricultural Affairs
> Foreign Agricultural Service
> U.S. Department of Agriculture
> Room 5092-S
> Washington, DC 20250-1000
> (202) 447-6138

The *U.S. Agricultural Counselors, Agricultural Attachés and Agricultural Trade Officers* contains contacts for 35 countries and is available at no charge from the FAS.

Contact
> Dick Welton, Deputy Assistant Administrator
>   for Foreign Agricultural Affairs
> Foreign Agricultural Service
> U.S. Department of Agriculture
> Room 5092-S
> Washington, DC 20250-1000
> (202) 447-3253

Export Development Offices

Through its network of overseas Export Development Offices, the Commerce Department is able to make available exhibition or conference space to individual U.S. firms, their agents, or trade associations on a first-come, first-served basis. When no regular exhibitions are scheduled, facilities can be used for sales meetings, conferences, seminars, or one-company product promotions, or they can be used as a temporary "base of operation" for U.S. business travelers. Arrangements for use of exhibition or conference space must be made at least 30 days in advance.

Export Development Offices with exhibition and/or meeting facilities are located in London, Mexico City, Milan, Seoul, Warsaw, Moscow and Tokyo.

Cost
Use of these facilities is based on specific services requested.

Contact

Far East: Wanda Ale	(202) 377-2997
Europe: Hans Amrhein	(202) 377-4909
Latin America: Peggy Kelleher	(202) 377-4406
Middle East/Africa: Al Sterling	(202) 377-1209

Japan Office for the U.S. Electronics Industries

The Japan Office is a project of the U.S. electronics industry, supported by the U.S. Department of Commerce's International Trade Administration (ITA). As a resource for U.S. electronics industries, the following services are provided:

A team of Japan trade experts advises and assists U.S. firms in entering the Japanese market, and solves problems common to the U.S. electronics industry in Japan.

One of the most comprehensive libraries of the Japanese electronics industry is maintained and made available to U.S. firms.

U.S. industry is represented to the Japanese government and Japanese trade groups.

Information is provided on governmental, trade, technical and marketing developments that affect the competitive position of the U.S. electronics industry.

Information collected in Japan is distributed to members of the industry in the U.S. through various publications.

Contact

John P. Stern, Senior Representative
U.S. Electronics Industry/AEA Japan Office
Nanbu Building, 3rd Floor
Kioicho 3-3
Chiyoda-ku, Tokyo
Japan 102
Telephone: 03/237-7195
Telex: 2322854 AEATYO
Facsimile: 03/237-1237

CHAPTER FIVE

JUDGING THE FEASIBILITY

After making a first trip and determining the general climate for doing business in a particular country, detailed information and an assessment of the commercial viability of the proposed operation are then required. These may involve a business plan, projections for cash flow and demand, materials and construction costs, and an estimate of operating expenses. There are several types of federal programs to provide funding and assistance for such feasibility studies. This chapter describes these programs, categorized into four broad areas:

Technology Transfer. Programs to provide funding to transfer technology to foreign countries.

Major Projects. Federal programs to help U.S. firms compete for major overseas contracts. These projects are typically government-to-government and involve infrastructure activity.

Specific Projects. Programs for funding feasibility studies on specific investments and export potential projects. These projects typically involve private partners.

Special Programs for Small Business. Government programs to help small businesses determine the feasibility of export operations.

TECHNOLOGY TRANSFER

Research and Development Funding

The Bureau of Science and Technology, within the Agency for International Development (AID), identifies ideas for productive technology transfer to developing countries.

Terms
The terms are determined on a project-by-project basis by the overseas mission in the developing country for which the technology is targeted.

Eligibility
Eligibility is determined by the respective AID overseas mission. The U.S. company must be committed to helping institutions in less developed countries develop and adapt technology.

Contact
Brad Langmaid, Deputy Assistant Administrator
for Science and Technology
U.S. Agency for International Development
Washington, DC 20523
(202) 647-4322

or the AID country officer in Washington, DC, (see appendix), to determine the appropriate contact in the overseas AID mission

Technology Transfer Information

The International Finance Corporation typically acts as a catalyst or advisor to donor and recipient firms involved with technology transfer. The Technology and Development Unit will identify suitable technologies, innovative concepts, products and processes, and adapt them as necessary for transfer to entrepreneurs in developing countries.

In addition, the IFC Technology and Development Unit provides contracting opportunities for consultants concerning feasibility studies.

100

TELECONSULT COMPANY

One objective of the U.S. Trade and Development Program (TDP) is to help developing countries utilize American high technology. West Germany and Japan are competing against U.S. firms to provide equipment and services to upgrade the Philippine telecommunications system. TDP has helped finance a feasibility study that will recommend standards for the Philippine government's Ministry of Telecommunications and Transportation to adopt. The U.S. firm conducting the feasibility study, the Teleconsult Company, will also prepare the standards for the tender documents associated with procuring goods and services for the project.

Contact

A. K. Bose, Technical Manager
Technology and Development Unit
International Finance Corporation
1818 H Street, NW
Washington, DC 20433
(202) 676-0551

MAJOR PROJECTS

Feasibility Study Funding

The U.S. Trade and Development Program (TDP) funds project planning to help U.S. companies compete for, and participate in, major public sector projects in developing countries. TDP also provides reimbursable grants to U.S. companies considering an equity investment in a project overseas. These grants enable a company to analyze the technical, economic, and financial aspects of a proposed investment project and to develop data for planning to enable it to determine whether or not the project should be developed.

Terms

TDP will provide a grant to a government of a developing country to finance planning services for a public-sector project on the condition that a U.S. firm is selected by that government to perform the study. For investor projects, TDP will provide up to 50 percent of the cost of the feasibility study, which must be reimbursed if the investment proceeds. TDP's participation usually ranges up to $500,000 for public-sector projects, and from $50,000 to $150,000 for investor projects.

Eligibility

1. The project must have the potential to generate substantial U.S. exports, usually equal to 50 to 75 times the value of the U.S. government's expenditure.

ARTHUR D. LITTLE

TDP funded two feasibility studies totalling $1,100,000 carried out by Arthur D. Little of Boston, Massachusetts. The studies evaluated the application of a nationwide telecommunications system including undersea fiber optics, rural cellular application, and radar. Based upon the recommendations of the study for a complete telecommunications system, TELECOM (the Colombian telecommunications agency) signed a $120 million telecommunications project.

LEMCO ENGINEERS, INC.

Through a TDP grant of $434,000 to the Royal Thai Government, LEMCO Engineers, Inc. of St. Louis, Missouri was hired in 1980 to perform a feasibility study on a high-voltage transmission line supplying Bangkok with much of its electricity. LEMCO was subsequently awarded follow-up contracts of $13 million for engineering, design, equipment specifications, and construction supervision of the project. Total U.S. exports to the project to date are $32 million.

2. The project must have high priority for the host country.
3. The project must be consistent with U.S. foreign policy goals.
4. U.S. government assistance must be critical to the project going forward.
5. The investor, if there is one, must be able to finance at least 40 percent of the project cost.

Contact
U.S. Trade and Development Program
International Development Cooperation Agency
Washington, DC 20523
(703) 875-4357

HARZA ENGINEERING COMPANY

TDP funded a feasibility study carried out by Harza Engineering Co. to examine the alternative design for the construction of a 58 meter low dam at Basus in the People's Republic of China. The study also recommended the construction of three 11 kilometers-long power tunnels between the dam and its power house. To build the tunnels the Chinese purchased two giant tunnel boring machines from S.A. Healy and the Robbins Company for $10.6 million. Robbins also sold $940,000 in cutters for tunnel excavation. Caterpillar Tractor Co. supplied $5.5 million in 35 ton trucks.

SPECIFIC PROJECTS

Export Feasibility Study Funding

Export-Import Bank

The Export-Import Bank (Eximbank) finances feasibility studies through its Direct Loan Program and its Exporter Credits, Guarantees and Insurance Programs. In the area of Direct Credits, Eximbank offers fixed-rate, medium-term loans to help finance project-related feasibility studies and preconstruction design and engineering services up to $10 million through its Engineering Multiplier Program. Loans to successful applicants will cover up to 85 percent of the U.S. costs. The Bank will also cover local costs up to 15 percent of the eligible U.S. costs through its Financial Guarantee.

Feasibility studies that cost over $10 million can be financed through a combination of the Engineering Multiplier Program and its regular direct lending terms. If Eximbank undertakes final project financing, loan payments can be tied into a long-term financial package.

Feasibility studies may also be financed through Eximbank's Exporter Credits, Guarantees, and Insurance Programs. Assistance is available through export credit insurance provided by the Foreign Credit Insurance Association, the Commercial Bank Guarantee Program, the Working Capital Guarantee Program, and either the Small Business or Medium Term Credit Program. The foreign borrower is not required to enter into a formal loan agreement with Eximbank under these programs.

Terms and Eligibility
(Refer to Eximbank's loan program in Chapter 7 of this book.)

Contact
John W. Wisniewski
Vice President for Engineering
Export-Import Bank of the U.S.
811 Vermont Avenue, NW
Washington, DC 20571
(202) 566-8802

Agricultural Export Marketing Assistance

Market Development Cooperators, which are agricultural nonprofit associations, work with the Foreign Agricultural Service to promote and expand overseas markets for U.S. products. More than 50 foreign agricultural associations, 7000 processors and handlers, and 1500 farm cooperatives representing several million farmers participate in this program. U.S. companies can receive assistance in expanding overseas markets for their food products by contacting the Market Development Cooperator for their respective industry.

Contact
William Davis, Assistant Administrator
Foreign Agricultural Service
U.S. Department of Agriculture
Room 5089-S
Washington, DC 20250
(202) 447-4761

TARGETED EXPORT ASSISTANCE PROGRAM

A second export related program administered by FAS is the Targeted Export Assistance (TEA) program. The program was authorized by the Food Security Act of 1985 and provides funds to help producers finance promotional activities for U.S. agricultural products disadvantaged by the unfair foreign trade policies of competitor nations. The program's funds are used to reimburse agricultural organizations conducting specified activities for eligible commodities in specified countries.

In cooperation with approximately 40 organizations, USDA has approved TEA programs for a wide variety of commodities in almost every region of the world. Among the commodities included in TEA programs are: fresh pears, wheat, wine, peanuts, canned peaches, feed grains, dry peas and lentils, table grapes, wood products, soybeans, dairy cattle, rice, meat, poultry and eggs, and frozen potatoes.

The Joint Venture Feasibility Fund

The Joint Venture Feasibility Fund (JVFF), sponsored by Agency for International Development, provides funding and technical assistance to firms in the U.S. and in Caribbean Basin Initiative (CBI) countries who are seeking to form joint or co-ventures. JVFF grants up to 50% of certain costs associated with feasibility studies, market research, technical assistance and travel necessary for venture development.

Contact
Judith Halleran, Project Director
Joint Venture Feasibility Fund
440 Middlesex Road
Darien, CT 06820
(203) 655-8613

Caribbean Project Assistance

The Caribbean Project Development Facility was established under the auspices of the U.N. Development Program with the International Finance Corporation acting as the Executing Agency. Funding and assistance for the Facility's activities in the Caribbean and Central America have been provided by a number of international and governmental developmental agencies.

The Facility will prepare the financial plan and project proposal for use by the sponsor in approaching financial institutions. Other

---

USDA: COOPERATOR PROGRAMS

Thanks to the Department of Agriculture's cooperator programs, Japan has become the largest market for U.S. farm exports. Demonstrations, marketing trips, and educational programs by American farm groups, sponsored by the Agriculture Department's Cooperator programs, have helped build a large poultry program that depends primarily on U.S. technology, feed grains and soybeans.

The Cooperator programs have also helped promote the use of U.S. feed grains and soybeans for Japanese swine as well as dairy and beef cattle. In addition, these programs have opened Japan as a major market for U.S. beef, chicken parts, turkeys, and egg solids as well as for wheat, fruit, and vegetables.

forms of support to the sponsor include completion of feasibility studies and technical assistance. The staff will facilitate linkages with sources of project finance, both debt and equity, from within and beyond the region.

Contact
Paul Hinchey, Manager
The Caribbean Project Development Facility
1818 H Street, NW
Room I-9-123
Washington, DC 20433
(202) 676-9137

Caribbean Agribusiness Grants

The Peace Corps offers feasibility study assistances to local businesses and farmers in determining the viability of small and medium-sized agribusiness projects in the Caribbean. Trained in-country volunteers work with local counterparts and outside experts to provide market, technical, and financial analyses as well as strategy planning for promising agribusiness ventures. The program operates in Antigua, Grenada, Belize, Barbados, Costa Rica, Dominica, Dominican Republic, Guatemala, Anguila, Haiti, Honduras, Jamaica, Montserrat, St. Lucia, St. Kitts-Nevis, and St. Vincent.

Terms
The Peace Corps pays for the cost of volunteers and outside commercial experts.

Eligibility
U.S. companies are eligible for this service if they are working to establish a joint-venture project with a local company or farm group. The project must create local jobs and a host-country agency must request assistance through the Peace Corps country director.

Contact
Richard Chavez
Inter-American Operations
U.S. Peace Corps
806 Connecticut Avenue, NW
Washington, DC 20526
(202) 254-9616

African Feasibility Study

The Private Enterprise Office (AFR/PRE) of the Africa Bureau within the Agency for International Development, provides reimbursable grants for feasibility studies intended to provide the basis for investment and financing decisions. The availability of this financing permits AFR/PRE to encourage investment in selected joint ventures in developing countries that have a high agency priority.

Terms
PRE will provide 50 percent of the total study cost, up to a maximum of $50,000. The project sponsor finances the original cost and is reimbursed after submitting an acceptable completed feasibility study. If the project goes forward, the sponsor must reimburse all AFR/PRE funds.

Eligibility
AFR/PRE will consider only ventures with substantial ownership by a company in the host country. Project sponsors must be host-country firms or citizens. Projects must show potential for substantial developmental impact in the host country by generating net employment; earning net foreign exchange; developing managerial, technical, or other skills; or transferring technologies.

Application Procedure
A feasibility study workplan and a business plan containing a project description, financing requirements, and a technical plan should be submitted to AFR/PRE. A detailed listing of points to be covered in the application is available.

Contact
Harthon Munson, Associate Assistant Administrator
Private Enterprise Office, Africa Bureau
Agency for International Development
New State Building Room 4527-A
Washington, DC 20523
(202) 647-7614

Egyptian Feasibility Study Funding

The Agency for International Development has awarded funding to the government of Egypt to enable U.S. businesses to investigate potential investment opportunities in Egypt.

Terms

For small or medium-sized companies, the funding covers 75 percent of the direct costs (up to a maximum of $200,000) for conducting a feasibility study on a specific joint-venture project to be proposed by the applicant and approved by the Investment Authority prior to the conduct of the survey. For Fortune 1000 companies, funding is limited to 50 percent of the direct costs of the feasibility study.

Small- and medium-sized U.S. companies can apply for Reconnaissance Trip Grants. Once the application is approved prior to the reconnaissance visit, the company can be reimbursed up to a maximum of $6000 for the direct costs involved.

Eligibility

The applicant must be a U.S. company or a majority-owned subsidiary of a U.S. corporation. Applicants must demonstrate their willingness to take a strong equity position if the project moves to the implementation phase. Firms with limited or no experience in Egypt or the Middle East are expected to participate in a reconnaissance visit prior to applying for a feasibility study.

Contact

Ayman Abdelghaffar, Economic and Commercial Counselor
Economic and Commercial Bureau
Embassy of the Arab Republic of Egypt
2232 Massachusetts Avenue, NW
Washington, DC 20008
(202) 265-9111
Telex: 64251 COMRAU WSH

or

Deputy Chairman
General Authority for Investment and Free Zones
8 Adly Street
P.O. Box 1007
Cairo, Arab Republic of Egypt
Telephone: 906796;906804
Telex: 92235 INVEST UN

SPECIAL PROGRAMS FOR SMALL BUSINESS

Management Assistance Programs

The following programs sponsored by the Small Business Administration (SBA) are available to U.S. businesses. In addition, SBA district offices offer free export counseling and co-sponsor export training programs.

The Service Corps of Retired Executives (SCORE) is an organization of retired business executives with many years of practical experience. Members with international trade expertise help small businesses assess their export potential and develop a basic export marketing plan. SCORE volunteers work in each SBA district office and their services are free (see appendix).

The Active Corps of Executives (ACE), which augments SCORE's services, consists of more than 2600 active executives from all major industries, professional and trade associations, educational institutions, and many other professions. ACE members volunteer their expertise whenever needed by a U.S. small business.

The Small Business Institute makes senior and graduate-level students of international business available to small companies to provide overseas marketing information and to develop export marketing feasibility studies. Students from more than 450 U.S. colleges and universities participate in this program.

Small Business Development Centers based at U.S. universities assist new exporters by providing counseling, market information, and training programs in international trade.

Export Workshops and Training Programs are conducted periodically by seasoned exporters and knowledgeable international traders under the co-sponsorship of SBA district offices, the U.S. Department of Commerce, and other agencies and institutions concerned with international trade development. The workshops discuss procedures and techniques involved in exporting, from identifying overseas markets to insuring the receipt of payment for exported goods and services.

The Call Contract Program utilizes professional management and technical consultants who can provide to eligible small and minority businesses marketing and production technology information and assistance. Specialized export assistance may be provided at no cost to an eligible client through this program.

Contact
nearest Small Business Administration district office (see appendix)

SBA: SMALL BUSINESS INSTITUTE PROGRAM

When a Sweet Home, Oregon electronics firm wanted advice on how to enter South American markets, it turned to a Small Business Administration-supported research program at Oregon State University. After Jim McCrary, president of McCrary Electronics, explained his needs, a team of Oregon State business students spent a semester working out a market plan that was financed by the university's Small Business Institute program. Working under a faculty adviser, the graduate and undergraduate team developed information—political and cultural background, trade and economic facts—on three Latin American countries. The plan also set out marketing strategies that McCrary might follow, as well as names of banks, export firms, and freight forwarders to help him execute the plan.

CHAPTER SIX

REGULATIONS AND REQUIREMENTS

Before undertaking an overseas venture, American firms should be aware of foreign country agreements that must first be obtained, host-country regulations regarding certain types of business, tax incentives and requirements, and general regulations affecting trade between the United States and foreign countries. These subjects are reviewed in this chapter, which is organized into four major subgroupings:

Overseas Agreements. How to locate information on investment treaties, trade barriers, and foreign government approvals.

Export-Import Regulations and Restrictions. Programs for assisting U.S. firms with trade disputes and product standards, and information on customs and export restrictions.

Taxation. Information on the taxation of U.S. individuals and companies abroad and on U.S. government incentives for operating overseas.

Host-Country Incentives. Existing investment incentives available in foreign countries for American businesses willing to invest in those countries including import duty exemptions, tax holidays, and training grants.

OVERSEAS AGREEMENTS

Treaties in Force

The State Department annually publishes the *Treaties in Force: A List of Treaties and Other International Agreements of the United States in Force on January 1, 1987*. It includes bilateral and multilateral agreements in effect as of January 1, 1987 and an appendix with a tabulation of documents affecting international copyright relations of the United States.

Cost

$16 per copy. Order no.: S/N 044-000-02183-8.

Contact

Superintendent of Documents
United States Government Printing Office
Washington, DC 20402
(202) 783-3238

The *Treaties and Other International Acts Series* contains the texts of agreements entered into by the United States with other nations.

Cost

Annual subscription $89.00 in U.S.; $111.25 foreign. Single copies are available and vary in price. Order no.: S/N 844-001-00000-2.

Contact

Superintendent of Documents
U.S. Government Printing Office
Washington, DC 20402
(202) 783-3238

Bilateral Investment Agreements

A Bilateral Investment Treaty (BIT) is a reciprocal agreement between the U.S. government and a foreign government, which outlines the treatment of investors in the two countries. For the U.S. investor abroad, such treaties are valuable. These treaties are ratified by the Senate so they create an international obligation for the U.S. and the treaty partner, and thus they supersede domestic law.

The U.S. Government seeks to negotiate BITs that contain the following major elements:

Most-favored-nation or national treatment (with limited exceptions), whichever is better, for the U.S. investor abroad.

Guarantees of prompt, adequate, and effective compensation for expropriation, as well as the right to transfer such compensation at the prevailing exchange rate on the date of expropriation.

The right of investors to make free transfers of currency in connection with the investment at the prevailing exchange rate.

A legal framework for the settlement of disputes between a firm and host country and between governments, based on prevailing standards of international law including the possibility of third-party arbitration.

A treaty of at least ten years' duration.

The Office of the United States Trade Representative can provide copies of BITS, which are pending Senate ratification, and a list of countries that have entered into BIT negotiations with the United States. Information on performance requirements and other investment restrictions in major host countries is also available.

Contact
Donald Eiss, Deputy Assistant
Office of Industry and Services
Office of the U.S. Trade Representative
600 17th Street, NW, Room 422
Washington, DC 20506
(202) 395-5656

Foreign Government Approvals

Before a U.S. overseas investment can receive political risk insurance or a loan guaranty from OPIC, the investor must secure a Foreign Government Approval (FGA) from the host country approving the project for purposes of OPIC coverage. FGAs are required by the bilateral agreements providing for operation of OPIC programs. Under many such agreements, approval is automatic in the case of the foreign government's own projects and projects which have complied with investment registration requirements of local law. The procedure for obtaining an FGA varies from country to country. A project must be registered with OPIC before the investor makes an irrevocable commitment to invest. (See description of OPIC programs in Chapter 8)

Contact

Jackie Crumpler, Central Records Officer
Overseas Private Investment Corporation
1615 M Street, NW
Washington, DC 20527
(202) 457-7059

USTR: NEGOTIATING ENTRY

Negotiating entry for a U.S. firm into a country that restricts foreign investment is a major duty of the Office of the United States Trade Representative (USTR). For example, the USTR recently assisted a Washington, DC high-technology company in investing in a neighboring country. For three years, meetings and negotiations had taken place between the company and the host government, but without success. If the firm's products were to be marketed successfully, an actual presence in the neighboring country was needed. The Trade Representative met with the other country's officials to clarify the nature of the proposed investment and to persuade the neighbor that the investment met its economic objectives. The investment was ultimately approved.

Foreign Business Practices

Foreign Business Practices: Materials on Practical Aspects of Exporting, International Licensing and Investing presents practical information about foreign business operations with the following subjects included: the use of foreign agents and distributors; treaties and laws which protect patents and trademarks in foreign countries; foreign licensing and joint venture arrangements; Foreign Sales Corporations; and antitrust exemptions for United States exporters. The latest publication is 1985.

Cost
$3.50 per copy. Order no.: S/N 003-009-00460-8.

Contact
Superintendent of Documents
U.S. Government Printing Office
Washington, DC 20402
(202) 783-3238

Business Counseling and Advice

The Office of Trade Finance of the Commerce Department provides counseling and advice on U.S. and foreign country laws, regulations, and practices affecting international trade and investment. Staff members offer information and help U.S. firms research laws on taxation; antitrust, patent, and trademark rights; licensing patents; foreign agents, distributors, and joint ventures; product liability; and other issues related to exporting and overseas investment.

Contact
James Walsh
Office of Trade Finance, Foreign Business Practices
U.S. Department of Commerce, Room 4420
Washington, DC 20230
(202) 377-4471

Business Assistance

The Office of Business and Export Affairs is a point of contact in the State Department for U.S. companies requiring assistance with international business.

Contact
Marshall Adair, Special Assistant
Commercial, Legislative, and Public Affairs
U.S. Department of State
Room 6822
Washington, DC 20520
(202) 647-1942

Patents and Trademarks

The U.S. Patent and Trademark Office (PTO) administers the patent and trademark laws of the U.S. After examining patent and trademark applications, PTO grants protection to qualified inventions and Federal registration to qualified trademarks. The U.S. PTO also provides information concerning international patents and trademarks.

Contact

Office of Legislative and International Affairs
U.S. Patent and Trademark Office
Box 4
Washington, DC 20231
(703) 557-3065

Foreign Trade Barriers

Published in October 1987, *The National Trade Estimate Report on Foreign Trade Barriers* examines the most significant barriers of United States trading partners. Each deterrent is examined in depth by country, with additional information on their effects and best counter measures. The information is provided by the Executive Office of the President, Office of the United States Trade Representative, Department of Agriculture, and Department of Commerce.

Cost

$17 per copy. Order no.: S/N 041-001-00326-6.

Contact

Superintendent of Documents
U.S. Government Printing Office
Washington, DC 20402
(202) 783-3238

Within the National Oceanographic and Atmospheric Administration, the National Marine Fisheries Service (NMFS) addresses trade problems affecting U.S. fishery exports. The Office of Trade Services works in coordination with the United States Trade Representative, the International Trade Administration, and the International Trade Commission. These activities support bilateral and multilateral trade negotiations and actions by U.S. industry under United States trade law.

Contact

for information on trade matters:

Office of Trade and Industry Services
National Marine Fisheries Services
1825 Connecticut Avenue, NW
Room 1025
Washington, DC 20235
(202) 673-5492; 673-5502

or the following Fisheries Services Division:

Fisheries Services Division
P.O. Box 1109
Gloucester, MA 01930
(617) 281-3600
Telex: 940007 NMFS GLOS

Fisheries Development Division
Duval Building
9450 Koger Boulevard
St. Petersburg, FL 33702
(813) 893-3394

Fisheries Development Division
300 South Ferry Street
Room 2016
Terminal Island, CA 90731
(213) 548-2478; 548-2597

Fisheries Development Division
P.O. Box 1668
Juneau, AK 99802
(907) 586-7224
Telex: 45377 NMFS AKR JNU

Fisheries Development Division
P.O. Box 1109
7600 San Point Way, NW
BIN C15700
Seattle, WA 98115
(206) 527-6117
Telex: 910-44-2786 NMFS SEA

Lowering Agricultural Trade Barriers

The Foreign Agricultural Service (FAS) identifies and works to reduce foreign trade barriers and practices that discourage the export
of U.S. farm products. Agricultural representatives play a major role
in trying to remove tariff or nontariff barriers affecting market access.
FAS has offices at the headquarters of the European Community in
Brussels and at the international negotiations center in Geneva. FAS
also maintains contact with the Food and Agricultural Organization
of the United Nations in Rome.

A company that has identified a barrier to exporting its products
to a foreign country should contact its Market Development Cooperator group (see Chapter 4, Agricultural Trade Offices). The
Cooperator and the Department of Agriculture will work together to
have the barrier removed. A company that believes it has been treated
unfairly by a foreign government in a trade issue, such as losing a
tender to a higher bidder, should also contact the Cooperator. Ex-

porters without Cooperator representation can contact the Agency directly.

Contact

Charles J. O'Mara
Foreign Agricultural Service
U.S. Department of Agriculture
Room 5057-S
Washington, DC 20250
(202) 447-6887

AGRITRADE INTERNATIONAL

When Agritrade International (ATI) of Portland, Oregon faced restrictions on the import of U.S. potatoes into Korea, ATI's president, Donald Hutchinson, contacted the Department of Agriculture's trade office in Seoul. Through the trade office, the firm made contact with Korean government agricultural officials. Today, the Portland company exports frozen baked potatoes to Korea. As the first potato exporter to Korea, the ATI company has opened the door to a new market for the United States.

EXPORT-IMPORT REGULATIONS AND RESTRICTIONS

Trade Agreements

The International Trade Commission's annual report, the *Operation of Trade Agreements Program*, includes information on the General Agreement on Tariffs and Trade (GATT), the Export-Import Bank, U.S. actions on imports, revisions of trade laws, and other information.

Cost
Free.

Contact
Office of Publications
International Trade Commission
500 E Street, SW
Washington, DC 20436
(202) 252-1807

Trade Dispute Assistance

The Department of Commerce assists in settling trade disputes between U.S. and foreign traders. Assistance is limited to informal, conciliatory efforts directed toward resolving misunderstandings between the two parties.

Only disputes related to a commercial transaction should be directed to the Commerce Department. The following types of cases should *not* be referred for investigation: disputes involving less than $500; collection cases; and disputes that the complainant has made no effort to settle.

Contact
nearest Commerce Department district office (see appendix)

Customs Requirements

Goods imported to the United States must be cleared by the U.S. Customs Service. The Service, with headquarters in Washington, has seven geographical regions that are further divided into districts with ports of entry. The Service is also responsible for administering the customs laws of the U.S. Virgin Islands and Puerto Rico.

121

The following free publications provide information on customs requirements for imports:

U.S. Import Requirements: General information on U.S. Customs requirements for imported merchandise.

Customs Rulings on Imports: How to obtain a binding U.S. Customs duty ruling on items before they are imported.

Importing into the United States: Customs and other requirements for importing merchandise into the United States.

Import Quota: Summary of import quotas administered by the Customs Service.

Notice to Masters of Vessels: Precautions that masters or owners of vessels should take to avoid penalties and forfeitures.

Notice to Carriers of Bonded Merchandise: Precautions that carriers and customhouse brokers should take to safeguard merchandise moving in-bond.

Drawback: How to obtain a duty refund on certain exports.

Foreign Trade Zones: Advantages, use, and customs requirements of foreign trade zones.

807 Guide: Details use of Item 807.00 in the U.S. Tariff Schedule, which permits a reduction in duty to reflect the value of components manufactured in the United States and assembled abroad.

Contact
appropriate U.S. Customs Service office:

Headquarters

Free Publications:	*For Business Matters:*
U.S. Customs Service	U.S. Customs Service
P.O. Box 7407	1301 Constitution Avenue, NW
Washington, DC 20044	P.O. Box 7407
(202) 566-8408	Washington, DC 20229
	(202) 566-8195

New York Region
6 World Trade Center
New York, NY 10048
(212) 466-4444

Northeast Region
#10 Causeway Street
Boston, MA 02222-1059
(617) 565-6210

North Central Region
55 East Monroe Street
Chicago, IL 60603-5790
(312) 353-6250

South Central Region
423 Canal Street
New Orleans, LA 70130
(504) 589-6324

Pacific Region
300 North Los Angeles Street
Los Angeles, CA 90053
(213) 894-5901

Southwest Region
5850 San Felipe Street
Houston, TX 77057
(713) 953-6843

Southeast Region
99 Southeast 5th Street
Miami, FL 33131
(305) 536-5952

The following publications are for sale:

Tariff Schedules of the United States Annotated: For use in classification of imported merchandise, for rates of duty, and for statistical purposes.

Cost
$56 in U.S.; $70 foreign. Order no.: S/N 949-005-00000-3.

Customs Regulations of the U.S.: Looseleaf volume of regulations interpreting many of the customs, navigation, and other laws administered by the U.S. Customs Service.

Cost
$36 in U.S.; $45 foreign. Order no.: S/N 948-006-00000-6.

Customs Bulletin: Weekly pamphlet containing proposed and final amendments to Customs Regulations, notices and administrative decisions of interest to the international trading community, and pertinent decisions of the U.S. Court of International Trade and the U.S. Court of Appeals for the Federal Circuit.

Cost
$62 in U.S.; $77.50 foreign. Single copy $1.50 in U.S.; $1.88 foreign.
Order no.: S/N 748-002-00000-6.

Contact
Superintendent of Documents
U.S. Government Printing Office
Washington, DC 20402
(202) 783-3238

International Mail Manual

The *International Mail Manual* provides information on correct international postal rates, prohibitions, restrictions, availability of insurance and other special services, as well as information on mailing to individual countries. Subscription service consists of three complete cumulative manuals per year.

Cost
$14 for annual subscription. Order no.: S/N 839-002-00000-9.

Metric Requirements

Metric Laws and Practices in International Trade: A Handbook for Exporters provides basic information to American exporters on foreign laws and regulations pertaining to metric requirements for imported products. The handbook, compiled by the Commerce Department, includes information on laws of 55 countries.

Cost
$4.75 in U.S.; $5.95 foreign. Order no.: S/N 003-009-00353-9.

Contact
Superintendent of Documents
U.S. Government Printing Office
Washington, DC 20402
(202) 783-3238

For other information, referrals and research reports on the role of metric in international trade:

Contact
G.T. Underwood, Director
Office of Metric Programs
U.S. Department of Commerce
Room 4816H, Hoover Building
Washington, DC 20230
(202) 377-0944

Binding Rates of Duty

U.S. companies may obtain from the U.S. Customs Service a decision on the tariff classification and rate of duty of specific merchandise before it is shipped to the United States. To obtain a decision, the following information must be provided:

1. Complete description of the goods, including samples, sketches, diagrams, and other illustrative material if the goods cannot be described adequately in writing.
2. Method of manufacture or fabrication.
3. Specifications and analyses.
4. Quantities and costs of the component materials.
5. Commercial designation and chief use in the United States.

Contact
Area Director of Customs
New York Seaport
6 World Trade Center, Room 423
New York, NY 10048
(212) 466-5817

or the U.S. Customs Service regional offices (listed previously in this chapter)

Export-Import and Sales Restrictions

Any venture involving coffee, tea, cocoa, sugar, jute, cotton, bananas, or hard fibers could be affected by restrictions in international commodities agreements. The Office of Food Policy provides information on these restrictions. At this time, the only commodities with food policy restrictions are cocoa and coffee.

Contact
Dave Stebbing, Chief, Food Policy Division
Office of Food Policy
Bureau of Economic and Business Affairs
U.S. Department of State
Room 3526
Washington, DC 20520
(202) 647-3036

Regulations Affecting Sensitive Exports

The Bureau of Export Administration of the Department of Commerce helps firms to meet the requirements of the Export Administration Act. The Act lists the licensing requirements for sensitive, high-technology equipment and data. For each listed commodity, it identifies the countries for which export license documents are required. The Export Administration Regulations are published in the *Federal Register* (codified in the *Code of Federal Regulations*: 15 CFR Parts 368-399). The following publications are available free of charge:

Exports by Mail
Denial Orders Currently Affecting Export Privileges
The Distribution License—A guide for Exporters
The Export License—How to fill out the ITA form 622P
The Export License and the ATA Carnet
Export License Checklist
Country Groups Color-Coded Map

Contact
Export Seminar Staff
Office of the Under Secretary
U.S. Department of Commerce
Room 1608
P.O. Box 273
Washington, DC 20044
(202) 377-8731

The Bureau of Export Administration offers a three-day comprehensive course on Export Administration Regulations each month. In offering both introductory and advanced information, the course is designed to teach exporters how to use and interpret U.S. administration regulations, including information on the use of commodity control lists, and how to complete export license applications. More detailed information is also provided on exports of strategic goods and technical data, distribution licensing and internal control programs, COCOM and country policies, anti-boycott complaints, export enforcement, etc.

Cost
$375.

Contact
Export Seminar Staff
Export Administration
U.S. Department of Commerce
Room 1608
P.O. Box 273
Washington, DC 20044
(202) 377-8731

The following publications are for sale:

The Export Administration Regulations 1987: A comprehensive list of the rules controlling exports of U.S. products and requirements for export licensing. An annual subscription includes Export Administration Bulletins, which explain recent policy changes and include updated regulations.

Cost
$77 in U.S.; $96.25 foreign. Order no.: S/N 903-012-00000-5.

Contact
Superintendent of Documents
U.S. Government Printing Office
Washington, DC 20402
(202) 783-3238

Exports Licenses Approved and Re-exports Authorized: A list of all licenses by general commodity description, dollar value, and country of destination. Issued daily.

Cost
Annual subscription $37.50

Contact
Processing Branch
U.S. Export Administration
P.O. Box 273
U.S. Department of Commerce
Room 2099
Washington, DC 20230
(202) 377-3000

Tracking Export License Applications

The Commerce Department's System for Tracking Export License Applications (STELA) enables the exporter to access the Export Control Automated Support System (ECASS) database using a push-button phone. The STELA system will respond with the current application status.

Cost
Free.

Contact
Director
ITA/Automated Information Staff
Room 3898
U.S. Department of Commerce
Washington, DC 20230
(202) 377-2752 push-button telephone
(202) 377-2753 exporter assistance staff

Standards and Certification Information

The National Center for Standards and Certification Information (NCSCI) serves as the central depository and inquiry point for standards and standards-related information in the United States. NCSCI responds to over 5,000 individual inquiries annually on identification and source availability of standards. NCSCI also prepares and issues indexes and directories for specialized standards information.

Contact
National Bureau of Standards
National Center for Standards and Certification
    Information
Room A-629 Administration Building
Gaithersburg, MD 20899
(301) 975-4040

Standards Hotline

The Inquiry Point at the National Bureau of Standards maintains a General Agreement on Tariff and Trade Hotline to provide current information on notifications of proposed foreign regulations.

The message includes product, country, closing date for comments, and Technical Barriers to Trade (TBT)/Notification number for each notification and the contact for additional information.

Contact:
Hotline
(301) 975-4041

Agricultural Product Standards

The Department of Agriculture's Foreign Agriculture Service (FAS) identifies, collects, and analyzes foreign proposals concerning agricultural product standards. Notifications of proposed foreign standards are published in Export Briefs, a weekly newsletter.

Cost
$75 per year.

Contact:
Philip Letarte
AIMS Coordinator
Foreign Agricultural Service
U.S. Department of Agriculture
Room 4649-S
Washington, DC 20250-1000
(202) 447-7103

FAS also solicits comments on proposed foreign standards from individuals and companies, U.S. government agencies, state departments of agriculture, exporter associations, and farm organizations. These comments are relayed to foreign countries.

Contact
Dr. Stanford N. Fertig, Director
Technical Office
U.S. Department of Agriculture
Building 1070 BARC-East
Beltsville, MD 20705
(301) 344-2651 or (301) 344-2846

USDA: GOING TO BAT FOR U.S. GROWERS

The Department of Agriculture makes a firm promise to farm product exporters: If your product meets U.S. health and safety standards, the Department will go to bat for you, should you meet trouble in a foreign market.

For instance, consider the case of Pioneer Overseas Corporation of Johnston, Iowa. Due to an oversight, four containers of a total shipment of 48 containers of hybrid corn seed bound for Greece were released without inspection or cleaning by customs officials in Houston, Texas. All were loaded aboard a vessel en route to Europe when the USDA alerted Pioneer of the threat of Khapra beetle infestation in the four containers. The USDA has the responsibility to notify any foreign country of prohibited pests that may be in products shipped from the United States. However, instead of immediately cabling the Greek authorities and running the risk of a misunderstanding on the severity of the possible contamination, Dr. Al Chock, USDA Animal and Plant Health Inspection Service Regional Director for Greece, flew to Athens. With Dr. Chock's assistance, only the four containers were detained for inspection and finally released with a clean bill of health.

Inspection Services

Seafood Export Inspection Services

The National Marine Fisheries Service conducts inspection and analyses of fishery commodities for export, and issues official U.S. Government certificates attesting to the findings. The U.S. Department of Commerce can provide bilingual certificates for shipments to France and trilingual certificates for shipments to Belgium.

The NMFS inspection and certification and/or analytical services are available on a fee-for-service basis for the following:

Origin and species of fish.
Sanitary condition of processing facilities.

Product inspection for wholesomeness, safety, and suitability for human consumption.
Chemical, biological, and physical tests for adulterants, contaminants, and microconstituents.
Quantity of contents-net and drained weight.
Appropriateness of labeling and packaging integrity.
Other (as requested by applicant, including factors related to quality and condition).

Contact
for assistance with product standards and fishery product inspection services:

National Marine Fisheries Service
1825 Connecticut Avenue, NW
Room 1027
Washington, DC 20235
(202) 673-5875

or the following Inspection Offices:

Northeast Inspection Office
P.O. Box 1188
Emerson Avenue
Gloucester, MA 01930
(617) 281-3600

Southeast Inspection Office
Duval Building
9450 Koger Boulevard
St. Petersburg, FL 33702
(813) 893-3155

Western Inspection Office
5600 Rickenbacker Road
Building No. 7
Bell, CA 90201
(213) 267-6734

Agricultural Products Inspection Services

The Department of Agriculture provides inspecting, certifying, weighing, and grading services for agricultural, meat, and poultry products. These services help assure U.S. exporters that exports comply with the requirements of the importing country.

If a food quality standard imposed by a foreign importing country appears to be an unnecessary barrier to international trade, the Standards Code encourages the countries involved to resolve the problem informally. The Foreign Agricultural Service's agricultural counselors and attachés stationed in U.S. embassies overseas can be of help in settling these disputes (see appendix).

In addition, USDA's Food Safety and Inspection Service inspects meat and poultry products intended for export to assure that the product is sound, properly labeled, U.S.-inspected and passed, and meets all special requirements of the intended importing country at the time of export certification. To protect U.S. consumers, the Service is responsible for the following:

Evaluation of laws and regulations governing the meat inspection systems in foreign countries that export meat and meat products to the United States, to assure that they are comparable with U.S. requirements.

On-site reviews of certified foreign systems and plants preparing meat and meat products for export to the United States.

Inspection of an imported product at the time it is offered for entry at U.S. ports.

Routine inspection of both imported and exported products is provided free of charge through the Service's Meat and Poultry Inspection Operations. However, exporters are liable for any reimbursable charges incurred for certifying standards other than those required by USDA.

Contact

Inquiries regarding routine inspection service should be directed to the appropriate Agricultural Department regional office:

North Central Region

Dr. Jerry Booth, Deputy Director
607 East 2nd Street
Des Moines, IA 50309
(515) 284-6300

Northeastern Region

Dr. C.E. Harmon, Director
1421 Cherry Street, 7th Floor
Philadelphia, PA 19102
(215) 597-4217

Southeastern Region

Dr. J.D. Willis, Director
1718 Peachtree Street, NW Room 299S
Atlanta, GA 30309
(404) 347-3911

Southwestern Region

Dr. M.A. Waguespack, Director
1100 Commerce Street
Room 5-F41
Dallas, TX 75242
(214) 767-9116

Western Region
Dr. James Harbottle, Director
620 Central Avenue
Building 2C, Room 102
Alameda, CA 9450l
(415) 273-7402

Meat and Poultry Export Information
Dr. Robert Fetzner, Director
Export Coordination Division/I.P.
U.S. Department of Agriculture/FSIS
14th and Independence Avenue, SW
Room 0036S
Washington, DC 20250
(202) 447-9051

Meat and Poultry Import Information
Patricia Stolfa, Deputy Administrator
International Programs
U.S. Department of Agriculture/FSIS
14th and Independence Avenue, SW
Room 341-E
Washington, DC 20250
(202) 447-3473

Live Animal and Plant Product Health Inspection

The Animal and Plant Health Inspection Service inspects and certifies that animals, plants, and agricultural products conform with health and sanitation requirements for import or export as prescribed by the United States and the country of destination. There is no charge for this service during working hours.

Contact
For information regarding inspection of live animals and poultry for export and import:

Import-Export, Operations Staff
U.S. Department of Agriculture/HIS/VS
6505 Belcrest Road
Room 764
Hyattsville, MD 20782
(301) 436-8383

For information regarding inspection of live plants for export and import:

Plant, Protection and Quarantine
Animal and Plant Health Inspection Service
U.S. Department of Agriculture
6505 Belcrest Road
Hyattsville, MD 20782
(301) 436-8537 (for exports)
(301) 436-8645 (for imports)

Export Grain Inspection

U.S. Grain for export must be officially inspected and weighed, except for land shipments to Canada and Mexico. The Federal Grain Inspection Service (FGIS), or one of the eight qualified delegated states, performs these inspection and weighing services. Fees for these services vary.

Cost

For services performed under a contract:

$29.20 per hour, Monday-Saturday
$39.80 per hour, Sunday and Holidays

For services performed without a contract:

$38.80 per hour, Monday-Saturday
$52.80 per hour, Sunday and Holidays

USDA: PROTECTING MARKETS

Inclement weather in the southeastern United States adversely affected the quality and appearance of much of the 1985 soybean crop. Soybean merchandising problems developed in 1986 resulting in an unusually large number of foreign complaints. The Federal Grain Inspection Service (FGIS) met with foreign buyers and conducted a series of collaborative studies to exchange samples and interpretive lines for damage in soybeans. As a result, the FGIS interpretive line for damage in soybeans was tightened which greatly increased buyer satisfaction and significantly reduced the number of foreign complaints on soybeans.

In addition to inspecting grain, the Service conducts other tests, such as testing protein content in wheat and aflatoxin levels in corn. It also tests processed grain products such as flour and cornmeal, and inspects certain related commodities such as rice, dry beans, peas, and lentils. The fees for these services vary.

Contact

To determine the appropriate person to contact in your area for the weighing and inspection of grain, processed grain products, and related commodities:

John Marshall, Director
Field Management Division
Federal Grain Inspection Service
U.S. Department of Agriculture
Room 1641-S
Washington, DC 20250
(202) 382-0228

This service also maintains an international monitoring staff to handle foreign buyer complaints about U.S. grain. Exporter complaints are ordinarily filed with the agricultural representative in the U.S. embassy of the foreign country (see appendix).

Cost
Free.

Contact

International Monitoring Staff
Federal Grain Inspection Service
United States Department of Agriculture
Room 1627-S
P.O. Box 96454
Washington, DC 20090-6454
(202) 382-0226

Registration is required of each firm that annually buys, handles, weighs, or transports 15,000 or more, metric tons of grain for sale in foreign commerce.

Cost
Annual registration $135 for firms engaged in exporting grain; $270 for firms engaged in exporting grain and that own 10% or more of another firm that is engaged in interstate commerce.

Contact
Joanne Peterson, Assistant to Director
Compliance Division
Federal Grain Inspection Service
U.S. Department of Agriculture
P.O. Box 96454
Washington, DC 20090-6454
(202) 447-8262

Agricultural Grading and Standardization Services

The Agriculture Department's Agricultural Marketing Service develops grade standards and carries out grading services for meat, cattle, swine, wool, poultry, eggs, dairy products, fruits, vegetables, cotton and tobacco. Upon request, the Service will evaluate samples of seed for export shipment. Standards for exported cotton are covered by the U.S. Cotton Standards Act.

The Service also provides food quality certification to foreign buyers to assure that any product shipped overseas meets contract specifications. Buyers must submit the specification or contract in advance. The Service reviews the contract and works with the buyers to write a contract or specification that can be certified. Requirements for Department of Agriculture certification can be made a part of the purchase agreement.

Cost
Varies based on usage.

Contact
for grading standards and services:

Product	Contact	Telephone
Cotton	Fred S. Mullins	(202) 447-2145
Tobacco	William O. Coats	(202) 447-7236
Dairy	Richard W. Webber	(202) 447-3171
Fruits and Vegetables		
—fresh	Carl E. Torline	(202) 447-5870
—processed		
products	Joe A. Fly	(202) 447-4693
Livestock		
—seed branch	James Triplett	(202) 447-9340

—meat grading and certification	Eugene M. Martin	(202) 382-1113
Poultry —standardization	D. Michael Holbrook	(202) 447-3506
—grading	Larry W. Robinson	(202) 447-3271
Wool	Keith Padgett	(303) 353-9750

Technical Assistance on Transportation of Agricultural Commodities

The Office of Transportation (OT) is the center within the Department of Agriculture for all domestic and international transportation matters. OT develops transportation policies and programs and represents the interests of agriculture and rural communities with other government agencies. In addition, the Office supplies technical assistance and information, identifies barriers, and estimates adverse effects on transport systems in agriculture. It also offers economic assistance and technical research and development.

Contact
James Snitzler, Director
International Division
Office of Transportation/TSD
U.S. Department of Agriculture
Auditors Building, Room 1405
Washington, DC 20250
(202) 653-6275

The Export Services Branch (ESB) provides technical services, information, and research on transportation and packaging problems encountered by exporters and shippers of agricultural products.

Contact
B. Hunt Ashby, Export Services Branch Chief
Office of Transportation-ID-ESB
U.S. Department of Agriculture
Auditors Building, Room 1405
Washington, DC 20250
(202) 653-6317

In addition, a European Marketing Research Center in Rotterdam, the Netherlands, provides technical assistance to U.S. exporters, including help with lost and damaged exports shipped to the European market. The Center also provides information on foreign requirements for packaging and labeling and spoilage tolerances.

Contact
Gordon K. Rasmussen, Director
European Marketing Research Center
USDA/Agricultural Research Service
c/o American Embassy
APO New York 09159
Phone: 011-31-10-476-5233

Contract Procedures in the Near East and North Africa

An Introduction to Contract Procedures in the Near East and North Africa is published for business representatives who are involved in major projects and equipment sales in the Near East and North Africa. It describes contract conditions, regulations, and procedures in each of the countries and gives tips on bargaining and negotiating contracts. Each country is covered separately. Of special interest are the introduction, containing an overview of the region, and the chapter on Islamic law and its commercial use.

Cost
$2.50 in U.S.; $3.15 foreign. Order no.: S/N 003-009-00336-9.

Contact
Superintendent of Documents
U.S. Government Printing Office
Washington, DC 20402
(202) 783-3238

TAXATION

Taxation and U.S. Corporations Operating Overseas

U.S. corporations are taxed on worldwide income. To assist international taxpayers, the Department of the Treasury's Internal Revenue Service (IRS) provides six publications:

No. 54,   *Tax Guide for U.S. Citizens and Resident Aliens Abroad*

No. 514,   *Foreign Tax Credits for U.S. Citizens and Resident Aliens*

No. 570,   *Tax Guide for U.S. Citizens Employed in U.S. Possessions*

No. 593,   *Income Tax Benefits for U.S. Citizens Who Go Overseas*

No. 686,   *Certification for Reduced Rates in Tax Treaty Countries*

No. 901,   *U.S. Tax Treaties*

Your state's IRS Forms Distribution Center can provide these publications.

The IRS provides service to U.S. citizens through Revenue Service representatives attached to U.S. embassies and consulates in Bonn, Caracas, Riyadh, London, Manila, Mexico City, Nassau, Ottawa, Paris, Rome, Sao Paulo, Singapore, Sydney, and Tokyo. The IRS also maintains offices in San Juan, Guam, and the Virgin Islands.

If your firm's accounting is done internally, you may want to purchase tax references developed by major publishers. Internal accountants should be fully aware of the regulations passed by the Financial Accounting Standards Board (FASB). Accountants with international interests should review FASB 52, a publication that describes the legally binding regulations affecting financial reporting of most companies operating abroad.

Cost
$5.50 per copy.

Contact
Financial Accounting Standards Board
Order Department
P.O. Box 3821
Stanford, CT 06150
Main Office: (203) 329-8401
Order Department (203) 356-1990

Taxation of U.S. Citizens Abroad

U.S. citizens and resident aliens who work or live abroad or receive certain types of foreign income or income from U.S. possessions fall under special categories for tax purposes and are granted special exclusions or deductions under certain circumstances. It is recommended that individuals consult a tax attorney or accountant to determine whether modifications to the rules have been enacted and their effect, if any, on taxes. See the publications previously listed.

Contact
For more information on taxes and exclusions, write or call your state's IRS Forms Distribution Center. Individuals in residence.abroad should contact:

Percy Woodard, Jr.
Assistant Commissioner—International
Internal Revenue Service
950 L'Enfant Plaza South, SW
Washington, DC 20024
(202) 447-1000

Operating Abroad: U.S. Income Tax Incentives

Major U.S. accounting firms offer comprehensive tax information for U.S. corporations, small businesses, and individuals engaged in international commercial transactions. They can provide detailed information on taxation of foreign operations, controlled foreign corporations, sale or liquidation of controlled foreign corporations, foreign tax credits, tax treaties, and special U.S. trade incentives, as well as tax incentives offered by host countries. The following summary was provided by the international accounting and consulting firm of Deloitte Haskins & Sells. All case studies in this section are hypothetical. This is a basic introduction to some of the more important tax aspects of foreign trade and investment. Because the tax subjects are complex, you are well advised to consult a knowledge-able tax advisor.

Tax Favored Export Entities

U.S. law allows for the establishment of certain entities which receive special tax benefits from the income earned through the export of qualifying goods and services. These are the FSC (Foreign Sales Cor-poration) and the Interest-Charge DISC (Domestic International Sales Corporation). The qualification requirements and associated benefits of the export incentives are as follows:

Foreign Sales Corporation. To qualify as an FSC, the corporation must be incorporated in a foreign country. It must maintain a "per-manent establishment" outside the United States, and have at least one director who also resides outside the United States. Additionally, the FSC must meet specified foreign management requirements, and perform certain economic processes outside the United States. If the corporation meets these and other technical requirements, up to 15/23 of its income (16/23 for non-corporate shareholders) may be exempt from U.S. tax, while the remainder will be taxed currently. The FSC rules also provide special pricing and income allocation techniques that help exporters get the maximum tax benefit from the use of this export vehicle.

Small FSC. Small exporters may elect to treat their FSCs as "small FSCs". The amount of export receipts receiving tax favored treatment is limited to $5 million for this class of FSC. In return, the admin-istrative and operating costs are reduced, as the "small FSC" is ex-empt from the offshore management and economic process requirements of "large FSCs" noted above.

Interest-Charge DISC. Rather than forming an FSC, exporters may establish an "interest-charge" DISC. In contrast to the FSC, this is a domestic entity. To qualify, a domestic corporation must derive at least 95% of its gross receipts from exporting activities and 95% of its assets must be export related. If the corporation meets these and other requirements, the DISC provisions of the tax code will allow the deferral (versus the FSC's exemption) of U.S. income taxes on up to 16/17 of export profits derived from a maximum of $10 million of gross receipts annually. Unlike the FSC, the "interest-charge"

DISC is not subject to U.S. tax. Its shareholders however, are taxed currently on: the 1/17 of export profits not eligible for deferral (whether distributed or not); any dividends the DISC actually remits from export profits previously deferred from U.S. income tax; and any profits derived from gross receipts in excess of the $10 million limit. In addition, the shareholders must also pay an interest charge on the deferred tax of the DISC. As with the FSC, the DISC rules also provide special pricing and income allocation techniques to maximize available tax benefits.

EXPORTCO

Exportco is an exporter, with taxable income qualifying for tax benefits in 1988 of $100,000

	Exportco FSC	Exportco IC-DISC
Qualifying Net Income	100,000	100,000
FSC Exempt Amount (15/23)	(65,217)	
IC-DISC Deferral (16/17)	—	(94,118)
Current Year Taxable Income	34,783	5,882
Tax Incurred by FSC (34%)	11,826	
Tax Incurred by IC-DISC Shareholder (34%)		2,000*

*Does not consider interest charge.

(Based on Corporate Limits and Tax Rates)

Licensing Technology to a Foreign User

If a U.S. business decides not to operate abroad but to make its technology available to a foreign user, royalties or other fees received for the use of the technology may be subject to withholding by the foreign country on the gross amount of the fee. Generally, when such a withholding is made, it is creditable against the U.S. income tax payable upon the fee. An income tax treaty between the U.S. and the foreign country may reduce or eliminate this withholding.

For some U.S. businesses that have neither the desire nor the capacity to set up operations overseas, licensing technology may provide a useful alternative. However, it may be best from a business standpoint to actually establish operations abroad. In that case, significantly different tax considerations come into play (See transfers of property to a foreign corporation).

FORCO

Assume that FORCO, a foreign corporation, pays a $100 fee in 1988 for the use of USCO's patents or technology. FORCO must withhold $20, which is the foreign income tax imposed on such fees. FORCO pays the $20 to the foreign tax authorities and $80 to USCO. USCO increases the net it receives by the $20 withheld and reports a fee of $100 on its U.S. tax return. The U.S. tax of $34 on this $100 fee is reduced to $14 because a credit is allowed for the $20 foreign tax withheld.

Operating within a Foreign Country

If a U.S. corporation or individual establishes a foreign corporation to carry on activities abroad, its income generally is not subject to U.S. tax until the corporation pays a dividend to the U.S. shareholder. Therefore, U.S. tax on such foreign income may be deferred, although the foreign corporation is wholly owned by a U.S. corporation or individual.

When a dividend is paid, the United States will allow a credit for withholding tax imposed by the foreign country on the dividend. In the case of a U.S. corporate shareholder owning at least 10 percent of the foreign corporation, a credit is also allowed for all or a portion of any foreign corporate income tax imposed on the foreign corporation.

USCO

Assume USCO establishes a wholly owned foreign subsidiary, FORCO, on January 1, 1988. In 1988, FORCO has operational income of $100 and pays income tax of $30. FORCO pays the remaining $70 as a dividend to USCO. However, the foreign country imposes a withholding tax of $4, therefore, only $66 reaches USCO. In addition to the withholding tax, if USCO elects to claim a credit for foreign tax, it is deemed to have paid $30 of the foreign taxes paid by FORCO. The dividends actually received must be increased by the amount of deemed-paid and withheld foreign taxes. Therefore, USCO reports a gross dividend of $100. The foreign taxes of $34 may be credited against the U.S. tax which USCO would otherwise pay on the dividend.

Operating Abroad through a branch of a U.S. Corporation or a Partnership or Joint Venture

A U.S. Corporation that has foreign source income through the operation of a branch incurs U.S. corporate taxes on that income as it is earned. If there are foreign losses, those amounts may be used to reduce its U.S. taxable income. If foreign income taxes are paid on the foreign source income, the foreign taxes may be credited against its U.S. taxes (subject to certain limitations if foreign losses have been used to offset U.S. income). U.S. partners or joint ventures, must include a share of foreign source income in their U.S. tax returns. U.S. tax is payable on this income, but a credit is allowed for a share of foreign income taxes incurred.

"S Corporations"

Certain provisions of the Internal Revenue Code allow a U.S. corporation that is owned by a small group of U.S. shareholders to elect to pay no U.S. corporate taxes. Instead, each shareholder is taxed on a share of the corporation's income as it is earned and may deduct a share of any losses. Since the corporation is not taxed, the usual double tax burden of operating in the corporate form (i.e., the corporation taxed and the shareholders taxed when dividends are re-mitted to them) is avoided. Foreign corporate income taxes paid by such a corporation that operates abroad are allowed as credits on the shareholders' U.S. individual tax returns.

Possessions Corporations

Some U.S. possessions, like Puerto Rico, may provide tax incentives for a U.S. corporation that organizes a business there including various tax holidays. If the U.S. corporation also elects to be taxed as a possessions corporation and complies with certain other requirements, the corporation will receive a special tax credit against its U.S. corporate income tax. The credit will equal the U.S. income tax that would have been levied on profits earned by that corporation in the possession. Thus, the corporation may pay no U.S. income tax on those profits. Also, if more than 80 percent of that corporation is owned by a U.S. parent company, any dividends received by that parent company from the possessions corporation will be exempt from U.S. income tax. A U.S. corporation can elect to be taxed as a possessions corporation if at least 80 percent of its gross income is from sources in a possession and 75 percent of that gross income is from the active conduct of business in the possession.

Exemption from Gross Income for Employees Based Abroad

Self-employed U.S. individuals or U.S. employees residing in a foreign country can exempt from U.S. income tax up to $70,000 of foreign earned income (income from the performance of personal services in the foreign country) after 1986. To qualify for this exemption, the employee or self-employed individual must be resident abroad for an entire tax year or be physically present abroad for at least 330 days during a 12-month period. An employee may also be exempt from U.S. income tax on amounts received from his or her employer to cover certain excess housing costs incurred in the foreign country.

Many employers take advantage of these exemptions by reducing the compensation of their overseas employees by an amount equal to the U.S. income tax that the employees would have paid had they remained in the United States.

Foreign Tax Credit Limitation

All U.S. taxpayers are permitted to credit against their U.S. income tax liability foreign income taxes paid or accrued during the taxable year on foreign-source income. In most instances, U.S. corporate

TAXES: TIM JONES

To illustrate the exemption from gross income for U.S. employees based abroad, assume that for all of 1988 Tim Jones is employed abroad by USCO and is in the 28 percent tax bracket. His salary of $50,000 is entirely excluded from his U.S. income tax return for 1988 because Jones meets either the "residence abroad" or "presence abroad" test. Jones is required to pay $5,000 of income taxes to the foreign country in which he resides. Pursuant to USCO's policy, USCO reduces Jones' wages by an amount equal to the U.S. income tax that Jones would have paid on wages if he had been based in the United States, but it reimburses Jones for the $5,000 of foreign income tax he pays to the foreign country.

taxpayers that receive dividends from a foreign subsidiary in which they own at least 10 percent of the voting stock are allowed to credit the corporate income taxes paid by that subsidiary on the earnings distributed. However, there are limitations on the credit designed to ensure that the foreign tax credit claimed will not exceed the U.S. income tax payable by the U.S. taxpayers on the foreign source income. To the extent the limitation prevents a U.S. taxpayer from crediting all of the foreign income tax paid or accrued, double taxation (U.S. plus foreign) or excessive taxation of the same income may result. Because of a variety of factors, including differences in U.S. and foreign concepts of income, it is not unusual for the amount of creditable foreign tax to be limited in a taxable year. A 2-year carryback and 5-year carryforward period is permitted for those credits so limited, subject to certain requirements.

Transfers of Property to a Foreign Corporation

When a U.S business organizes a foreign corporation to do business abroad, it often transfers to that foreign corporation tangible property that has appreciated in value (such as equipment or foreign currency), or intangible property that will give rise to future income (such as patents or technical know-how, customer lists, etc.), necessary to the conduct of that business. Any such transfer must be reported to the IRS. The gain realized on a transfer to a subsidiary company would ordinarily not be taxed by the U.S. at the time of transfer. However, since the foreign corporation's income may not be currently subject to U.S. income tax, it would be possible for that corporation to subsequently sell or use that property and avoid any U.S. income tax. To prevent such avoidance, when applied to transfers of property to a foreign corporation, the general rule is that the amount of gain or income to be earned will be recognized and subject to tax. Certain exceptions to this rule exist, including nonrecognition of gain if tangible assets transferred will be used in the active conduct of a trade or business outside the U.S.

Passive Foreign Investment Company (PFIC)

A PFIC is any foreign corporation if, for any taxable year, 75% or more of its gross income consists of passive income, or if at least 50% of the average value of its assets produce (or are held to produce) passive income. Ownership percentage by U.S. persons is not a determinant of PFIC status. A PFIC can elect to be treated as a Qualified Electing Fund (QEF) or a Non-Qualified Electing Fund (NonQEF). A U.S. shareholder in a PFIC electing QEF status must currently include in income his pro rata share of the QEF's net capital gain and other earnings and profits (subject to the taxpayer's election to defer payment of tax and incur an interest charge). A U.S. shareholder in a PFIC which does not elect QEF status must pay tax and an interest charge on the deferred portion of any gain on disposition of PFIC stock and on certain distributions from the PFIC.

The Closely Held Foreign Corporation—Passive Income

As discussed previously, if a U.S. individual organizes a foreign corporation to conduct activities abroad, the income earned by that corporation will normally not be subject to U.S. income tax until the U.S. corporation pays dividends to that individual. However, if more than 50% of the corporation's gross income is passive income, e.g., interest, dividends, etc., and more than 50% in value or voting power of the corporation's stock is owned by or for 5 or fewer U.S. citizens or residents, the corporation will be a "Foreign Personal Holding Company". As such, the corporation's net income will be taxed directly to its U.S. shareholders although not actually distributed to those shareholders as dividends.

Controlled Foreign Corporations

Because the income of a foreign corporation is generally not taxed by the United States until distributed as dividends to its U.S. shareholders, some taxpayers sought to shift income currently taxable by the U.S. to a foreign subsidiary to defer U.S. income tax. The Internal Revenue Code attempts to prevent this by requiring shareholders of so-called controlled foreign corporations (CFC) to pay tax currently on the following types of income earned by the CFC even though such income has not been distributed to the shareholders:

Foreign Personal Holding Company Income. Passive income realized by the CFC such as dividends, interest, rentals, royalties, foreign currency gains, gains from the sale of property that does not generate active income and certain commodity gains.

Foreign Base Company Sales Income. Income realized by the CFC from the purchase of personal property from a related person and its sale to any person, or the purchase from any person and sale to a related person, if the property is both manufactured and sold for use outside the country in which the CFC is organized.

Foreign Base Company Services Income. Income realized by the CFC from performing services outside its country of incorporation "on behalf of" its U.S. parent or for a related person.

Insurance Income. Income realized by the CFC from insuring or reinsuring property, people, or products situated outside the country in which the CFC is organized.

Investment of Earnings in U.S. Property. To avoid paying taxable dividends to its U.S. parent, the CFC invests its earnings in bonds, stock, or other property of its U.S. parent.

Foreign Base Company Shipping Income. Income derived from the use of any aircraft or vessel in foreign commerce, whether or not the income is earned from a related party.

Foreign Base Company Oil Related Income. Income realized from "downstream activities" (transportation, refining, etc.) of petroleum products, by major oil producers, unless extracted in the CFC's country of incorporation or if the products are sold for use in such country.

Non-Arm's-Length Dealing with a Foreign Corporation

If a U.S. corporation deals with its foreign subsidiary in other than an "arm's-length" fashion, the IRS may adjust the U.S. taxpayer's income as if parties were unrelated. Thus the arm's-length standard requires a related taxpayer to report its income and expenses from transactions with its parent as if it were not related to its parent. (It is, therefore, extremely important that the basis for any intercompany pricing be carefully documented.)

Gain on Disposition of Foreign Subsidiary by U.S. Parent Taxed as Ordinary Income

If a U.S. corporation sells or exchanges (including liquidation) stock of a foreign subsidiary that is a controlled foreign corporation (CFC), any gain recognized by the U.S. corporation on the stock sale will be taxable as dividend income to the extent the gain does not exceed the foreign corporation's earnings and profits attributable to the stock which have not been previously taxed by the U.S.

USCO

Suppose USCO, the U.S. parent, sells its 100 percent Controlled Foreign Corporation, FORCO, at a gain of $90. FORCO has accumulated earnings and profits of $80 not previously taxed by the United States while USCO held its stock. Up to $80 of USCO's gain will be taxable to USCO as dividend income, and the remaining $10 is taxable as a capital gain. Under the 1986 Tax Reform Act, the $10 is taxed at ordinary rates, but retains its character as capital gain. To the extent gain is recharacterized as dividend income, the corporate shareholder is entitled to a "deemed paid" foreign tax credit. The availability of this credit to offset U.S. taxes may make dividend treatment more desirable.

Bribe- and Boycott-Related Income

U.S. taxpayers who use foreign corporations to make illegal bribes or other payments to foreign officials or who participate in economic boycotts against Israel (or other designated countries) may be denied credits for foreign income taxes, deferral from U.S. tax on the foreign subsidiary's income, and FSC benefits.

Denial of the Foreign Tax Credit with Respect to Certain Foreign Countries

In general, the foreign tax credit is denied when income is attributable to activities conducted:

1. in a country that the Secretary of State has designated as one repeatedly supporting terrorism, or

2. in a country with which the U.S. does not have diplomatic relations, or

3. in a country the government of which the U.S. does not recognize.

In addition, U.S. shareholders of such a CFC will be taxed currently on the corporation's income attributable to activities conducted in one of the above described countries.

Miscellaneous U.S. Tax Disincentives to Operating Abroad

Special accelerated cost recovery tables are applicable to property used primarily outside the United States, so that the depreciation deductions are smaller on this property than on comparable property used in the United States. With limited exceptions, a foreign corporation cannot file a consolidated U.S. income tax return with its U.S. parent. Also, there are extensive and complicated tax reporting requirements for foreign operations.

HOST-COUNTRY INCENTIVES

The following is a checklist, provided by Deloitte Haskins & Sells, of some incentives offered by countries to attract investment. Of course, the "package" of incentives given varies with the country and may vary significantly within a country, depending on how attractive a particular investment is to the country's economy. The most attractive investment would have some of the following attributes:

Be a large employer of local labor.
Earn hard currencies from exports.
Use local raw materials.
Train local managers and technicians.
Help develop locally-owned suppliers.
Make a maximum reinvestment of profits in the local company.
Provide goods that are a substitute for imports.

1. Tax and Tariff Incentives

Income Tax Incentives

Corporate income tax holidays (exemptions from income tax) that may be limited or unlimited in time and amount.
Accelerated depreciation.
Investment tax credit in addition to depreciation.
Tax exemption or rebate of taxes to the extent funds are used to acquire public bonds.
Increased deduction allowed for business entertainment in connection with export sales.
"Double deduction" of export promotion expenses.
Royalty or fee income of a foreign transferor of technology may be free of withholding of income tax.
Foreign contractor's taxable income may be determined by a favorable formula.
Reduced personal taxation of foreign managers and technicians.
Reduced withholding of income tax on dividends to foreign shareholders from approved investment.

Other Tax Incentives

Exemption from excise taxes on imported machinery and equipment.
Exemption from registration duties, stamp taxes, or capital taxes upon incorporation.
Exemption from property taxes.
Exemption from sales, value added, and excise taxes with respect to export sales.

Tariff Incentives

Waivers on import of machinery, equipment, and raw materials.
Access to regional common markets.
Tariff-free foreign trade zones.

2. Non-Tax Incentives

Financial Assistance

Grants for purchase of land, buildings, and machinery.
Grants for expenditure of export market development.
Grants to aid research and feasibility studies.
Government land provided for factory sites.
Low-cost rentals in government-owned industrial parks.
Low-cost financing.

Other

Assistance in locating plant sites, employees, suppliers, and markets.
Preference in purchases by government agencies.
Protection of market from competition.
Purchase of government-owned raw materials (e.g., oil and gas) at less than market price.
Guarantee of availability of foreign exchange to purchase equipment and raw materials and to pay interest, fees for technology, and dividends.
Work permits granted to imported technicians and managers.
Employee training provided.

The foregoing checklist is intended only to make you aware of a variety of incentives that are offered by host countries, many of which are negotiable during the preinvestment stage. A prospective investor's market and investment feasibility study should include a very thorough investigation of the tax and non-tax incentives, as well as the disincentives to doing business in a particular country. Further information can be obtained from major accounting firms, foreign ministries, U.S. embassies, and financial institutions abroad, as well as government agencies in the United States.

CHAPTER SEVEN

FINANCING THE DEAL

The final decision to invest or do business in a country may depend on the availability of financing for the project. This chapter describes the sources of government financing in three categories:

Investment Capital. Programs for establishing and funding an investment overseas.

Export Financing. Funding assistance for the export of goods and services. In addition, these financial programs may be used to create and develop overseas markets for products and services that are associated with investment projects.

Special Finance Programs. Government programs for funding operations such as financial institutions, foreign procurement contracts, and other service-related groups.

155

INVESTMENT CAPITAL

OPIC Project Financing

The Overseas Private Investment Corporation (OPIC) provides medium- to long-term financing for U.S. business ventures in some 100 developing countries. Two types of loan programs are available:

Direct Loans

These loans from OPIC funds generally range up to $6,000,000 and are reserved exclusively for projects sponsored by or significantly involving U.S. "small businesses" or cooperatives. A "small business" is defined in 1987 as a manufacturing firm having revenues less than $120 million or a non-industrial firm with a net worth less than $42 million. This definition is subject to annual adjustment.

Guaranteed Loans

OPIC also issues loan guarantees, under which funding can be obtained through U.S. financial institutions. These loan guarantees, which cover both commercial and political risks, are available for projects having significant U.S. involvement. OPIC loan guarantees can be as large as $50 million. This program is available for projects sponsored by any U.S. company, regardless of the size. The loans may be arranged on either a fixed or floating rate basis.

Eligibility
OPIC's criteria are the same whether it makes a direct loan in dollars or issues a loan guarantee. The project must be commercially and financially sound, and it must be sponsored by an investor having a proven record of success in a closely related business. Eligible enterprises include, but are not limited to, manufacturing, agricultural production, fishing, forestry, mining, energy development, processing, storage, and certain service industries involving significant capital investment.

OPIC's financing is available for new ventures or expansion of existing enterprises in those developing countries where the agency operates. The project must contribute to the economic and social development of the host country, be consistent with the economic interests of the United States and not have a significant adverse effect on the U.S. economy or employment.

Terms

Repayment of both direct loans and loan guarantees is usually made in equal, semiannual principal payments following a suitable grace period, with a final maturity of five to twelve years or more. The length of the grace period is generally contingent upon the time needed by the project to generate a positive cash flow. Direct loan interest rates generally parallel the commercial equivalent. Interest rates on guaranteed loans are comparable to those of other U.S. government guaranteed issues for similar amounts and maturities. In addition, OPIC charges the borrower a guarantee fee ranging from 1.75 to 3 percent. Commitment and facility fees are also charged. OPIC's financing commitment may range up to 50 percent of total project costs for a new venture and up to 75 percent for the expansion of an existing successful operation.

Application Procedure

The sponsor of a potential project should provide OPIC with the following preliminary information:

Name, location, and business of the proposed project.

Identity, background, and financial statements of the principal sponsors.

Planned sources of supply, anticipated output and markets, distribution channels, and the basis for projecting market share.

Summary of costs and sources of procurement of capital goods and services.

Proposed financing plan, including the amount of OPIC participation anticipated, and financial projections.

Brief statement of the contribution the business is expected to make to local economic and social development.

Contact

Finance Department
Overseas Private Investment Corporation
1615 M Street, NW
Washington, DC 20527
(202) 457-7037
(800) 457-7037
(Toll-Free outside greater Washington, DC Metropolitan Area)

For direct loans:
Suzanne Goldstein
(202) 457-7196

For loan guarantees:
John Andrews
(202) 457-7196

JAMAICA BROILERS, LTD.

Small business companies can turn to the Overseas Private Investment Corporation's direct loan program to consolidate and expand ongoing operations. Jamaica Broilers, Ltd. took out a $1 million loan from OPIC to build and equip a fully integrated poultry breeder farm at White Marl, Jamaica. The following year the company obtained an additional $750,000 to expand its blast freeze and cold room capacity and to purchase new incubators for its hatchery. Today its facilities are among the largest and most efficient in the Caribbean. At the same time, to increase production, the company has contracted with 250 farmers within 40 miles of its Kingston processing plant to raise poultry.

Jamaica Broilers now produces about 60 percent of the poultry consumed in the country or about 40 million pounds of dressed broilers annually. As a result, chicken, an important source of protein for Jamaicans, is available at a reasonable cost. Jamaica Broilers, as it has from the start, continues to buy equipment, breeder eggs, and feed grain from the United States.

IFC Project Financing

The International Finance Corporation (IFC), the private sector affiliate of the World Bank, invests in private ventures in developing countries by means of equity financing and loans without government guarantees, in collaboration with other investors. Always a minority partner, IFC seeks partners from industrial countries and from developing countries with whom the corporation can form joint enterprises.

IFC investment projects range from $4 million to several hundred million dollars in over 90 member countries throughout the developing world.

IFC will share in project financing, up to 25 percent of a project's cost in a variety of forms—loans, equity, and debentures, depending on the needs of the project. IFC can put financial packages together, unite partners and arrange syndications with banks.

IFC staff and consultants can design a project, appraise its prospects and help to secure cost savings and efficient management. They will assess the technical and market aspects of the project, but will not undertake feasibility studies.

Application Procedure

There is no standard application form for IFC financing. However, the Corporation does need certain preliminary information to help determine if a project qualifies for consideration. This information should include a description of the project, information about sponsorship, management and technical assistance and basic market information.

A review of the technical feasibility and an estimate of investment requirements, project financing and expected returns will be required.

Contact

Judhrir Parmar, Vice President
Investment Operations
International Finance Corporation
1818 H Street, NW
Washington, DC 20433
(202) 676-0385

or the following regional leads:

Region	Director	Phone
Europe & Middle East	Donald Gustafson	(202) 676-0571
Asia One (East Asia & Pacific)	Thorstein Stephansen	(202) 676-0601
Asia Two (South Asia)	Wilfried E. Kaffenberger	(202) 676-9093
Latin America & Caribbean One (Mexico, Central America, Caribbean)	Helmut Paul	(202) 676-0701

Latin America &
    Caribbean Two   Guillermo Schultz   (202) 676-0896

Africa One
(Northern &
    Western Africa)   Andre G. Hovaguimian   (202) 676-0511

Africa Two
(Southern &
    Eastern Africa)   M. Azam K. Alizai   (202) 676-0513

Agribusiness and Small Manufacturer Financing

The Bureau for Private Enterprise within AID will consider market-term financing for projects in developing countries through its Private Sector Revolving Fund.

Eligibility

Although projects in many industries are eligible, agricultural, health, and exporting projects are given high priority. For loans or loan guarantees, the Bureau will consider only private enterprises with substantial local ownership. Sponsors must be either host-country nationals, U.S. firms, or U.S. citizens. Projects must have a substantial developmental impact by generating net employment opportunities; earning net foreign exchange; developing managerial, technical or other skills; or transferring technologies. Loans may be used to capitalize a new enterprise and/or expand an existing enterprise. Revolving Fund managers give priority to innovative and financially viable projects benefiting mainly smaller businesses in developing countries and which can serve as models for replication in other countries. Increasingly, Bureau financing is made in conjunction with AID field mission financing.

Terms

The Bureau has flexibility in negotiating terms and conditions depending on the nature, risk, and developmental impact of the project. Financing is available up to $3 million with emphasis in the range of $250,000 to $1,000,000 but not for more than 25 percent of total project cost. Maximum term of the loan is 10 years with a negotiable grace period for principal. There are no fixed or minimum requirements for collateral. Repayment is on a semi-annual or annual basis.

Application Procedure

If sponsors can demonstrate that they meet these criteria, a business plan should be submitted to the Bureau for Private Enterprise. The plan should include:

A. Project Description

1. Brief background, description, and present status of the project.
   a. If an established firm: company name, ownership, management, joint venture agreement, articles of incorporation, and other legal arrangements; brief history and background of firm and owners.
   b. If a proposed venture: proposed legal arrangement; name, ownership, management; source of funds; and experience with indigenous or foreign enterprises.
2. Expected development impact

B. Financing Requirements (from all sources)

1. Total costs, itemized by project requirement.
2. Proposed financial structure, including source of funds and anticipated terms, and critical factors affecting investment opportunity.

C. Technical Plan

1. Technology to be used—its appropriateness, feasibility, and source.
2. Ease of incorporating the technology given existing levels of management and technical skills.
3. Advisory assistance and training requirements and how they will be provided.
4. Sources of raw materials, equipment, and labor.
5. Location in relation to markets and suppliers.
6. Relationship between activity and production.

D. Marketing Plan

1. Market and customer profile.
2. Transportation and distribution.
3. Pricing.
4. Competition.

E. Financial Plan

1. Source and application of funds statement (five years).
2. Projected pro forma income statement and balance sheet (five years).
3. Projected cash flow analysis and/or rate of return.

F. Legal Requirements

1. Legal impediments and requirements that will affect project success.
2. Import and export duties.
3. Tax implications (e.g., dividends and profits, interest payments).
4. Foreign exchange restrictions and regulations on repatriation of dividends, profits, interest, and principal repayments.
5. Ownership and management requirements.
6. Barriers to free market private enterprise activities.

G. Management Plan

1. Structure.
2. Skills (existing and needed).
3. Training requirements.

H. Implementation Plan

As much detail as possible should be given under each of the major topic areas described above. Any other factors or commitments critical to project success should also be described.

Contact
Sean P. Walsh, Director
Office of Investment
Bureau for Private Enterprise
Agency for International Development
Room 3214 NS
Washington, DC 20523
(202) 647-9842

Distributorship Financing

The Overseas Private Investment Corporation's distributorship program provides ongoing financing for the sale and service of U.S. equipment in eligible developing countries. The program helps to increase U.S. exports and fosters local skills in the distribution of goods and service/maintenance capabilities. It also provides an important transitional step between exports to overseas markets and actual investment. The program enables companies to test the market and their ability to service the product before committing to an overseas manufacturing operation.

Eligibility

The criteria for eligibility are generally the same as for other OPIC financing programs discussed earlier in this chapter. Where the foreign distributor is wholly owned by local interests, OPIC requires that the U.S. manufacturer and/or exporter be significantly at risk and subordinated to OPIC in the financing of the project.

Terms

The distributorship program provides medium-term commercial financing for up to 50 percent of the cost of a new dealer facility or 75 percent of the cost for expanding an existing operation. For additional information on terms, refer to the OPIC Finance Program described earlier in this chapter.

Contact

Graham Williams
Financial Services and Product Development
Overseas Private Investment Corporation
1615 M Street, NW
Washington, DC 20527
(202) 457-7105

BELIZE CEMCOL LTD.

The Overseas Private Investment Corporation guaranteed a $420,000 loan to Belize Cemcol Ltd. to help it establish a dealership for Caterpillar Tractor equipment in Belize. The sales agency, owned by Caterpillar's Honduran dealer, sells equipment and spare parts; its repair center, the only one of its kind in the country, trains skilled mechanics to repair and maintain Caterpillar machinery used primarily in construction and farming.

Small Business Investment Company

Small Business Investment Companies (SBICs) are limited partnerships or corporations certified under state law that are licensed and regulated by the Small Business Administration. The primary purpose of an SBIC is to provide equity capital and long-term financing to small business concerns for growth, expansion, and modernization.

Eligibility

Generally, an SBIC finances small businesses located in the United States. However, funds may be provided to small business concerns for use outside the United States if the funds are used: to acquire materials abroad for its domestic operations; for its foreign branch operations and foreign joint ventures or; for transfer to a foreign subsidiary it controls. If used for a foreign branch or subsidiary operation, or for foreign joint ventures, the major portion of the assets and activities of the concern must remain in the United States. This means that the SBIC cannot finance a foreign corporation directly even if there is some U.S. small business ownership. The entity receiving the financing must be a domestic company with a majority of its assets and activities in the United States. However, that entity may use SBIC funds for its foreign branch operations or for relending to its foreign subsidiaries and foreign joint ventures.

Terms

An SBIC finances small firms in two ways:

Direct Loans

Although most SBICs want an opportunity to share in the growth and potential profits of the small companies they finance, some make loans that involve no equity participation. The interest rate on a loan, determined by negotiation between the SBIC and the small business, must be within SBA's regulatory maximum and may be subject to the state's legal limit. Collateral requirements, terms of repayment, and other parts of the loan agreement are also determined by negotiation, within the boundaries of the regulations.

Equity Investments

Loans with Warrants. In return for a loan, the small business issues warrants enabling the SBIC to purchase common stock in the company, usually at a favorable price, during a specified period of time.

Convertible Debenture. The SBIC loans money to a company and in return receives a debenture. The SBIC then either can accept repayment of the loan or can convert the debenture into an equivalent amount of common stock of the small business.

Common Stock. The SBIC purchases common stock from the small business.

An SBIC may invest up to 20 percent of its private capital in a single business. Several SBICs may participate in financing the same business and thereby increase the maximum investment.

Contact

John Edson, Program Assistant
Investment Division
U.S. Small Business Administration
Washington, DC 20416
(202) 653-2806

EXPORT FINANCING

Direct Loans, Intermediary Loans, and Guarantees

The Export-Import Bank provides financing assistance for U.S. exports of capital equipment and services that are normally financed on a term of more than one year. Eximbank's financing takes the form of a direct loan to a public or private buyer overseas, a loan to a financial intermediary who then makes a loan to the overseas buyer, or a guarantee of a private credit to an overseas buyer. Reviews of requests for financing include appraisal of the financial, economic, and technical aspects of the transaction, as well as analysis of the degree of foreign government subsidized export credit competition for the sale. Reviews also consider the effect the transaction will have on the U.S. economy.

Eligibility

For direct or intermediary loans, there must be evidence of foreign, officially-supported export credit competition, except for loans of less than $2.5 million for the sale of products produced by a small business. The applicant must submit the best information available regarding the existence of foreign, officially-supported competition, preferably including the name of the foreign suppliers, the terms, and interest rates they are offering. When the specific identity of the foreign competitor or its financing offer is not known, other means of indirectly establishing subsidized official export credit competition will be pursued by Eximbank. If the sale involves an invitation to bid, a copy of the bid document must accompany the application for financing.

Eximbank follows the small business definitions established by the U.S. Small Business Administration.

Terms

Eximbank will provide credit or guarantee for up to 85 percent of the U.S. export value of each transaction. It requires a 15 percent cash payment to the U.S. seller from the foreign buyer. Financing from private lenders may be denominated in dollars or an acceptable foreign currency. Repayment of principal and interest is scheduled in equal semiannual installments, normally beginning six months from the date of product delivery or project completion. Repayment terms usually range between one and ten years based on the type of product or project and the official OECD country classification. Repayment terms do not exceed those which are customary in international trade, and usually follow the schedule below:

Contract Value

Medium Term	Maximum Term
Up to $50,000	2 years
$50,000–$100,000	3 years
$100,000–$200,000	4 years
$200,000 or more	5 years (Exceptionally up to 7 years)

Long-term
Over 7 years usually not to exceed 10 years.

Eximbank's guarantee is available for fixed or floating interest rate export loans. In the event of a claim, Eximbank interest on dollar loans will be guaranteed at the following rates:

For fixed rate: the lesser of the rate on the note minus 50 basis points or the Treasury rate at the time of loan pricing for a comparable term plus 50 basis points.

For floating rate: the lesser of the rate on the note minus 50 basis points or a rate determined on the basis of one of the following options, such option to be selected by the guaranteed party at the time of entering into the transaction:

Prime rate less 200 basis points
LIBOR less 25 points
Treasury rate plus 50 basis points

Rates and Fees

Interest rates on Eximbank's loans are fixed for the life of the loan at the time of authorization. Interest rates are based on the international arrangement among the members of the Organization for Economic Cooperation and Development (OECD) and are reviewed every six months. Effective July 1987, these OECD rates are as follows:

Country Classification	2-5 years	more than 5 years
I. Relatively rich	9.55	9.80
II. Intermediate	8.25	8.75
III. Relatively poor	7.40	7.40

For medium-term intermediary loans, Eximbank's rates to a financing institution unrelated to the exporter are as follows:

Loan Value	Eximbank's Rate
Below $1 million	OECD rate—1.5%
$1–5 million	OECD rate—1.0%
Over $5–10 million	OECD rate—0.5%

For Direct Loans, Long-term Intermediary Loans, and Medium-term Intermediary Loans to other responsible parties, Eximbank will charge the OECD rate. The intermediary must charge the OECD rate.

Eximbank charges a one-time processing fee of $100, due with each application for a Preliminary Commitment (PC) and for a Final Commitment that is not a conversion of a PC fee of 0.5 percent per year to the borrower on the undisbursed amount of each direct loan and charges the lender a fee of 0.125 percent for the undisbursed amount of each guaranteed loan. No commitment fee is charged for a medium-term intermediary loan; however, if a medium-term intermediary loan is combined with a guarantee covering the intermediary's loan to the foreign borrower, a 0.5 percent per annum commitment fee is charged on the undisbursed balance of the guaranteed loan.

Eximbank also charges a front-end exposure fee to the exporter, assessed on each disbursement of a loan made or guaranteed. Exposure fees vary according to the repayment term of the loan, the classification of the borrower or guarantor and the borrower's country.

Repayment Assurance
To assure repayment, Eximbank may require a repayment guarantee by a financial organization in the buyer's country. Frequently a central bank, finance ministry, or government development bank will provide this guarantee. In some cases, larger commercial banks or parent firms are acceptable.

Application Procedure
An application form for the loan and guarantee programs can be obtained by contacting the Export-Import Bank Office of Public Affairs. Requests for assistance can take two forms, depending on the state of development of the transaction being financed:

Preliminary Commitments

These are used when the project or product sale is in an early stage of negotiation, but U.S. exporters need to include a financing package as part of their marketing efforts. Eximbank's Preliminary Commitment (PC) outlines the amount, terms, and conditions of financial assistance it is prepared to offer to purchasers of U.S. equipment and services. The duration of a PC is normally 180 days. Once the foreign buyer decides to purchase U.S. goods, and before the PC expires, the buyer must apply to Eximbank to convert the PC to a loan and/or guarantee. Applications for PCs may be submitted by the overseas buyer, a U.S. exporter, a U.S. or foreign bank involved in the transaction, or any other responsible applicant. The application must include sufficient information to permit Eximbank to appraise the financial, economic, and technical aspects of the transaction.

Final Loan/Guarantee Applications

These must be submitted by the prospective borrower or lender. The application must be supplemented by information that is sufficient for Eximbank to appraise the financial, economic, and technical aspects of the transaction.

Contact
> James R. Sharpe, Senior Vice-President, International Lending
> Export-Import Bank of the U.S.
> 811 Vermont Avenue, NW
> Washington, DC 20571
> (202) 566-8187

Private Export Funding Corporation

The Private Export Funding Corporation (PEFCO), acting as a supplemental lender to traditional financing sources, works with Eximbank in using private capital to finance U.S. exports. PEFCO makes loans to public and private borrowers located outside of the United States who require medium- and/or long-term financing of their purchases of U.S. goods and services. It also purchases from Lenders or Noteholders the Eximbank guaranteed obligations of foreign importers who have financed the purchase of U.S. goods and services through traditional lenders or suppliers.

In all cases, the loans made by PEFCO or the foreign importer notes purchased from others by PEFCO must be covered by the compre-

Theodore Lownik Library
Illinois Benedictine College
Lisle, Illinois 60532

hensive guarantee of repayment of principal and payment of interest by Eximbank.

Project and Product Buyer Credits

PEFCO lends funds to foreign buyers of capital equipment or expensive products where the amounts are larger and repayment periods are longer than traditional lenders make for their own account.

Eligibility
a) Eximbank Comprehensive Guarantee must be available.
b) Amount must exceed $1,000,000.
c) Fixed Interest Rate is required.
d) Final maturity must be over 5 years.
e) Loan must be in U.S. dollars.
f) Payment net of any local or withholding taxes.
g) The Loan request must come through a commercial bank.

Terms
PEFCO loans have ranged from $1 to $225 million, for 5 years to 22 years and have been sponsored by domestic and foreign banks. Occasionally PEFCO loans have been made to commercial or special purpose lessors or "borrowers of convenience" with the actual users of the equipment being obligors of the intermediaries. Terms and conditions of PEFCO offers will be reflective of current market conditions and will be responsive to special requirements of borrowers.

Application Procedure
PEFCO should be approached through a commercial bank. When contacted, PEFCO will provide an indication of the terms of its potential credit promptly, provided it knows the amount, appropriate disbursement and repayment schedules. Thereafter, a firm offer can be made available for a period of up to 45 days. If the offer is accepted, a Credit Agreement will be negotiated among the Borrower and PEFCO, Eximbank and any other lender or guarantor in the normal manner.

Note Purchase Facility

The PEFCO Note Purchase Facility (NPF) was designed to provide assured liquidity to traditional lenders who utilize the Eximbank medium term program. Under this facility, PEFCO will make offers to purchase from Lenders or Noteholders, or prospective Lenders the Eximbank Guaranteed foreign importer notes being used to finance U.S. goods and services.

Eligibility
Security—Eximbank comprehensive guarantee
Amount—Not in excess of $10,000,000
Repayment—7 years or less
Interest rate—Either fixed or floating with Eximbank guarantee on same basis
Prepayment—Requires Noteholders consent
Taxes—Payment net of any and all foreign local or withholding taxes
Source—Any existing Lender or Noteholder or potential Lender

Terms
PEFCO offers will be based on then current market conditions. Purchase will be without recourse to seller. Offers on existing notes carrying fixed or floating interest rates will be available for up to two days pending response. Offers for pending commercial transactions may be made available to commercial banks on fixed or floating rate terms for extended periods for additional fees. Accepted offers would be settled in no less than five business days. PEFCO would require possession of Note and Eximbank guarantee Agreement.

Application Procedure
Potential lender, lender or noteholders can request an offer from PEFCO by letter or telephone.

Contact
John A. Deuchler/William Ekberg
Private Export Funding Corporation
280 Park Avenue
New York, New York 10017
(212) 557-3100

Working Capital Guarantee Program

Eximbank's Working Capital Guarantee Program provides exporters access to export-related working capital loans from financial institutions. The guarantees are available only if the working capital would not be provided without Eximbank's support and if the ex-

PHILIPPINE LONG DISTANCE TELEPHONE

The fiber optic submarine cable system between the Philippines, Guam and Japan is an integral part of the worldwide project linking major world trading partners with an echo-free, secure and delay-free communications system with digital capabilities.

The Philippine share of the $772 million multinational cable project amounts to about $115.6 million. The Philippine Long Distance Telephone Co. (PLDT) borrowed a major portion of the cost of approximately $66,200,000 U.S. goods and services from Private Export Funding Corporation. Additional funds for the balance of U.S. goods and services were borrowed by PLDT from the Asian Development Bank and investors who purchased obligations guaranteed by the Overseas Private Investment corporation.

porter would not be able to support its exports sales through other means. Most of the working capital loans guaranteed by Eximbank are expected to support exports from small- to medium-sized businesses, especially new-to-export or new-to-market producers.

Eligibility

Eximbank will issue its guarantee to the lender if, in its judgement, the eligible exporter is creditworthy for the loan or line of credit to be guaranteed. Generally, a financial institution or other public or private creditor will be eligible to apply for Eximbank's Loan Guarantee. If Eximbank has no working experience with the creditor, two years of full financial data, including balance sheets, income statements, corporate ownership, and a brief corporate history, are required. An eligible lender must be able to demonstrate the ability to perform and service loans to exporters. Eligible loans for this program are specific loans or revolving lines of credit advanced by an eligible lender to an exporter for export-related activities. The applicant must demonstrate to Eximbank's satisfaction that the loan would not be made without its guarantee.

Terms

The terms of the guaranteed loan generally will be up to 12 months but may be longer if required. The guarantee will be for 90 percent of the principal amount of the loan, plus interest up to the U.S. Treasury rate plus 1%. The lender will be at risk for 10 percent of the principal amount of the loan, interest in excess of the guaranteed rate, and late interest, if any. Eximbank requires that the eligible lender be secured with inventory of exportable goods or accounts receivable on goods or services already exported, or other acceptable collateral. Such security must have a value, as determined by the lender and Eximbank, of not less than 90 percent of the outstanding loan balance. Eximbank will not impose any interest rate or fee ceiling on the lender for guaranteed loans. However, it will monitor rates and fees being charged.

Fees

Eximbank charges a $100 processing fee as well as an up-front facility fee of .5% of the loan amount and a quarterly usage fee of a .25%.

Application Procedure

Eximbank requires the following information from each exporter for the requested loan guarantee:

A summary of the exporter's business plan and history of activities.*

Two years of financial statements with cash flow projections.

At least two credit or blank reports.

A summary of management's experience in related and non-related fields.

*For newly formed trading companies or other exporters, an opening balance sheet in addition to other pertinent financial data may be submitted in lieu of this information.

Copies of the application form are available upon request from Eximbank. The application and attachments provide Eximbank with the information on which it will decide whether the request meets the program guidelines and offers a reasonable assurance of repayment. If the applicant is the Lender, they are required to submit their own credit analysis and describe how they will control disbursement and application of funds, payment procedures, etc.

Contact
James W. Crist, Vice President
Working Capital Guarantee Program
Export-Import Bank of the U.S.
811 Vermont Avenue, NW
Washington, DC 20571
(202) 566-8819

Small Business Advisory Service

The Small Business Advisory Service is a special office of Eximbank which provides information and materials on the availability and use of export financing to encourage small businesses to sell overseas.

Contact
Larry Luther, Senior Business Affairs Officer
Office of Business Affairs
Export-Import Bank of the U.S.
811 Vermont Avenue, NW
Washington, DC 20571
(800) 424-5201 (in Washington, DC, (202) 566-8860)

Lease Financing

The Overseas Private Investment Corporation (OPIC) offers financial assistance to foreign leasing companies in which there is a significant U.S. private business interest. The funds are used to encourage U.S. exports of productive equipment for projects that contribute to host-country development.

Eligibility
The borrowing company or U.S. sponsor must be an established leasing company with a history of successful leasing operations. Companies must demonstrate the capability to proceed with the proposed leasing plan. Leases should be made to private companies on a medium- to long-term basis. On a case-by-case basis, OPIC will also consider financing a portion of the equipment costs of a single cross-border lease.

Terms
Terms of the guarantees are typically from four to seven years, with appropriate grace periods before principal repayment begins. U.S. dollar loans are provided by a U.S. lender under an OPIC guarantee, which covers 100 percent of all lender risks. The loans can carry

fixed or floating rates geared to U.S. Treasury obligations. The borrower also pays an annual guarantee fee to OPIC in the range of 1.5 to 3 percent.

In addition to guaranteed loans, direct loans from OPIC are available to foreign companies or projects in which a U.S. small business has a significant interest. Small business is defined in 1987 as a manufacturing firm with revenues of less than approximately $120 million or a non-industrial firm with a net worth less than $42 million. This definition is subject to annual adjustment. OPIC lends up to $6 million per project at a fixed rate priced at prevailing U.S. government agency rates of comparable maturity.

Security for the loans may include first liens on the assets financed and/or other collateral or pledges as required to adequately secure OPIC's financing.

Contact
Graham Williams
Financial Services and Product Development
Overseas Private Investment Corporation
1615 M Street, NW
Washington, DC 20527
(202) 457-7105

Small Contractor's Guarantee Program

OPIC administers a Small Contractors Guarantee Program to assist small business construction and service contractors.

Eligibility
The program is limited to small business contractors having a net worth less than $42 million (in 1987). This definition is subject to annual adjustment.

Terms
OPIC will guarantee an eligible financial institution for up to 75 percent of an on-demand standby letter of credit or other form of performance or advance payment guarantee issued on behalf of a contractor. The contractor may also apply for OPIC's political risk insurance for up to 90 percent of that portion of the letter of credit not guaranteed by OPIC. (See discussion of OPIC insurance programs in Chapter 8.)

Contact
Brian Treadwell
Financial Services and Product Development
Overseas Private Investment Corporation
1615 M Street, NW
Washington, DC 20527
(202) 457-7179

Small Business Export Loan Guarantees

The Small Business Administration (SBA) may guarantee up to $500,000 of commercial financing to firms wishing to establish or expand their export operations.

Eligibility

For loan programs, SBA defines a "small business" as a concern (including its affiliates) that is independently owned and operated, not dominant in its field, and falls within employment or sales standards developed by the agency. For most industries, the standards are as follows:

Manufacturing. Maximum number of employees ranges from 250 to 1500, depending on the industry in which the applicant is primarily engaged.

Wholesaling. Maximum number of employees not exceeding 500.

Services. Annual receipts not exceeding $3.5–17 million.

Construction. Annual receipts between $9.5–21.5 million, depending on the type of construction.

Retailing. Annual sales or receipts not exceeding $3.5–13.5 million, depending on the industry.

Agriculture. Annual receipts not exceeding $3.5 million.

Terms

If the loan is $100,000 or less, the guarantee is not less than 90 percent. If the loan is more than $100,000, the guarantee may not be less than 70 percent, unless such a guarantee would be necessary to insure that the guaranteed portion of the loan would not exceed $500,000. The maximum guarantee percentage for loans or portions of loans that refinance prior indebtedness may not exceed 80 percent. Interest rates are negotiated between the borrower and lender with the maximum set by the SBA. At present, the maximum allowable rate for loans with maturities of up to 7 years is 2.25 percent above the prime rate. For maturities longer than 7 years, the maximum allowable rate is 2.75 percent above prime. Certain additional one-time fees may also be charged by the lender in accordance with allowable SBA limits.

Contact
nearest SBA district office (see appendix)

Small Business Export Revolving Line of Credit Loan Program

The SBA's Export Revolving Line of Credit (ERLC), available only under the loan guarantee program, helps small businesses export their products and services. The request for the SBA to participate in the ERLC financing must come from the applicant's bank or lending institution. Any number of withdrawals and repayments can be made, as long as the dollar limit of the credit line is not exceeded and the disbursements are made within the stated maturity period. Proceeds can be used only to finance labor and materials needed for manufacturing or wholesaling for export and to develop foreign markets. Professional export marketing advice or services, foreign business travel, and participation in trade shows are examples of eligible expenses to develop foreign markets. Funds may not be used to pay existing obligations or to purchase fixed assets, nor can the SBA provide funds to establish overseas joint ventures. A cash flow projection depicting monthly activity and cash balances, covering expected activity during the term of the line of credit, must be submitted with the application.

Eligibility
Applicants must qualify under the SBA's size standards and meet the other eligibility criteria applicable to all SBA loans. In addition, an applicant must have been in business (not necessarily in exporting) for at least 12 full months prior to filing an application. The business must be current on all payroll taxes and have a depository plan for the payment of future withholding taxes.

Terms
The SBA can guarantee up to 90 percent of a bank line of credit to a small business exporter. An applicant may have other SBA loans in addition to loans under this program, as long as the SBA's share of the total outstanding balance of all loans does not exceed $500,000.

The maturity of an Export Revolving Line of Credit is based on an applicant's business cycle but cannot exceed 18 months, including all extensions. No provisions exist for renewals, but borrowers can reapply for a new credit line when their existing line of credit expires. A new credit line may not be used to pay off an existing line of credit. The rate of interest that may be charged by the lender will be the same as for other SBA-guaranteed loans. Interest may be up to 2.25 percent greater than the prime rate for loans maturing in 12 months or less, 2.75 percent greater than the prime rate for loans greater than 12 months.

Lenders must also pay a guarantee fee to the SBA, based on the length of maturity for the loan. For maturities of 12 months or less, the fee is .25 percent of the guaranteed portion of the loan. For maturities exceeding 12 months, the fee is 1 percent of the guaranteed portion of the loan.

The lender may also charge the borrower a commitment fee equal to .25 percent of the loan amount, or a $200 minimum. This fee cannot be charged until the SBA approves the line of credit. Collateral may include accounts receivable, inventories, assignments of contract proceeds, and bank letters of credit. Only collateral that is located in the United States and its territories and possessions—or other assets under the jurisdiction of U.S. courts—is acceptable. SBA may not guarantee a letter of credit nor may loan proceeds be used to secure a letter of credit.

Contact
nearest SBA district office (see appendix)

Agricultural Export Credit Guarantee Program

The Export Credit Guarantee Programs (GSM-102 and GSM-103) of the Commodity Credit Corporation (CCC) are designed to expand U.S. agricultural exports by stimulating U.S. bank financing of foreign purchases. The Programs operate in cases where credit is necessary to increase or maintain U.S. exports to a foreign market and where private financial institutions would be unwilling to provide financing without a guarantee. These Programs guarantee letters of credit from foreign financial institutions against default.

GSM-102 (Export Credit Guarantee Program) provides to the exporter the guaranteed repayment of 6-month to 3-year loans made to banks in eligible countries that purchase U.S. farm products. Twenty-six countries participated in the fiscal 1986 program. Any agricultural commodity may be covered. The 1985 Farm Bill directs that a minimum of $5 billion in GSM-102 guarantees be made available each fiscal year through fiscal 1990.

GSM-103 (Intermediate Credit Guarantee Program), established in July 1986, is similar to GSM-102 except that it guarantees loans from 3-10 years. The 1985 Farm Bill directs CCC to make a minimum of $500 million available in such guarantees during fiscal 1987 and 1988 and a maximum of $1 billion available in fiscal 1989 and 1990.

Eligibility

Eligible countries are those for which the guarantees are necessary to secure financing of the exports and where the destination country has the foreign exchange to make the scheduled payments. Commodities are reviewed on a case-by-case basis to determine eligibility.

Contact

Melvin E. Sims, General Sales Manager and
    Associate Administrator
Foreign Agricultural Service
U.S. Department of Agriculture
14th and Independence Avenue, NW
Room 4071
Washington, DC 20250
(202) 447-5173

SPECIAL FINANCE PROGRAMS

Foreign Bank Loans

The Agency for International Development (AID) has funded a number of foreign development and commercial banks that can provide project financing for joint ventures between U.S. and host-country investors. AID has allocated funds to banks in Costa Rica, Haiti, Jamaica, the Eastern Caribbean, Kenya, and Peru.

Eligibility
U.S. Businesses that enter into joint-venture arrangements with indigenous firms may be eligible for this financing.

Terms
Established by each bank.

Contact
U.S. companies seeking project financing should consult the appropriate AID country officer in Washington (see appendix) to determine whether a development bank in a particular country has received AID funds.

Revolving Loan Fund

The Bureau for Private Enterprise within AID may provide loans at market terms or loan guarantees to help capitalize private intermediate credit institutions which serve the private sector in developing countries. The financing mechanism is AID's Private Sector Revolving Fund, which gives priority to innovative and financially viable projects primarily benefitting smaller businesses and which can serve as models for replication in other countries.

Eligibility
U.S. companies such as venture capital firms which operate abroad and work with developing country firms may be eligible for loans or guarantees as well as host-country institutions. Joint ventures between U.S. and host-country firms may also be eligible to receive loans from institutions capitalized by this program.

Contact
Sean P. Walsh, Director
Office of Investment
Bureau for Private Enterprise
Agency for International Development
Room 3214NS
Washington, DC 20523
(202) 647-9842

Dairy Export Incentive Program

Commodity Credit Corporation (CCC) will make payments (either in cash or CCC-owned commodities) on a bid basis to entities selling U.S. dairy products for export. Such sales must be additional and not displace commercial export sales.

Contact
Lawrence T. McElvain
Commodity Credit Corporation
Operations Division
U.S. Department of Agriculture
Room 4503-S
Washington, DC 20250-1000
(202) 382-9150

Export Enhancement Program

The Export Enhancement Program (EEP) of the Department of Agriculture's Foreign Agricultural Service (FAS) enables U.S. exporters to meet prevailing world prices for targeted commodities and destinations. The Commodity Credit Corporation's (CCC) government-owned commodities are used to provide bonuses to U.S. exporters to help them expand sales in selected markets.

The program has facilitated the sale of $2.1 billion worth of U.S. agricultural products since its inception in May, 1985. Sixty-nine initiatives have been made available to 45 countries for 12 commodities.

Eligibility
U.S. commodities are eligible for inclusion in the EEP, as long as program criteria are met: increased U.S. exports above what would have occurred without the program; each proposal targeting a specific market to challenge only the competitors who overtly subsidize their exports; a net plus to the overall economy and; not increasing

budget outlays beyond what would have occurred in the absence of the program.

For information on the qualifications for participation in the program:

Contact
Larry McElvain, Director
Commodity Credit Corporation
Operations Division
14th and Independence Avenue, SW
Washington, DC 20250
(202) 382-9150; 382-9240

Multilateral Procurement Opportunities

The World Bank

The World Bank, through its financial and technical assistance to developing countries, provides contracting opportunities for suppliers of goods and services that are eligible to participate in Bank-approved procurement projects. Bidding opportunities are internationally competitive and are advertised globally through a number of publications and data systems.

Contact
Carol Stitt, Business Relations Specialist
Office of Public Affairs
The World Bank
1818 H Street, NW
Washington, DC 20433
(202)477-5322

The Inter-American Development Bank

The Inter-American Development Bank (IDB) offers contract opportunities for suppliers of goods and services needed to complete IDB procurement projects. To ensure efficient utilization of its lending resources, the Bank requires competitive international public bidding for such projects.

Contact
Joseph Hinshaw, Deputy Associate External Relations Advisor
Office of External Relations
Inter-American Development Bank
1300 New York Avenue, NW
Washington, DC 20577
(202) 623-1369

Procurement Contracts

The Agency for International Development (AID) operates two types of programs in which U.S. companies can benefit as exporters. AID's Commodity Import Programs finance the procurement of basic commodities needed in developing countries. Under this program, funds are allocated by the recipient government to its ministries to provide for exchange needed to purchase machinery, industrial chemicals, farm equipment, medical supplies and other products. Another opportunity for U.S. businesses to export to the developing world is created by AID-financed projects, such as construction of irrigation facilities, rural health networks, and disease control programs.

Contact
Jack Warner, Chief
Overseas Branch
Office of Procurement/Commodity Support
U.S. Agency for International Development
Washington, DC 20523
(703) 875-1058

Region	Contact	Telephone
Asia/Near East	James Politte	(703) 875-1219
Latin America & Caribbean	Judith Johnson	(703) 875-1091
Africa & Europe	Stephen Dean	(703) 875-1060

Consulting Contracts

The Indefinite Quantity Contracts (IQC) is a special method by which preliminary agreement can be reached between AID and a contractor on general work descriptions and company qualifications, saving the time and individual negotiations otherwise necessary to contract for specific short-term requirements. The resulting IQC specifies the services which can be performed using a "work order" arrangement. The work order provides for short-term technical services, normally 120 days or less. IQC contracts are usually for a two-year period, which may be renewed or extended as necessary.

Contact

Jean Hacken, Chief Contracting Officer
Office of Procurement
Room 1571
U.S. Agency for International Development
Washington, DC 20523
(202) 875-1170

Business Brokering

The Agency for International Development's Bureau for Science and Technology, under its Market and Technology Access Project (MTAP), provides cost-sharing contracts to firms engaged in brokering collaborative business ventures involving U.S. and developing country enterprises.

Eligibility

U.S. businesses engaged in providing trade and investment promotion or brokering services involving U.S. and developing country firms will be eligible to respond to any Request for Proposal that may be issued under this project.

Contact

Michael Farbman, Chief
Employment and Small Enterprise Division
S&T/RD
U.S. Agency for International Development
Washington, DC 20523
(703) 235-8881

CHAPTER EIGHT

PROTECTING THE DEAL

Any overseas venture involves a certain amount of risk. The programs discussed in this chapter are designed to protect your interests by providing insurance to cover the common commercial and political risks of doing business overseas. Included are discussions on insurance for three types of overseas enterprises:

Investment Insurance. Government insurance programs to protect U.S. businesses with fixed-asset overseas investments against losses due to expropriation, currency inconvertibility, political violence, and business interruption.

Export Insurance. Government insurance programs to protect U.S. exporters against the risk of nonpayment by foreign buyers because of commercial or political reasons.

Special Programs. Government insurance programs similar in coverage to those above, but designed for U.S. firms whose overseas operations are of a specialized nature, such as leasing, contracting, and servicing.

AMF CORPORATION

OPIC insured AMF Corporation's investment of $950,000 in a Chinese venture for the production of sports equipment. AMF is providing machinery, equipment, and technical assistance for the project, which will produce volleyballs, soccer balls, and basketballs. The agreement is for 10 years.

AMF's associates in the venture include Shanghai Light Industrial Products, Shanghai Rubber Industrial Corporation, and Shanghai Leather and Leather Products Corporation.

AMF will purchase all of the balls manufactured on its machinery, with the price based on a formula involving labor, material costs, and market conditions. Under the terms of the agreement, AMF will export the products to markets in the Far East, Southeast Asia, Europe and South America.

The project will employ approximately 70 persons and is expected to earn significant foreign exchange for the People's Republic of China.

The new China facility will make AMF more competitive, enabling it to open new world markets. The project is expected to generate initial U.S. exports of machinery, equipment, and materials estimated at $1 million. Annual remittances to the United States are projected at $100,000.

INVESTMENT INSURANCE

The Overseas Private Investment Corporation (OPIC) offers a number of insurance programs designed to encourage U.S. private investment in the developing countries of the world.

Insurance Program

OPIC insures investments in qualified projects in friendly, less developed countries against loss caused by certain political risks. Insurance is provided against four major types of political risk:

Inability to convert into dollars local currency received by the investor as profits or earnings or return on the original investment.

Losses due to expropriation, nationalization, or confiscation by action of a foreign government.

Loss due to political violence such as war, revolution, insurrection, or civil strife.

Loss of business income due to interruption of the business caused by political violence or expropriation.

Eligible Investors. OPIC's charter requires that its insurance be issued only to "eligible investors." OPIC may thus insure an investment by an eligible investor in a project controlled by foreign interests, but it is only the eligible investor's investment that is insured, not the entire project. Eligible investors are:

Citizens of the United States.

Corporations, partnerships, or other associations created under the laws of the United States, or of any state or territory of the United States, which are substantially beneficially owned by U.S. citizens.

Foreign businesses at least 95 percent owned by investors eligible under the preceding criteria.

187

OPIC recognizes a corporation organized under the laws of the United States or of any state or territory of the United States to be substantially benefically owned by U.S. citizens if more than 50 percent of each class of its issued and outstanding stock is owned by U.S. citizens either directly or beneficially.

Eligible Countries. OPIC programs are available to cover U.S. private investments in over 100 countries defined as "less developed friendly countries and areas," with which the United States has agreements for the operation of the OPIC programs. A list of eligible countries is available from OPIC. The availability of OPIC insurance is generally restricted to investments in countries with per capita GNPs lower than $3887 (in 1983 dollars). In countries with higher GNP levels, insurance is available for investments sponsored by U.S. small businesses or cooperatives, projects involving minerals or energy (except oil and gas exploration in OPEC countries), construction projects, projects using OPIC's letter of credit or contractors coverage, and other projects that OPIC's Board of Directors determines to merit insurance, such as those offering exceptionally significant developmental or trade benefits. Small businesses are defined as a manufacturing firm having 1987 revenues less than $120 million or a non-industrial firm with a 1987 net worth less than $42 million. This definition is subject to annual adjustment.

Eligible Investment. OPIC insures not only new investments, but also those used for the enlargement or modernization of existing plant and equipment as well as additional working capital in an expanded business. It may, in some cases, include the cost of acquiring an existing business. The investor should apply for insurance sufficient to cover possible project cost overruns. Coverage is available not only for conventional equity investments and loans but also for investment or exposure of funds and goods or services under various contractual arrangements. To be eligible for insurance, an investor must apply for and receive an OPIC Registration Letter before the investment is made or irrevocably committed. This letter does not commit OPIC to offer insurance, nor does it commit the investor to accept it.

Other Criteria. Investors are asked to supply data on a project's developmental effect on the host country, including information relating to job creation, skill development, balance of payments effects, taxes and host-government revenues, and contribution to basic human needs.

OPIC will deny coverage for investments that are likely to have a negative effect on U.S. domestic employment. It may also refuse coverage for investments in projects that are likely to have adverse effects on the U.S. balance of payments and those used primarily to finance the procurement of goods or services for a particular project in other industrialized countries.

OPIC's agreements with the governments of countries in which OPIC programs are offered require that the foreign government specifically approve each individual project for purposes of OPIC's insurance of investment in the project. Insurance coverage cannot begin until OPIC receives an acceptable Foreign Government Approval (FGA) covering the investment. (See Chapter 6).

Coverage

Inconvertibility. Inconvertibility coverage assures that earnings, capital, principal and interest, and other eligible remittances, such as payments under service agreements, can continue to be transferred into U.S. dollars. The insured will be compensated for currency blockage whether it is active (when host-country authorities deny access to foreign exchange on the basis of new, more restrictive regulations) or whether it is passive (when the monetary authorities fail to act within a specified period on an application for foreign exchange-usually 60 days). In either case, OPIC makes dollar payments upon receipt of the local currency.

Expropriation. OPIC insurance contracts define the insurable event of "expropriatory action" to include not only a direct taking of property but also a variety of situations that might be described as "creeping expropriation." An action taken by the host-country government which has a specified impact on either the properties or operations of the foreign enterprise or on the rights or financial interests of the insured investor may be considered expropriatory. For an action to be considered expropriatory, it must continue for at least one year for most investments, six months for contracts covering oil and gas projects, and three months or less for contracts covering institutional loans.

OPIC compensation for expropriatory actions is based on the net book value of the investor's insured interest in the foreign enterprise.

War, Revolution, Insurrection, and Civil Strife (political violence). Coverage extends to losses from actions taken to hinder, combat, or defend against hostile action during war, revolution, insurrection, or civil strife. Civil strife includes politically motivated violent acts by a group or individual, including acts of terrorism and sabotage. A loss caused by an individual or group acting primarily to achieve demands of labor or students, however, would be excluded from the coverage. Civil strife coverage is optional and the premium rate is reduced if the coverage is not selected.

Business Income Coverage. OPIC covers loss of profit and continuing normal operating expenses during a period when operations are interrupted due to an event of damage caused by political violence. Losses are covered for a period of up to one year or until the damaged property could reasonably have been repaired or replaced, whichever is sooner. OPIC also pays compensation for necessary expenses incurred to the extent that the expenses reduce the business income loss otherwise payable.

Terms
OPIC insurance contracts generally require the insurance premium to be paid annually in advance. Premiums are computed for each type of coverage on the basis of a contractually stipulated maximum insured amount chosen by the investor on a yearly basis. The current insured amount represents the insurance actually in force during any contract year. The difference between the current insured amount and maximum insured amount for each coverage is called the *standby amount*. The major portion of the premium is based on the current insured amount, with a reduced premium rate being applicable to the standby amount. For expropriation and war coverages, the insured must maintain current coverage at a level equal to the amount of investment at risk.

Premiums
Annual base rates for manufacturing, agribusiness, and services projects are given in the following list. Note that these rates vary for different industries and are discussed in greater detail in this chapter.

Coverage	Current (%)	Standby (%)
Inconvertibility	0.30	0.25
Expropriation	0.60	0.25
Political Violence	0.60	0.25
Political Violence with civil strife	0.75	0.30
Business Income (Political Violence)	0.45	0.25
Business Income with civil strife	0.60	0.30

Rates applied to individual investments may vary by as much as one-third from these base rates, depending on the risk profile of a specific project. Rates for natural resource and hydrocarbon projects or very large projects may vary by more than one-third of the base rates. OPIC insurance contracts (except for those covering institutional loans and certain service contracts) contain provisions that allow for an increase in the initial current coverage rate by up to 50 percent during the first 10 years of the contract period and another 50 percent during the second 10 years of the contract period.

Contact

Leigh Hollywood
Overseas Private Investment Corporation
1615 M Street, NW
Washington, DC 20527
(202) 457-7047

Special Insurance Programs

Minerals Insurance

OPIC offers specialized coverage for investments in mineral exploration and development (including processing where it is an integral part of a development project). OPIC will cover up to 90 percent of the initial investment plus an equal amount of retained earnings. The percentage of investment and retained earnings insured will depend on OPIC's assessment of risk factors in the project, including the extent of multinational equity and/or debt participation.

SMITH KLINE & FRENCH
INTERNATIONAL COMPANY

OPIC issued $2.8 million in insurance to Smith Kline & French International to cover its investment in a Bangladesh project for manufacturing a number of its pharmaceutical products. Twenty-five percent of the project is owned by Bangladesh nationals.

The project establishes a ready source of critically needed pharmaceutical products in one of the world's poorest countries. It is expected to supply hospitals and consumers with reasonably priced products in place of costly imports, thus contributing to improved health standards.

The project will employ 122 local workers. Anticipated returns to the host country are estimated at $100,000 annually during the first five years of operation, and $400,000 annually thereafter.

Coverage
Exploration. Insurance will be provided against all four covered risks (described earlier in this chapter) during the exploration phase for intangible costs as well as tangible assets.

Breach of Specified Government Contractual Obligations. Special additional coverage may be provided against losses resulting from the breach of certain host-government undertakings identified by the project sponsor at the outset as vital to the successful operation of the project. Such special coverages will be individually rated.

Political Violence. In addition to standard political violence coverage, insurance may be offered to cover consequential loss due to closing of operations for a period of at least six months. This loss may be directly caused by political violence events in the project country or by specified political violence events in another country.

Premiums
Annual base rates for natural resource projects other than oil and gas are as follows:

Coverage	Current (%)	Standby (%)
Inconvertibility	0.30	0.25
Expropriation	0.90	0.25
Political Violence	0.60	0.25
Political Violence with civil strife	0.75	0.30

Contact

B. Thomas Mansbach
Overseas Private Investment Corporation
1615 M Street, NW
Washington, DC 20527
(202) 457-7045

Energy Insurance

OPIC provides insurance for most types of investment in energy exploration, development and production. This includes investments made pursuant to traditional concession agreements, production-sharing agreements, service contracts, risk contracts, and other agreements with host-country governments.

Coverage

Coverage is available for up to 90 percent of the investment and generally does not exceed $100 million per project. OPIC's insurance for energy investments includes coverage against inconvertibility, expropriation, political violence, and interference with operations due to political violence.

Coverage for oil and gas projects is issued for a maximum term of 12 years with an extension of 8 years after the original insured period at OPIC's discretion. Insurance covering the construction period plus 10 years may be issued for coal mining projects, while projects involving the development of alternative energy sources may be insured for up to 20 years.

OPIC insurance is not available for investments in oil and gas exploration, development, and production projects in member countries of the Organization of Petroleum Exporting Countries (OPEC). However, projects in OPEC countries involving investments in petroleum service operations and downstream petrochemical projects, as well as investments in other energy and mineral sources, may be eligible.

Premiums

Premium rates are determined by the risk profile for a particular project. The annual base rates for oil and gas projects are as follows:

Coverage	Exploration Period (%)	Development/ Production Period (%)
Inconvertibility	0.30	0.30
Expropriation	0.40	1.50
Political Violence	0.60	0.60
Political Violence and Civil Stife	0.75	0.75
Interference with operations caused by political violence	0.40	0.40
Interference with operations caused by political violence with civil strife	0.55	0.55

The rates are applied to sums actually invested, beginning with the quarter in which each incremental investment is made. Coverage can be assured for future investments in the project by the payment of the modest standby premiums.

The base rates for other types of energy projects vary in accordance with the type of project and the method of investment.

Contact

B. Thomas Mansbach
Overseas Private Investment Corporation
1615 M Street, NW
Washington, DC 20527
(202) 457-7045

Insurance for Financial Institutions

OPIC offers U.S. banks and other financial institutions a number of services particularly designed to meet their needs.

Coverage

OPIC can cover a bank's capital investment in foreign branches and affiliated institutions. Typically, it will provide coverage for up to 270 percent of a capital infusion for protection of both the investment and attributable earnings. OPIC also is able to provide up to

UNION OIL COMPANY OF CALIFORNIA

The Union Oil Company of California took out a $100 million political risk insurance policy with the Overseas Private Investment Corporation on its investment in a natural gas venture in Thailand. The project involved developing and producing from an offshore natural gas field. The gas produced by the insured project is transported by an underwater pipeline, built and owned by the Petroleum Authority of Thailand and partially funded by the World Bank, to supply natural gas to two Bangkok power plants. The project will help Thailand begin to attain energy self-sufficiency and will produce significant foreign exchange savings.

100 percent coverage for loans made by a financial institution to an unrelated foreign private enterprise.

Premiums
Annual base rate for institutional loans is as follows:

Coverage	Current (%)	Unused Commitment (%)
Inconvertibility	0.25	0.20
Expropriation	0.30	0.20
Political Violence	0.60	0.20
Political Violence with civil strife	0.70	0.22
Inconvertibility and expropriation (combined)	0.50	0.30
Inconvertibility, expropriation, and political violence (combined)	0.90	0.50
Inconvertibility, expropriation, political violence with civil strife (combined)	1.00	0.52

Contact

Leigh Hollywood
Overseas Private Investment Corporation
1615 M Street, NW
Washington, DC 20527
(202) 457-7047

EXPORT INSURANCE

Eximbank Guarantee Program

Under Eximbank's Guarantee Program, the Export-Import Bank guarantees the repayment of medium-term (181 days to 7 years) and long-term (7-10 years) export obligations acquired by U.S. financial institutions from U.S. exporters. The purpose of this program is to increase U.S. exports of capital and quasi-capital goods by assuming commercial and political risks associated with international trade financing.

Terms

Eximbank requires that the buyer make a 15 percent cash payment to the exporter. Most guarantees provide comprehensive coverage of both political and commercial risks. In addition, a guarantee covering only political risks is also available for transactions with private or nonsovereign public buyers, and is the only type of guarantee available where there is common ownership between the supplier (or exporter) and the overseas buyer (or guarantor). Repayment terms do not exceed those which are customary in international trade, and usually follow the schedule below:

Contract Value

Medium-term	Maximum Term
Up to $50,000	2 years
$50,000-$100,000	3 years
$100,000-$200,000	4 years
$200,000 or more	5 years (Exceptionally up to 7 years)

Long-term
Over 7 years usually not to exceed 10 years.

Coverage

Floor-Plan Coverage. When Eximbank guarantees a revolving line of credit involving repeat sales to dealers/distributors, a floor-plan period of up to 270 days is also eligible. Products not resold to an end user during the floor-plan period are then financed under a medium-term debt obligation.

Switch-Cover Option. This feature permits U.S. equipment that has been exported to a dealer/distributor to be guaranteed in the name of the end user.

Bank-to-Bank Lines. In nonindustrial countries, Eximbank offers its guarantee to cover revolving medium-term lines of credit established by a U.S. bank with a foreign bank.

Preshipment Coverage. When the export product is specially fabricated or requires a lengthy manufacturing period, Eximbank may issue its guarantee to the exporter, effective from the date of contract rather than date of shipment.

Foreign Currency Guarantees. Transactions may also be denominated in selected foreign currencies.

Small Business Commercial Coverage

Commercial risk coverage is increased from 90 percent to 95 percent for products manufactured by a small business as defined by the SBA. Commercial risks include losses from a buyer's insolvency or failure to pay within six months after the due date of an insured obligation.

Contact

James W. Crist, Vice President
Loans and Guarantees
Export-Import Bank of the U.S.
811 Vermont Avenue, NW
Washington, DC 20571
(202) 566-8990

Foreign Credit Insurance Association

The Foreign Credit Insurance Association (FCIA) is a group of U.S. marine, property, and casualty insurance companies. FCIA helps U.S. exporters compete on favorable terms with exporters from other countries. FCIA also helps expand U.S. exports. FCIA, as agent for Eximbank, insures U.S. exporters against the risk of nonpayment by foreign buyers for commercial and political reasons. Commercial risks include losses from a buyer's bankruptcy or failure, due to insolvency, to pay within six months after the due date of an insured obligation. Political risks are losses from dollar transfer delays, war, revolution, license revocation, diversion of goods, and similar politically related incidents occurring in the buyer's country that cause a loss to the U.S. company. The credit insurance can cover 90 percent of the commercial risks and 100 percent of the political risks or 95 percent of all risks; a choice that is made by the policyholder.

FCIA works in cooperation with the Export-Import Bank and markets and issues the credit insurance on behalf of Eximbank.

Eligibility

Any company, corporation, partnership, or similar entity registered to do business in the United States and engaged in the export or export financing of U.S. products is eligible to participate in FCIA programs. A qualified U.S. exporter may obtain FCIA coverage by becoming a policyholder directly or by working through an FCIA policy held by a commercial bank. Coverage is available when at least 50 percent of the value of a product consists of labor and materials exclusively of U.S. origin.

Virtually any product can be insured, though there are some exceptions:

Military or defense-related equipment generally is not eligible for coverage (exceptions require advance approval).

Cattle or livestock and used equipment require the completion of a special questionnaire with each application for coverage.

Insured products usually are shipped from the United States. However, coverage is available for sales made either from an exporter's consigned stock in a foreign country or from the insured's wholly owned subsidiary overseas, provided the U.S. content requirement is met.

Terms

FCIA covers transactions using credit terms that generally do not exceed those recognized internationally as customary for the products in question. Short-term products (such as consumer goods and spare parts) carry maximum repayment terms of 180 days. Repayment terms for medium-term products (capital and quasi-capital goods) can range from 181 days to five years.

SOLAREX CORPORATION

The Export-Import Bank approved both guarantee protection and discount loan support for a $300,000 export sale to a Colombian utility of American-made solar power generating equipment. The sale was made against competition from suppliers in France, Germany, and Japan.

The Solarex Corporation of Rockville, Maryland, which manufactures solar power equipment, worked with Eximbank to arrange the financing of the sale.

The purchaser, Empresas Departamentales de Antioquia, will use the solar generators to power a telecommunication system for 99 small villages.

Programs for New Exporters

New-to-Export Policy

The New-to-Export policy, sponsored by FCIA, provides companies just beginning to export, or with limited export volume, with enhanced commercial risk protection for the first two years of a policy's life which includes 95 percent commercial coverage, 100 percent political coverage and no deductible.

Eligibility

Companies must not have had direct Association coverage for two years preceding the date of application, and the following documentation must be submitted to FCIA.

1. satisfactory references from a credit-reporting agency, two suppliers, and a commercial bank;

2. signed financial statements or annual report for the latest fiscal year, or start-up statements which reveal a positive net worth;

3. a sales history showing average annual export credit sales during the preceding two fiscal years not exceeding $750,000 (together with affiliates and exclusive of sales made on terms of confirmed irrevocable letters of credit or cash in advance. In

the case that the preceding fiscal year was the firm's first year of exporting, sales may not exceed $1,000,000).

Umbrella Policy

For the company just beginning to export that needs some outside expertise in operating under a policy, the Umbrella policy is available. An Umbrella policy is issued to a qualified entity such as an insurance broker, bank, state or municipal government agency, etc., as the policy administrator; the administrator then seeks to market the insurance policy to local exporters. In so doing, the administrator agrees to qualify the exporter and its buyers for the insurance and also agrees to report shipments and all overdues. The administrator acts as the Insured's representative regarding communications with and reporting to FCIA and Eximbank.

Eligibility
1. signed financial statements or annual report for the latest fiscal year, or start-up statements which reveal a positive net worth.

2. average annual export sales history during the preceding two fiscal years not exceeding $2,000,000 (together with affiliates and exclusive of sales made on terms of confirmed irrevocable letters of credit or cash in advance).

Short-Term Single-Buyer Policy

The Short-Term Single-Buyer Policy is custom written to recognize the sales contract and payment terms. Since the policy is structured for single sale transactions, the standard policy period during which shipments can be made is 3 months. FCIA can issue a policy for up to 12 months to accommodate multiple shipments under a sales contract.

Under the Short-Term Single-Buyer policy there is no requirement to insure a spread of business, thus providing an opportunity for exporters to selectively insure transactions with or without linking them to bank financing. Exporters may access FCIA insurance either on a multibuyer basis or selectively. In general, however, exporters will not be able to have both policies simultaneously.

Coverage applies to credit sales to a foreign buyer, or export letters of credit opened by a foreign buyer, or export letters of credit opened by a foreign issuing bank, for U.S. goods produced and shipped from the U.S. during the policy period. Cover is generally provided for credit terms up to 180 days. On a case-by-case basis, agricultural commodities, capital equipment and quasi-capital equipment may be insured on terms up to 360 days.

Percentages of cover are equalized for commercial and political risks: for sovereign obligors, 100%; private sector and other nonsovereign obligors, 90%; letter of credit transactions, 95%; bulk agricultural transactions, 98%.

There is no first loss deductible provision in the policy; however, the policyholder must stay at risk for the amount exceeding the insured percentage.

The policy utilizes a risk-based pricing system. A disciplined formula provides a premium rate that reflects the major risk elements of each transaction. Premium is paid on the total volume amount to be insured.

Short-Term Multi-Buyer Policy

The Short-Term Multi-Buyer Policy is generally written to cover shipments during a one-year period and insures a reasonable spread of an exporter's eligible sales. It enables premiums to be lowered, helps the exporter to make quicker credit decisions (providing faster service to overseas buyers) and reduces paperwork.

The exporter can obtain financing and can offer competitive credit terms to attract and retain buyers around the globe, even in higher-risk markets. This policy insures short-term sales with repayment terms generally up to 180 days.

At the inception and each annual renewal of the Short-Term Multi-buyer policy, the exporter may choose to cover 90% of commercial risks and 100 percent of political risks, or choose equalized cover at 95% for both commercial and political risk. For short-term transactions, this coverage applies to the gross invoice amount and in many cases to interest at FCIA specified rates.

Medium-Term Policy

The Medium-Term policy covers capital and quasi-capital goods of U.S. manufacture sold in international trade on terms from six months to five years (occasionally longer). Policies are written on a case-by-case basis. The exporter may insure either a single sale or repetitive sales to the same buyer and is not required to insure all of his medium-term transactions.

The foreign buyer must make a 15 percent cash payment on or before due date of first installment. The remaining financed portion is to be covered by a promissory note requiring payment in approximately equal installments on a monthly, quarterly or semiannual basis.

The policy generally covers interest charges up to specified limits as well as principal due. Coverage is normally 90 percent of a commercial and 100 percent of a political loss.

A Combination Medium-Term policy is utilized mainly to protect exporters in transactions with overseas dealers and distributors. It protects against risk in three areas:

1. parts and accessories on terms up to 180 days;

2. inventory financing, where the exporter may ship goods under a "floor plan" arrangement. Initial coverage is up to 270 days with no down payment required;

3. receivables financing, with terms typically up to three years following the minimum cash payment upon resale by the dealer, or at the end of the inventory period.

For medium-term transactions, the buyer must pay the normal 15 percent cash payment and coverage is on the remaining financed portion, plus interest, as described earlier.

Contact

Your insurance broker or:

Headquarters

New York

Foreign Credit
  Insurance Association
40 Rector Street
11th Floor
New York, NY 10006
(212) 306-5000

Chicago

Foreign Credit
  Insurance Association
20 North Clark Street
Suite 910
Chicago, IL 60602
(312) 641-1915

Houston

Foreign Credit
  Insurance Association
Texas Commerce Tower
Suite 2860
600 Travis
Houston, TX 77002
(713) 227-0987

Miami

Foreign Credit
  Insurance Association
80 Southwest 8th Street
Miami, FL 33130
(305) 372-8540

Los Angeles

Foreign Credit
  Insurance Association
Crocker Center
Suite 2580
333 South Grand Avenue
Los Angeles, CA 90071
(213) 687-3890

Washington, DC

Foreign Credit
  Insurance Association
811 Vermont Avenue, NW
Washington, DC 20571
(202) 566-8111

SPECIAL PROGRAMS

Leasing Program

OPIC offers political risk insurance coverage for cross-border operating and capital lease transactions with terms of at least 36 months. OPIC's insurance for assets leased under an operating lease provides coverage for the original cost of the leased assets (including duties, freight, and installation) incurred by the lessor. Insurance for capital leases covers the stream of payments due under the lease agreement. OPIC's insurance provides coverage against the following:

The inability to convert into dollars local currency received as lease payments.

Loss due to expropriation, nationalization, or confiscation by action of the host government.

Loss due to political violence.

Coverage is also available for equity investments in, and loans to, offshore leasing companies, for management and maintenance agreements involving leasing companies, and for consigned inventory.

Eligibility
See the description of OPIC's insurance program discussed earlier in this chapter.

Premiums
Premium rates are determined by the risk profile of a particular project. Annual base rates for leasing insurance are as follows:

Coverage	Current (%)
Inconvertibility	0.30
Expropriation	0.60
Political Violence	0.60
Political Violence with civil strife	0.75

205

Contact
Leigh Hollywood
Overseas Private Investment Corporation
1615 M Street, NW
Washington, DC 20527
(202) 457-7047

OPIC Contractors and Exporters Program

OPIC insures letters of credit or on-demand bonds required as bid, performance, advance payment, custom bonds, and other guarantees against arbitrary drawings. OPIC also provides contractors or exporters with political risk protection against losses resulting from currency inconvertibility, expropriation, political violence, and unresolved disputes with the owner.

Eligibility

The project must benefit host-country development, and there must be reasonable assurance of adequate project funding. Military projects and projects harmful to U.S. economic interests are not eligible. Imported goods and services associated with the contract should be primarily either of U.S. origin or from developing countries.

Coverage

Bid, Performance, and Advance Payment Guarantees. Through its insurance program, OPIC indemnifies the contractor or exporter for losses resulting from a foreign government owner's "arbitrary" drawing of a letter of credit or on-demand bond issued as a bid, performance, advance payment, or other guarantee. This insurance is also available to sub-contractors and others who are not the prime contractor but who must post a guarantee for a particular project. The insurance policy provides coverage for up to 90 percent of any loss; the balance of the political risk must be borne by the contractor. OPIC does not indemnify if the guarantee is drawn because of the contractor's failure to perform its contractual obligations or if the contractor provokes or agrees to the drawing.

OPIC may issue bid guarantee coverage before a contract is in force but without obligating itself to insure against the arbitrary drawing of the performance or advance payment guarantee which may be required if the contractor is the successful bidder.

Coverage also is available to contractors who post guarantees in favor of private parties. In these cases, an arbitrary drawing is defined as a drawing that is not justified by the terms of the contract and is directly caused by the host government or is followed by host government action that thwarts the proper functioning of the decisional procedure.

OPIC also offers the following coverages for certain additional risks incurred by U.S. contractors and exporters in the underlying contract:

Currency Inconvertibility. Inconvertibility coverage provides contractors with protection against the inability to convert local currency payments from the sale or other disposition of the insured party's property into U.S. dollars.

Expropriation. Coverage is available against the loss of the contractor's tangible assets and bank accounts maintained in the project country in connection with the underlying contract. This loss may result from confiscation by the host government that continues uninterrupted for a period of six months.

Political Violence. Under this coverage, the contractor is compensated for loss or damage to assets that results directly from hostile actions occurring within the project country.

Disputes. Disputes coverage compensates the contractor for losses sustained when a government owner fails to honor an arbitration award in favor of the contractor for a period of at least three months. Compensation is calculated at 90 percent of the portion of the award the government owner has failed to pay.

The coverage also provides for compensation when a government owner refuses, for a period of at least six months, to submit a dispute for resolution as outlined in the contract. OPIC will also provide compensation to the contractor if resort to the decisional procedure would be futile, impracticable, or hazardous to the physical safety of the insured's personnel due to changed conditions in the project country. In such cases OPIC's indemnity is based on the cost of goods, services, and materials provided under the contract, and which are the subject of the dispute. In the event the insured party's contract is with a private entity, OPIC will compensate the contractor only if nonpayment is directly caused by the host government or if the host government thwarts the proper functioning of the decisional procedure.

Judicial Requirements

Insurance against arbitrary drawings of letters of credit provided as performance and advance payment guarantees, and disputes coverage, are available only where the underlying construction, sales, or services contract provides a decisional procedure to settle disputes between the owner and the contractor; local law and practice indicate that the procedure would be followed in the event of a dispute; and experience suggests that the procedure is likely to be fair and impartial.

Terms

The term of the insurance policy generally coincides with the term of the guarantee or the duration of the contract, but the minimum premium payment is for six months.

Premiums

The annual base rate for contractors' and exporters' guarantee coverage is as follows:

Coverage	Current (%)	Standby (%)
Inconvertibility	0.30	0.25
Expropriation	0.60	0.25
Political Violence	0.60	0.25
Political Violence with civil strife	0.75	0.30
Disputes	0.80	0.25
Bid, performance, advance payment, and other guarantees	0.60	0.25

Contact

Benjamin Erulkar
Overseas Private Investment Corporation
1615 M Street, NW
Washington, DC 20527
(202) 457-7061

SOILTEST, INC.

In 1987, Soiltest, Inc., an Evanston, Illinois business, signed a contract with INECEL, the Electrical Institute of Ecuador, a government agency. The contract covered Soiltest's sale of soil and rock testing equipment to INECEL, part of a World Bank-financed nationwide electrification feasibility study in Ecuador. The Overseas Private Investment Corporation issued insurance totalling about $250,000 to Soiltest covering the risk of wrongful calling of a standby letter of credit. First Illinois Bank of Evanston had posted the letter of credit in favor of INECEL on behalf of Soiltest, to guarantee Soiltest's contractual obligations.

FCIA Special Programs

Coverage

Preshipments. FCIA provides preshipment coverage for exporters which dates from the execution of the sales contract rather than the date of shipment. This coverage is pertinent to specially fabricated goods or those requiring up to 18 months factory lead time. Transactions requiring payment in the buyer's currency may be eligible for coverage and political-only coverage for export sales may also be obtained.

Service Sales. Management consultants, engineering service firms, transportation companies and similar businesses may obtain protection for payments made by foreign customers. Coverage is offered to companies wishing to extend prudent terms to gain a greater share of the services market.

Equipment Leasing. Insurance coverage is available on operating and finance leases to cover defaulted lease payments against commercial and political loss (up to the point when the lease requires the return of the asset due to protracted default). Coverage is also available for the expropriation of the leased products. This coverage is available to any financially responsible leasing company, manufacturer, bank, trust, partnership or other domestic or foreign entity that leases or participates in the financing of U.S. export leases. Lease transactions may be either cross-border or international. Leased equipment can be either new or used, but must be of U.S. manufacture. Payments may be in dollars or other hard currencies.

Contact

Your insurance broker or FCIA offices listed previously in this chapter.

Eximbank Protection

The Export-Import Bank is prepared to consider issuing its guarantee for either a cross-border or international lease of U.S. manufactured goods or equipment. Eximbank will consider large and unusual lease transactions which FCIA normally cannot. For example, an operating or finance lease of a new commercial jet aircraft, offshore drilling rig or other export of significant value would be considered by Eximbank.

Eligibility

An Eligible Lessor is defined as any leasing company, manufacturer, bank, trust, partnership or other entity foreign or domestic that leases or participates in the financing of leases of U.S. manufactured equipment and services outside the United States.

Eximbank's lease guarantee will apply to new or used U.S. manufactured equipment and services. If the lessor is located offshore, it must be demonstrated to Eximbank's satisfaction that Eximbank support of the lease will result in an export of U.S. goods and services from the United States for the products or services being leased.

Eximbank will consider issuing its guarantee or insurance to support two basic contractual lease types. The guarantee and insurance may be applied to 1) an Export Operating Lease (Rental Contract), or 2) an Export Finance Lease (Full Payout Lease).

The leased asset may be new or used capital equipment manufactured in the United States, the title to which is owned by the U.S. lessor or will be purchased by the offshore lessor in connection with the Eximbank lease guarantee or insurance.

Terms

There is no cash payment required on an Export Operating Lease. For an Export Finance Lease, Eximbank will require a 15% cash payment of the lease contract. The lease payments may be calculated on a level payment basis (annuity basis) or on a standard loan repayment basis (equal principal installments with declining interest).

Contact

James W. Crist
Vice President
Loans and Guarantees
Export-Import Bank of the U.S.
811 Vermont Avenue, NW
Washington, DC 20571
(202) 566-8990

Export-Credit Information Services

The Export-Import Bank will provide credit information to an applicant on any buyer who has previously done business with the Bank.

Contact

C. Trujillo, Jr.
Vice-President of Information Management
Export-Import Bank of the U.S.
811 Vermont Avenue, NW
Room 1045
Washington, DC 20571
(202) 566-8911

CHAPTER NINE

TRAINING, ADVICE, AND ASSISTANCE

Once the decision has been made to begin operations abroad, several U.S. government programs are available to assist in the start-up phase. Government programs also can provide assistance when a business is expanded at a later date. Additional programs are available for handling the typical needs faced by a U.S. enterprise overseas. This chapter discusses three types of programs:

Training. Assistance for training and educating employees and others as part of an overseas business effort.

Advice. How to benefit from the large pool of experienced business executives, government officials, and industry specialists willing to help.

Special Assistance. Information and assistance with problems or questions that might arise with an overseas venture as well as promotional assistance for the export of agricultural products.

TRAINING

Technical and Managerial Skills Training

The U.S. Telecommunications Training Institute is a joint venture between the U.S. telecommunications industry and the U.S. government. The goal of this collaborative effort is to share U.S. communications advances globally by providing a comprehensive array of free telecommunications and broadcast training courses for qualified individuals from developing countries of the world. These courses are held in the laboratories, training facilities, and factories of major U.S. corporations and government agencies.

Contact
Judith Sparrow, Director
U.S. Telecommunications Training Institute
1255 23rd Street, NW
Suite 400
Washington, DC 20037
(202) 862-3857

Agricultural Education and Training

USDA International Training Division

The Agriculture Department's International Training Division offers a variety of courses to develop the skills of foreign agriculturalists. These courses include Animal Science and Natural Resources; Economics and Policy; Management, Education, and Human Resource Development; and Production and Technology.

The courses are open to agricultural and rural development technicians, scientists, trainers, administrators, and policymakers from developing nations. Courses are held in the Washington area, at universities in over 20 states, and in foreign countries. Applications for course enrollment must be submitted no later than two months before a course begins. For most courses, enrollment is on a space-available basis. Organizations sponsoring participants include the Agency for International Development, the Food and Agriculture Organization of the United Nations, international development banks, developing country governments, foundations, and private organizations. In addition, there are opportunities for foreign agriculturalists to participate in research in over 200 subject areas. This research is conducted in laboratories operated by the Agricultural Research

214

United States
Telecommunications
Training Institute   1988 Course Catalog/Annual Report

Global Growth Through Telecommunications Sharing

Cover page of United States Telecommunications Training Institute
(USTTI), 1988 course catalog and Annual Report. USTTI promotes
the transfer of telecommunications technology around the world by
providing free training to operators of broadcast and telephone systems throughout the world.

215

Service for Science and Education Administration. This allows foreign scientists to update, increase, and refine their research skills while working together with U.S. scientists in ongoing research programs.

Contact
Valdis Mezainis, Director
International Training Division
Office of International Cooperation and Development
U.S. Department of Agriculture
Room 232-MCG
Washington, DC 20250
(202) 653-8320

Middle Income Country Training Program

The Office of International Cooperation and Development funds the training of agriculturalists from middle income countries. Training opportunities are for senior and mid-level specialists and administrators concerned with agricultural trade, management, and marketing from the public and private sectors. The program offers short term training opportunities ranging from one week to six months. Scholarship recipients may attend university classes, meet with professionals in their fields, visit experiment stations and industry sites, and/or receive on-the-job training.

Contact
Charles Aanenson, Coordinator of Special Projects
Office of International Cooperation and Development
U.S. Department of Agriculture
Room 203 McGregor Building
International Training Division
Washington, DC 20250
(202) 653-8320

USDA Graduate School

The Graduate School of the U.S. Department of Agriculture is a nonprofit, self-supporting educational institution established by the U.S. government in 1921. The Graduate School has trained over 400,000 people at the international, national, state, and local levels. The International Programs Division provides training and technical assistance for participants from other countries. Training areas include financial and industrial management, economics, business administration, energy, human resource development, computer sciences, statistics, marketing, employment, forestry, agricultural and rural development, transportation, telecommunications, appropriate technology, cultural and museum management, and health and nutrition. Courses are taught in English, French, Spanish, Arabic, and Portuguese, and they are offered both in the United States and overseas.

The Graduate School also offers cross-cultural education, English-language training, and custom-designed programs to meet specific needs of an organization. In cooperation with other U.S. universities, a masters degree program in international management development is offered.

Contact

Lilia Parsons, Program Director
International Programs
The Graduate School
U.S. Department of Agriculture
600 Maryland Avenue, SW,
Suite 134
Washington, DC 20024
(202) 447-7476

Participant Training Program

The Participant Training Program (PTP), funded by the Agency for International Development, is a comprehensive training program for developing country nationals, administered by the Office of International Training. PTP utilizes training resources provided by universities and colleges, businesses, laboratories, agricultural concerns, labor organizations, state and local governments, and community organizations.

Contact

Mary Kay Williams
Office of International Training
U.S. Agency for International Development
Room 215 SA-16
Washington, DC 20523
(202) 875-4114

International Development Law Institute

The Bureau for Private Enterprise within AID provides a grant to the International Development Law Institute (IDLI) in Rome, Italy, to train developing country private lawyers. The grant provides for fellowships to attend courses and seminars focusing on developing country policy constraints to private enterprise development. Training under this grant strengthens the negotiating, drafting and administrative capacities of lawyers to address the concerns of both foreign investors and local businesses. It also helps resolve the current shortage of developing country arbitrators qualified to handle commercial and investment disputes.

Contact

Russell Anderson, Director
Office of Project Development
Bureau for Private Enterprise
Agency for International Development
Room 3208 NS
Washington, DC 20523
(202) 647-5806

ADVICE

In-Country Management Advice

The International Executive Service Corps (IESC), which is funded by the Bureau for Private Enterprise in AID, U.S. private contributors and service fees, provides technical assistance and managerial know-how to mainly small and medium-sized businesses in the developing world. IESC draws on a skills pool of about 9,500 retired American business volunteers who travel to host countries on short-term assignments. A secondary IESC role is to provide linkages between American businesses and Third World businesses which may lead to joint ventures.

Contact
Thomas Carroll, President
International Executive Service Corps
8 Stamford Forum
P.O. Box 100S
Stamford, CT 06904-2005
(203) 967-6000

Specialized Management Counseling

The Active Corps of Executives (ACE) and the Service Corps of Retired Executives (SCORE), with the support of the Small Business Administration, offer free management counseling by more than 13,000 members. The members are executives from major industries, professional and trade associations, educational institutions, and other professions. They volunteer their specialized expertise on request by a U.S. business.

Contact
nearest Small Business Administration district office (see appendix)

INTERNATIONAL EXECUTIVE SERVICE CORPS

A group of Philippine businessmen provided the necessary funding for establishment of a small project involving the design and production of ceramics. Their goal was to establish an enterprise that would create local employment and whose profits would be used to provide an ongoing source of revenue to the families of patients at a leprosarium located not far from the plant.

Recognizing that the ultimate success of the project would depend to a great extent on management expertise and knowledge of the ceramics industry, the investors sought help from the International Executive Service Corps (IESC). In response, the corporation sent John Lux, retired vice-president of a Buffalo, New York porcelain-ceramics company, to Manila, where he spent two months working shoulder-to-shoulder with the plant manager and employees.

The teamwork paid off. Just one year later, the project had doubled its sales and added 100 new employees to the original staff of 60. By the end of the second year, annual enrollment in its training school had risen to 45, and more recently a major building program for the construction of production line and electric kiln housing was completed.

SPECIAL ASSISTANCE

Expropriation Assistance

The State Department's Office of Investment Affairs is a point of contact in the U.S. government for multinational corporations. In addition to its role in expropriation matters, it formulates State Department policy on bilateral investment treaties. The Office assesses the investment climate for U.S. businesses in developing nations by monitoring host-country investment policies and regulations. In the event a country's legislation or other government actions threaten the integrity of its commitments to investors, the interagency group on expropriation, chaired by the Office of Investment Affairs, recommends an appropriate policy. The office also develops and coordinates U.S. policy concerning investment and multinational corporation issues, consults with Congress on investment issues, and maintains formal liaison with the U.S. business community on developments in international investment policy.

Contact
Marilyn A. Meyers, Director
Office of Investment Affairs
U.S. Department of State
Room 2533A
Washington, DC 20520
(202) 647-1128

Patents, Trademarks, and Copyrights

The State Department's Office of Business Practices is responsible for policies relating to the foreign protection of U.S. patents, trademarks, and copyrights. It closely follows developments that might lead to the erosion of this protection, especially in developing nations. It also works with the U.S. Patent and Trademark Office and the Copyright Office. The Office provides consultation and assistance to U.S. companies faced with possible patent, trademark, or copyright problems.

Contact
Harvey J. Winter, Director
Office of Business Practices
U.S. Department of State
Room 3531A
Washington, DC 20520
(202) 647-1486

221

International Telecommunications Information

The Office of International Affairs under the direction of the National Telecommunications & Information Administration works to minimize unnecessary U.S. and foreign government interference in the efficient functioning of international telecommunications markets. It also seeks to identify and, where feasible, diminish foreign obstacles to U.S. trade in telecommunications and information services and products.

Contact
Richard Beaird, Associate Administrator
National Telecommunications and Information Administration
Office of International Affairs
U.S. Department of Commerce
14th & Constitution Avenue, NW
Washington, DC 20230
(202) 377-1304

Communications Services and Regulations

The Federal Communications Commission (FCC) provides information concerning telecommunications rates, services, and regulations governing communications from the U.S. to points worldwide.

Contact
George Li, Chief
International Facilities Division
Federal Communications Commission
1919 M Street, NW Room 846
Washington, DC 20554
(202) 632-7834

Commerce Business Liaison

The Office of Business Liaison (OBL) serves as the focal point for contact between the Department of Commerce and the business community. The OBL is especially interested in creating an awareness of its business assistance services to small and medium-sized businesses. OBL staff answer questions on government policies, programs and services and provide information on a variety of published materials.

Contact

Gordon Schmidt, Trade Specialist
Office of Business Liaison
U.S. Department of Commerce
Room 5898-C
Washington, DC 20230
(202) 377-3176

Policy and Economic Climate

The Bureau for Private Enterprise in the Agency for International Development provides technical assistance to AID field missions and host governments. It is designed to improve the environment in developing countries for investment and private enterprise activity, domestic and foreign.

Financial Markets Development. The Bureau's Financial Market Development Project provides technical assistance to improve the institutional capability of developing countries to mobilize private capital for productive uses. Experts are provided to host countries to recommend changes in policy to remove barriers to capital market development, help establish financial market systems, and work with AID field missions in developing relevant projects.

Contact

James Dry
Office of Project Development
Bureau for Private Enterprise
U.S. Agency for International Development
Room 3208 NS
Washington, DC 20523
(202) 647-5806

Center for Privatization. The Center provides policy, strategic and tactical assistance in the transfer of state-owned or controlled enterprises or functions to the private sector. This includes technical expertise needed by AID missions to prepare country-specific and sector-specific divestiture strategies; assistance in policy dialogue with host country public and private sector leaders; and implementation of privatization actions in selected countries.

Contact
Louis Faoro
Office of Project Development
Bureau for Private Enterprise
U.S. Agency for International Development
Room 3208 NS
Washington, DC 20523
(202) 647-5806

Private Enterprise Development Support (PEDS). This project provides support to AID field missions and other agency units to develop broad private enterprise strategies geared to Third World economic growth. Contractors provide long- and short-term consultancies to missions and develop business training materials and courses for host country personnel.

Contact
Dr. Thomas Nicastro
Office of Project Development
Bureau for Private Enterprise
U.S. Agency for International Development
Room 3208 NS
Washington, DC 20523
(202) 647-5806

International Partnership Information

International Partnerships for the Commercialization of Technology (INPACT), sponsored by the U.S. Department of Commerce, provides information and counseling for countries that show interest in linking their smaller firms with U.S. counterparts. The INPACT program includes development and execution of bilateral agreements, training and project screening, and aid in identifying networks of potential partners and resources in the U.S.

INPACT companies are smaller, non-defense firms which are making use of novel applications of existing technology. Joint ventures formed through INPACT must adhere to existing laws and regulations in the participating countries, including U.S. trade regulations and export controls.

Contact
G.T. Underwood, Director
International Operations
Office of Productivity, Technology, and Innovation
U.S. Department of Commerce
Room 4816 HCHB
Washington, DC 20230
(202) 377-0944

Labor Information

The Department of Labor provides a number of services to Americans interested in doing business abroad, including information on the labor climate in certain countries and on foreign projects for which technical assistance is sought. The Department has made the Caribbean Basin a high-priority area and offers current information on labor conditions in countries in this region.

Contact
Christopher Hankin
Acting Deputy Under Secretary for International Affairs
Bureau of International Labor Affairs
Department of Labor
200 Constitution Avenue, NW
Washington, DC 20210
(202) 523-6043

Agricultural Export Promotion

The Department of Agriculture's Export Incentive Program assists private U.S. firms in promoting agricultural consumer products overseas. Under this program, the Foreign Agricultural Service reimburses firms for up to 50 percent of their export promotion expenditures. The amount of reimbursement is determined by the level of growth in export sales (around 5 percent of the growth in sales) and the extent of the company's promotional activities. The criteria for program approval include probable success in maintaining or increasing consumption of U.S. products, long-range contributions to U.S. agricultural exports and balance of payments, and competition in the export markets. The following products are currently being promoted under the program: wine, green peppers and other fresh vegetables, almonds, walnuts, canned corn, processed vegetables, cranberries, frozen peas, celery, citrus, and prunes.

This program is available only when at least one-half to two-thirds of the members of an industry seek assistance together. However, at the suggestion of a single firm, the Foreign Agricultural Service will contact others who might be willing to join. This program is not available when the industry's Cooperator group is active in the same market.

Contact

Frank Piason
Deputy Assistant Administrator
  for Commodity and Marketing Programs
Foreign Agricultural Service
U.S. Department of Agriculture
Room 5807-S
Washington, DC 20250
(202) 447-7791

CHAPTER TEN

A FINAL NOTE

When operating abroad, not all problems or opportunities can be anticipated. Special situations requiring special remedies may arise. The U.S. government, as your partner, stands ready to support American investors overseas not only through management advice and training programs, but also through all the programs described in this book.

AGRO-TECH INTERNATIONAL, INC.

To initiate its poultry operations in the Dominican Republic, the Miami-based Agro-Tech International, Inc. turned to OPIC for an $800,000 loan. The company, founded by Francisco Hernandez, used the OPIC loan to begin enlarging its poultry breeding and broiler farm capacity. But Hurricane David severely damaged the incomplete project, causing Agro-Tech to return to OPIC the following year for an additional $400,000 loan and an extension of its first loan OPIC granted. Sales for Agro-Tech and its subsidiaries, which supply farm equipment, feed grains, and technical services abroad, in addition to its feed and poultry operations, have increased by 50 percent.

APPENDIX

U.S. DEPARTMENT OF COMMERCE DISTRICT OFFICES

ALABAMA

Birmingham—Gayle C. Shelton, Jr., Director, Rm. 302 2015 2nd Avenue, North 3rd Floor, Berry Bldg., 35203 (205) 731-1331

ALASKA

Anchorage—Richard Lenahan, Director, 701 C Street, P.O. Box 32, 99513 (907) 271-5041

ARIZONA

Phoenix—Donald W. Fry, Director, Federal Bldg. & U.S. Courthouse 230 North 1st Avenue, Rm. 3412, 85025 (602) 261-3285

ARKANSAS

Little Rock—Lon J. Hardin, Director, Suite 811, Savers Federal Building, 320 W. Capitol Avenue, 72201 (501) 378-5792

CALIFORNIA

Los Angeles—Daniel J. Young, Director, Room 800, 11777 San Vicente Boulevard, 90049 (213) 209-6705

Santa Ana—116-A W. 4th Street, Suite #1, 92701 (714) 836-2461

San Diego—Richard Powell, Director, 6363 Greenwich Drive, 92122 (619) 293-5395

San Francisco—Betty D. Neuhart, Director, Federal Building, Box 36013, 450 Golden Gate Avenue, 94102 (415) 556-5860

COLORADO

Denver—(Vacant), Room 119, U.S. Customhouse, 721-19th Street, 80202 (303) 844-3246

CONNECTICUT

Hartford—Eric B. Outwater, Director, Room 610-B, Federal Office Building, 450 Main Street, 06103 (203) 240-3530

DELAWARE

Serviced by Philadelphia District Office

DISTRICT OF COLUMBIA

Washington, D.C. (Baltimore, Md. District)—Rm. 1066 HCHB, Department of Commerce, 14th & Constitution Avenue, N.W., 20230 (202) 377-3181

FLORIDA

Miami—Ivan A. Cosimi, Director, Suite 224, Federal Building, 51 S.W. First Avenue, 33130 (305) 536-5267

Clearwater—128 North Osceola Avenue, 33515 (813) 461-0011

Jacksonville—Independence Square, Suite 3205C, 32202 (904) 791-2796

Orlando—75 East Ivanhoe Boulevard, 32802 (305) 425-1234

Tallahassee—Collins Bldg., Rm. 401, 107 W. Gaines Street, 32304 (904) 488-6469

231

GEORGIA

Atlanta—George T. Norton, Director, Suite 504, 1365 Peachtree Street, N.E., 30309
(404) 347-7000

Savannah—James W. McIntire, Director, 120 Barnard Street, A-107, 31402
(912) 944-4204

HAWAII

Honolulu—George Dolan, Director, 4106 Federal Building, P.O. Box 50026, 300 Ala Moana Boulevard, 96850
(808) 541-1782

IDAHO

Boise—(Denver, Colorado District) Statehouse, Room 113, 83720
(208) 334-2470

ILLINOIS

Chicago—Michael Simon, Acting Director, 1406 Mid Continental Plaza Building, 55 East Monroe Street, 60603
(312) 353-4450

Palatine—W.R. Harper College, Algonquin & Roselle Rd., 60067
(312) 397-3000, x-532

Rockford—515 North Court Street, P.O. Box 1747, 61110-0247
(815) 987-8123

INDIANA

Indianapolis—Mel R. Sherar, Director, 357 U.S. Courthouse & Federal Office Building, 46 East Ohio Street, 46204
(317) 269-6214

IOWA

Des Moines—Jesse N. Durden, Director, 817 Federal Building, 210 Walnut Street, 50309
(515) 284-4222

KANSAS

Wichita (Kansas City, Missouri District)—River Park Place, Suite 565, 727 North Waco, 67203
(316) 269-6160

KENTUCKY

Louisville—Donald R. Henderson, Director, Room 636B, Gene Snyder Courthouse and Customhouse Building, 601 West Broadway, 40202
(502) 582-5066

LOUISIANA

New Orleans—Paul L. Guidry, Director, 432 World Trade Center, No. 2 Canal Street, 70130
(504) 589-6546

MAINE

Augusta (Boston, Massachusetts District)—77 Sewell Street, 04330
(207) 622-8249

MARYLAND

Baltimore—LoRee P. Silloway, Director, 415 U.S. Customhouse, Gay and Lombard Streets, 21202
(301) 962-3560

MASSACHUSETTS

Boston—Francis J. O'Connor, Director, World Trade Center, Suite 307 Commonwealth Pier Area, 02210
(617) 565-8563

MICHIGAN

Detroit—William Dolan, Director, 1140 McNamara Bldg. 477 Michigan Avenue, 48226
(313) 226-3650

Grand Rapids—300 Monroe N.W., Rm. 409, 49503
(616) 456-2411

MINNESOTA

Minneapolis—Ronald E. Kramer, Director, 108 Fed. Bldg. 110 S. 4th Street, 55401
(612) 348-1638

MISSISSIPPI

Jackson—Mark E. Spinney, Director, 328 Jackson Mall Office Center, 300 Woodrow Wilson Boulevard, 39213
(601) 965-4388

MISSOURI

St. Louis—Donald R. Loso, Director, 7911 Forsyth Boulevard, Suite 610, 63105, (314) 425-3302-4

Kansas City—James D. Cook, Director, Room 635, 601 East 12th Street, 64106 (816) 374-3141

MONTANA

Serviced by Denver District Office

NEBRASKA

Omaha—George H. Payne, Director, 1113 "O" Street, 68137
(402) 221-3664

NEVADA

Reno—Joseph J. Jeremy, Director, 1755 E. Plumb Lane, #152, 89502
(702) 784-5203

NEW HAMPSHIRE

Serviced by Boston District Office

NEW JERSEY

Trenton—Thomas J. Murray, Director, 3131 Princeton Pike Bldg. 4D, Suite 211, 08648
(609) 989-2100

NEW MEXICO

Albuquerque—(Vacant) 517 Gold, S.W. Suite 4303, 87102
(505) 766-2386

NEW YORK

Buffalo—Robert F. Magee, Director, 1312 Federal Building, 111 West Huron Street, 14202
(716) 846-4191

Rochester—121 East Avenue, 14604
(716) 263-6480

New York—Joel Barkan, Director, Fed. Office Bldg., 26 Federal Plaza, Foley Square, 10278
(212) 264-0634

NORTH CAROLINA

Greensboro—Samuel P. Troy, Director, 324 West Market Street, P.O. Box 1950, 27402
(919) 333-5345

NORTH DAKOTA

Serviced by Omaha District Office

OHIO

Cincinnati—Gordon B. Thomas, Director, 9504 Federal Office Building, 550 Main Street, 45202
(513) 684-2944

Cleveland—Toby Zettler, Director, Room 668, 666 Euclid Avenue, 44114
(216) 522-4750

OKLAHOMA

Oklahoma City—Ronald L. Wilson, Director, 5 Broadway Executive Park Suite 200, 6601 Broadway Extension, 73116
(405) 231-5302

Tulsa—440 S. Houston Street, 74127
(918) 581-7650

OREGON

Portland—Lloyd R. Porter, Director, Room 618, 1220 S.W. 3rd Avenue, 97204
(503) 221-3001

PENNSYLVANIA

Philadelphia—Robert E. Kistler, Director, 9448 Federal Building, 600 Arch Street, 19106
(215) 597-2850

Pittsburgh—John A. McCartney, Director, 2002 Federal Building, 1000 Liberty Avenue, 15222
(412) 644-2850

PUERTO RICO

San Juan (Hato Rey)—J. Enrique Vilella, Director, Room 659-Federal Building, 00918
(809) 753-4555

RHODE ISLAND

Providence (Boston, Massachusetts District)—7 Jackson Walkway, 02903
(401) 528-5104, ext. 22

SOUTH CAROLINA

Columbia—Edgar L. Rojas, Director, Strom Thurmond Fed. Bldg., Suite 172, 1835 Assembly Street, 29201
(803) 765-5345

Charleston—17 Lockwood Drive, 29401
(803) 724-4361

SOUTH DAKOTA

Serviced by Omaha District Office

TENNESSEE

Nashville—Jim Charlet, Director, Suite 1114, Parkway Towers, 404 James Robertson Parkway, 38103-1505
(615) 736-5161

Memphis—555 Beale Street, 38103
(901) 521-4137

TEXAS

Dallas—C. Carmon Stiles, Director, Room 7A5, 100 Commerce Street, 75242
(214) 767-0542

Austin—410 East 5th Street, Room 304, 78711
(512) 472-5059

Houston—James Cook, Director, 2625 Federal Courthouse, 515 Rusk Street, 77002
(713) 229-2578

UTAH

Salt Lake City—Stephen P. Smoot, Director, Room 340 U.S. Courthouse, 350 S. Main Street, 84101
(801) 524-5116

VERMONT

Serviced by Boston District Office

VIRGINIA

Richmond—Philip A. Ouzts, Director, 8010 Federal Bldg., 400 North Street, 23240
(804) 771-2246

WASHINGTON

Seattle—C. Franklin Foster, Director, 3131 Elliott Avenue, Suite 290, 98121
(206) 442-5616

Spokane—West 808 Spokane Falls Boulevard, Room 623, 99201
(509) 456-4557

WEST VIRGINIA

Charleston—Roger L. Fortner, Director, 3402 New Federal Building, 500 Quarrier Street, 26301
(304) 347-5123

WISCONSIN

Milwaukee—Patrick A. Willis, Director, Fed. Bldg., U.S. Courthouse, 517 E. Wisc. Ave., 53202 (414) 291-3473

WYOMING

Serviced by Denver District Office

U.S. SMALL BUSINESS ADMINISTRATION DISTRICT OFFICES

ALABAMA

2121 8th Avenue North
Suite 200
Birmingham, AL 35203-2398
(205) 731-1344

ALASKA

8th and C Streets
Anchorage, AK 99513
(907) 271-4022

ARIZONA

2005 N. Central Avenue
5th Floor
Phoenix, AZ 85004
(602) 261-3732

ARKANSAS

320 W. Capitol Avenue
Room 601
Little Rock, AR 72201
(501) 378-5871

CALIFORNIA

2202 Monterey Street
Suite 108
Fresno, CA 93721
(209) 487-5189

350 S. Figueroa Street
6th Floor
Los Angeles, CA 90071
(213) 894-2956

880 Front Street
Room 4S29
San Diego, CA 92188
(619) 293-5440

211 Main Street
4th Floor
San Francisco, CA 94105
(415) 974-0642

COLORADO

721 19th Street
Room 407
Denver, CO 80202
(303) 844-2607

CONNECTICUT

330 Main Street
2nd Floor
Hartford, CT 06106
(203) 240-4700

DISTRICT OF COLUMBIA

1111 18th Street, N.W.
6th Floor
Washington, DC 20036
(202) 634-4950

FLORIDA

1320 S. Dixie Highway
Suite 501
Coral Gables, FL 33146
(305) 536-5521

400 W. Bay Street
Room 261
Jacksonville, FL 32202
(904) 791-3782

GEORGIA

1720 Peachtree Road, N.W.
6th Floor
Atlanta, GA 30309
(404) 347-4749

HAWAII

300 Ala Moana
Room 2213
Honolulu, HI 96850
(808) 541-2990

236

IDAHO

1020 Main Street
Suite 290
Boise, ID 83702
(208) 334-1696

ILLINOIS

219 S. Dearborn Street
Room 437
Chicago, IL 60604-1779
(312) 353-4528

INDIANA

575 N. Pennsylvania Street
Room 578
Indianapolis, IN 46204
(317) 269-7272

IOWA

373 Collins Road, N.E.
Room 100
Cedar Rapids, IA 52402-3118
(319) 399-2571

210 Walnut Street
Room 749
Des Moines, IA 50309
(515) 284-4422

KANSAS

110 E. Waterman Street
1st Floor
Wichita, KS 67202
(316) 269-6571

KENTUCKY

600 Federal Place
Room 188
Louisville, KY 40202
(502) 582-5976

LOUISIANA

1661 Canal Street
Suite 2000
New Orleans, LA 70112
(504) 589-6685

MAINE

40 Western Avenue
Room 512
Augusta, ME 04330
(207) 622-8378

MARYLAND

10 N. Calvert Street
3rd Floor
Baltimore, MD 21202
(301) 962-4392

MASSACHUSETTS

10 Causeway Street
Room 265
Boston, MA 02114
(617) 565-5590

1550 Main Street
Room 212
Springfield, MA 01103
(413) 785-0268

MICHIGAN

477 Michigan Avenue
Room 515
Detroit, MI 48226
(313) 226-6075

300 S. Front Street
Marquette, MI 49885
(906) 225-1108

MINNESOTA

100 N. 6th Street
Suite 610
Minneapolis, MN 55403
(612) 349-3550

MISSISSIPPI

100 W. Capitol Street
Suite 322
Jackson, MS 39269
(601) 965-0121

MISSOURI

1103 Grand Avenue
6th Floor
Kansas City, MO 64106
(816) 374-3419

815 Olive Street
Room 242
St. Louis, MO 63101
(314) 425-6600

MONTANA

301 S. Park
Room 528
Helena, MT 59626
(406) 449-5381

NEBRASKA

11145 Mill Valley Road
Omaha, NE 68154
(402) 221-4691

NEW HAMPSHIRE

55 Pleasant Street
Room 210
Concord, NH 03301
(603) 225-1400

NEW JERSEY

60 Park Place
4th Floor
Newark, NJ 07102
(201) 645-2434

NEW MEXICO

5000 Marble Avenue, N.E.
Room 320
Albuquerque, NM 87100
(505) 262-6171

NEW YORK

26 Federal Plaza
Room 3100
New York, NY 10278
(212) 264-4355

100 S. Clinton Street
Room 1071
Syracuse, NY 13260
(315) 423-5383

NORTH CAROLINA

222 S. Church Street
Room 300
Charlotte, NC 28202
(704) 371-6563

NORTH DAKOTA

657 2nd Avenue North
Room 218
Fargo, ND 58102
(701) 237-5771

OHIO

1240 E. 9th Street
Room 317
Cleveland, OH 44199
(216) 522-4180

85 Marconi Boulevard
Room 512
Columbus, OH 43215
(614) 469-6860

OKLAHOMA

200 N.W. 5th Street
Suite 670
Oklahoma City, OK 73102
(405) 231-4301

OREGON

1220 S. W. Third Avenue
Room 676
Portland, OR 97204
(503) 423-5221

PENNSYLVANIA

231 St. Asaphs Road
Suite 400-E
Philadelphia, PA 19004
(215) 596-5889

960 Penn Avenue
5th Floor
Pittsburgh, PA 15222
(412) 644-2780

PUERTO RICO

Carlos Chardon Avenue
Room 691
Hato Rey, Puerto Rico 00918
(809) 753-4002

RHODE ISLAND

380 Westminister Mall
5th Floor
Providence, RI 02903
(401) 528-4586

SOUTH CAROLINA

1835 Assembly Street
Room 358
Columbia, SC 29201
(803) 765-5376

SOUTH DAKOTA

101 S. Main Avenue
Suite 101
Sioux Falls, SD 57102
(605) 336-2980

TENNESSEE

404 James Robertson Parkway
Suite 1012
Nashville, TN 37219
(615) 736-5881

TEXAS

1100 Commerce Street
Room 3C36
Dallas, TX 75242
(214) 767-0605

10737 Gateway West
Suite 320
El Paso, TX 79935
(915) 541-7586

222 E. Van Buren Street
Room 500
Harlingen, TX 78550
(512) 427-8533

2525 Murworth
Suite 112
Houston, TX 77054
(713) 660-4401

1611 Tenth Street
Suite 200
Lubbock, TX 79401
(806) 743-7462

727 E. Durango Street
Room A513
San Antonio, TX 78206
(512) 229-6250

UTAH

125 S. State Street
Room 2237
Salt Lake City, UT 84138
(801) 524-5800

VERMONT

87 State Street
Room 205
Montpelier, VT 05602
(802) 828-4474

VIRGINIA

400 N. 8th Street
Room 3015
Richmond, VA 23240
(804) 771-2617

VIRGIN ISLANDS

Veterans Drive
Room 210
St. Thomas, VI 00801
(809) 774-8530

WASHINGTON

915 Second Avenue
Room 1792
Seattle, WA 98174
(206) 442-5534

W. 920 Riverside Avenue
Room 651
Spokane, WA 99201
(509) 456-3783

WEST VIRGINIA

168 W. Main Street
5th Floor
Clarksburg, WV 26301
(304) 623-5631

WISCONSIN

212 E. Washington Avenue
Room 213
Madison, WI 53703
(608) 264-5261

WYOMING

100 East B. Street
Room 4001
Casper, WY 82602
(307) 261-5761

WASHINGTON, D.C. COUNTRY OFFICERS

Country	U.S. Dept. of State Washington, DC 20520 State Officer/Phone*	U.S. Dept. of Commerce Washington, DC 20230 Commerce Officer/Phone*	Agency for Intl. Development Washington, DC 20523 AID Officer/Phone*
Afghanistan	James Bruno/647-9552	Stan Bilinski/377-2954	Jeffrey Malick/647-3516
Albania	Tom Countryman/647-3298	Karen Ware/377-2645	**
Algeria	Kathleen Fitzpatrick/647-4680	Jeffrey Johnson/377-4652	**
Andorra	Christopher Dell/647-1412	Christine Sloop/377-4508	**
Angola	Michael McKinley/647-9429	John Crown/377-0357	Jonathan Conly/647-4228
Anguilla	Eugenia Davis/647-2621	Thomas Klotzbach/377-2527	**
Antigua and Barbuda	Eugenia Davis/647-2621	Thomas Klotzbach/377-2527	Peter Kolar/647-2116
Argentina	John Caulfield/647-2401	Mark Siegelman/377-1548	Marvin Schwartz/647-4376
Australia	Susan Keogh-Fisher/647-9690	Gary Bouck/377-3647	**
Austria	William Millan/647-2005	Philip Combs/377-2920	**
Bahamas, The	Nancy Lees/647-2621	Americo Tadeu/377-2527	**
Bahrain	David Ostroff/647-6572	Claude Clement/377-5545	Ann McDonald/647-3516
Bangladesh	Siria Lopez/647-9552	Polly Holcombe/377-2954	Peter Kolar/647-2116
Barbados	Eugenia Davis/647-2621	Thomas Klotzbach/377-2527	**
Belgium	Eleanor Raven-Hamilton/647-6664	Boyce Fitzpatrick/377-5401	**
Belize	Michele Sison/647-2205	Kirsten Baumgart/377-2527	Ed Campbell/647-3446
Benin	Don Hester/647-3391	Reginald Biddle/377-4388	Mable Meares/647-6154
Bermuda	Charlie Peacock/647-8027	Vacant/377-2527	Peter Kolar/647-2116
Bhutan	John Lister/647-2141	Sean Gallagher/377-2954	**
Bolivia	Vicki Huddleston/647-3076	Ann Beard/377-2521	Penelope Farley/647-4376
Botswana	June Perry/647-8434	Frank Stokelin/377-5148	Leonard Pompa/647-4289
Brazil	David Beall/647-6541	Robert Bateman/377-1744	Helen Soos/647-4376
British Virgin Islands	Eugenia Davis/647-2621	Thomas Klotzbach/377-2527	**

* Area code 202
** AID does not operate in country

241

Country	State Officer/Phone	Commerce Officer/Phone	AID Officer/Phone
Brunei	Michael Bellows/647-3278	George Paine/377-3647	**
Bulgaria	Thomas Countryman/647-3298	Karen Ware/377-2645	**
Burkina Faso	Deborah Odell/647-2865	Amy Friedheim/377-4564	Ronald Daniel/647-9207
Burma	Robert Loftis/647-7108	Kyaw Win/377-5334	Chris Brown/647-9136
Burundi	Kevin Brown/647-3138	John Crown/377-0357	Warren Rush/647-9762
Cambodia	Anthony Kolankiewicz/647-3133	JeNelle Matheson/377-2462	**
Cameroon	Thomas Shannon/647-4965	Ian Davis/377-0357	Abbe Fessenden/647-7986
Canada	Robert Homme/647-3135	William Cavitt/377-3101	**
Cape Verde	Ronald Trigg/647-3391	Philip Michelini/377-4388	Louise Werlin/647-8125
Cayman Islands	Eugenia Davis/647-2621	Vacant/377-2527	**
Central African Republic	Kevin Brown/647-3138	Ian Davis/377-0357	Abbe Fessenden/647-7986
Chad	John Dobrin/647-3138	Ian Davis/377-0357	Ronald Daniel/647-6039
Chile	Peter DeShazo/647-2407	Brian Hannon/377-1495	Marvin Schwartz/647-4376
China	Robert Goldberg/647-6796	Jeffrey Lee/377-3583	**
Colombia	Nancy Mason/647-3023	Herbert Lindow/377-4303	Penelope Farley/647-4376
Comoros	Eunice Reddick/647-8913	James Robb/377-4564	Jose Rivera/647-9763
Congo	Earl Irving/647-4965	Ian Davis/377-0357	Dean Burnius/647-9809
Cook Islands	Ann Kambara/647-3546	Gary Bouck/377-3647	Chris Brown/647-9137
Costa Rica	Brian Dickson/647-4980	Brigit Helms/377-2527	Donald Enos/647-5101
Cuba	Kenneth Skoug/647-9272	Ted Johnson/377-2527	**
Cyprus	Richard Fisher/647-6953	Ann Corro/377-3945	Christine Adamcyzk/647-9114
Czechoslovakia	Daniel Smith/647-3187	Kate Scanlan/377-2645	**
Denmark	Ken Kolb/647-5669	Maryanne Lyons/377-3254	**
Djibouti	John Berntsen/647-8852	James Robb/377-4564	Richard Eney/647-8145
Dominica	Eugenia Davis/647-2621	Thomas Klotzbach/377-2527	Peter Kolar/647-2116
Dominican Republic	Philip Carter/647-4195	Kirsten Baumgart/377-2527	Peter Kolar/647-2116
Ecuador	Michael Meigs/647-3338	Herbert Lindow/377-4303	Marvin Schwartz/647-4376
Egypt	Teresita Schaeffer/647-2365	Jeffrey Johnson/377-4652	Rick Handler/647-9114
El Salvador	James Callahan/647-3681	Brigit Helms/377-2527	Richard Nelson/647-8525
Equatorial Guinea	Earl Irving/647-4965	John Crown/377-0357	Abbe Fessenden/647-7986
Estonia	Nadia Tangour/647-3187	Val Zabijaka/377-4655	**

Country	State Officer/Phone	Commerce Officer/Phone	AID Officer/Phone
Ethiopia	John Berntsen/647-8852	James Robb/377-4564	Richard Eney/647-8145
Fiji	Ann Kambara/647-3546	Gary Bouck/377-3647	Chris Brown/647-9136
Finland	George Boutin/647-5669	Maryanne Lyons/377-3254	**
France	Deborah Graze/647-2632	Maria Aronson/377-8008	**
French Antilles (or French Guiana)	Eugenia Davis/347-2621	Americo Tadeu/377-2527	**
French Polynesia	Ann Kambara/647-3546	Gary Bouck/377-3647	**
Gabon	Thomas Shannon/647-4965	Ian Davis/377-0357	Abbe Fessenden/647-7986
Gambia, The	Anthony Benesch/647-2865	Philip Michelini/377-4388	Yvonne John/647-6049
Germany, East	Charlie Skinner/647-2005	Naomi Norden/347-2645	**
Germany, West	Jim Savage/647-2155	Velizar Stanoyevitch/377-2434	**
Ghana	Donald Hester/647-3391	Reginald Biddle/377-4388	Rudolph Thomas/647-7985
Gibraltar	Howard Perlow/647-8027	Robert McLaughlin/377-3748	**
Greece	Jim Jeffrey/647-6113	Ann Corro/377-3945	David Jones/647-1563
Greenland	Ken Kolb/647-5669	Maryanne Lyons/377-3254	**
Grenada	Eugenia Davis/647-2621	Thomas Klotzbach/377-2527	Peter Kolar/647-2116
Guadeloupe	Eugenia Davis/647-2621	Americo Tadeu/377-2527	**
Guatemala	Richard Dotson/647-3681	Americo Tadeu/377-2527	Thomas Cornell/647-5221
Guinea	Leslie Bassett/647-3066	Philip Michelini/377-4388	Mable Meares/647-6154
Guinea-Bissau	Leslie Bassett/647-3066	Philip Michelini/377-4388	Mable Meares/647-6154
Guyana	William Moore/647-4195	Thomas Klotzbach/377-2527	Ed Campbell/647-3446
Haiti	Jack Felt/647-2280	Americo Tadeu/377-2527	Robert MacAlister/647-2116
Honduras	Rose Litkins/647-4980	Brigit Helms/377-2527	Emily Leonard/647-5101
Hong Kong	Robert Goldberg/647-6796	JeNelle Matheson/377-2462	**
Hungary	Nadia Tongour/647-3187	Karen Ware/377-2645	**
Iceland	Kenneth Longmyer/647-6071	Maryanne Lyons/377-3254	**
India	Grant Smith/647-2141	Richard Harding/377-2954	Bill Sugrue/647-4516
Indonesia	Bronson Percival/647-3277	Don Ryan/377-3875	Helene Kaufman/647-9136
Iran	Lisa Paiscik/647-6111	Claude Clement/377-5545	**
Iraq	Philip Remler/ 647-5692	Thomas Sams/377-5767	**

243

Country	State Officer/Phone	Commerce Officer/Phone	AID Officer/Phone
Ireland	Kenneth Longmyer/647-6071	Brenda Hogan/377-4104	**
Israel	John Hirsch/647-3672	Elise Kleinwaks/377-4652	Philip Gary/647-7367
Italy	Anna Borg/647-2453	Noel Negretti/377-2177	**
Ivory Coast	Leslie Bassett/647-3066	Philip Michelini/377-4388	Rudolph Thomas/647-7985
Jamaica	Dale Schaffer/647-2620	Kirsten Baumgart/377-2527	Paul Wenger/647-3448
Japan	Charles Cohen/647-2912	Ed Leslie/377-4527	**
Jordan	George Malleck/647-1022	Thomas Sams/377-5767	Ben Hawley/647-9000
Kampuchea (see Cambodia)			
Kiribati	Ann Kambara/647-3546	Gary Bouck/377-3647	**
Kenya	Jim Entwistle/647-8913	James Robb/377-4564	Nedra Huggins-Williams/647-9762
Korea, North	Joseph Mussomeli/647-7717	Liliana Monk/377-3583	**
Korea, South	Edward Kloth/647-7717	Karen Chopra/377-4958	**
Kuwait	Mark Foulon/647-6562	Thomas Sams/377-5767	**
Laos	Anthony Kolankiewicz/647-3133	JeNelle Matheson/377-2462	**
Latvia	Terry Snell/647-3187	Val Zabijaka/377-4655	**
Lebanon	Joseph LaBaron/647-1030	Thomas Sams/377-5767	Marx Sterne/647-9001
Lesotho	June Perry/647-8434	Fred Stokelin/377-5148	Leonard Pompa/647-4289
Liberia	Ned McMahon/647-3395	Philip Michelini/377-4388	Carol Steele/647-7988
Libya	Sharon Wiener/647-4675	Simon Bensimon/377-5737	**
Liechtenstein	William Millan/647-2005	Philip Combs/377-2920	**
Lithuania	Nadia Tongour/647-3187	Val Zabijaka/377-4655	**
Luxembourg	Steven Candy/647-6664	Boyce Fitzpatrick/377-5401	**
Macau	Robert Goldberg/647-6796	JeNelle Matheson/377-2462	**
Madagascar	Eunice Reddick/647-8913	John Crown/377-0357	Jose Rivera/647-9763
Malawi	John Ordway/647-8252	Fred Stokelin/377-5148	Robert Wrin/647-4328
Malaysia	Michael Bellows/647-3278	Gary Bouck/377-3875	Chris Brown/647-9136
Maldives	Steve Blake/647-2351	Vacant/377-2954	**
Mali	Deborah Odell/647-2865	Amy Friedheim/377-4564	Louise Werlin/647-8125
Malta	Marcie Ries/647-2453	Robert McLaughlin/377-3748	Christine Adamcyzk/647-9114
Marshall Islands, Republic of	James Berg/647-0108	Gary Bouck/377-3647	**
Martinique	Eugenia Davis/647-2621	Americo Tadeu/377-2527	**

Country	State Officer/Phone	Commerce Officer/Phone	AID Officer/Phone
Mauritania	Anthony Benesch/647-2865	Amy Friedheim/377-4564	Willy Saulters/647-9207
Mauritius	Eunice Reddick/647-8913	John Crown/377-0357	**
Mexico	John St. John/647-9894	Melissa Coyle/377-2527	Penelope Farley/647-4376
Micronesia, Federated States of			**
Monaco	James Berg/647-0108	Gary Bouck/377-3647	**
Mongolia	Deborah Graze/647-2633	Maria Aronson/377-8008	**
Montserrat	Ken Jarrett/647-9141	Liliana Monk/377-3583	**
Morocco	Eugenia Davis/647-2621	Thomas Klotzbach/377-2527	Marx Sterne/647-9001
Mozambique	Ralph Winstanley/647-4675	Simon Bensimon/377-5737	Jonathan Conly/647-4228
Namibia	Greg Fergin/647-9429	Fred Stokelin/377-5148	Jonathan Conly/647-4228
Nauru	Michael McKinley/647-9429	Emily Solomon/377-5148	**
Nepal	Stanley Ifshin/647-3546	Gary Bouck/377-3647	David Garms/647-4516
Netherlands	Milton Charlton/647-1450	Stan Bilinski/377-2954	**
Netherlands Antilles	Eleanor Raven-Hamilton/647-6664	Boyce Fitzpatrick/377-5401	**
New Caledonia	Eugenia Davis/647-2621	Vacant/377-2527	**
New Zealand	Ann Kambara/647-3546	Gary Bouck/377-3647	**
Nicaragua	Ravic Huso/647-9691	Gary Bouck/377-3647	Richard Nelson/647-8525
Niger	Robert Witajewski/647-2205	Ted Johnson/377-2527	George Jones/647-9206
Nigeria	Deborah Odell/647-2865	Amy Friedheim/377-4564	Rudolph Thomas/647-7985
Norway	Robert Procter/647-3406	Reginald Biddle/377-4388	**
Oman	Ken Kolb/647-5669	James Devlin/377-4414	Peter Deinken/647-9000
Pacific Islands	Kathleen Allegrone/647-6571	Claude Clement/377-5545	**
Pakistan	Stanley Ifshin/647-3546	Gary Bouck/377-3647	Robert Dakan/647-3517
Palau, Republic of	Robert Boehme/647-9823	Stan Bilinski/377-2954	**
Panama	James Berg/647-0108	Gary Bouck/377-3647	Thomas Cornell/647-5221
Papua-New Guinea	Vincent Mayer/647-4986	Brigit Helms/377-2527	Helen Kaufman/647-9137
Paraguay	Stanley Ifshin/647-3546	Gary Bouck/377-3647	Marvin Schwartz/647-4376
Peru	Deborah Bolton/647-2296	Mark Siegelman/377-1548	Helen Soos/647-4376
Philippines	Edward Vazquez/647-3360	Ann Beard/377-2521	William Nance/647-9139
Poland	Geraldeen Chester/647-1221	George Paine/377-3875	**
	Daniel Fried/647-1070	Edgar Fulton/377-2645	

Country	State Officer/Phone	Commerce Officer/Phone	AID Officer/Phone
Portugal	John Caswell/647-1412	Ann Corro/377-3945	Christine Adamcyzk/647-9114
Puerto Rico	Eugenia Davis/647-2621	Ted Johnson/377-2527	**
Qatar	David Ostroff/647-6572	Claude Clement/377-5545	**
Reunion Island	Deborah Graze/647-2632	Gary Bouck/377-3647	**
Romania	Paul Schlamm/647-32989	William Winter/377-2645	**
Rwanda	Kevin Brown/647-3138	John Crown/377-0357	Warren Rush/647-9762
Samoa (see Western Samoa)			
San Marino	Anna Borg/647-2453	Noel Negretti/377-2177	**
Sao Tome and Principe	Thomas Shannon/647-4965	John Crown/377-0357	Abbe Fessenden/647-7986
Saudi Arabia	John Riddle/647-7550	Cynthia Anthony/377-4652	**
Senegal	Anthony Benesch/647-2865	Philip Michelini/377-4388	Helen Vaitaitis/647-8124
Seychelles	Dale Dean/647-5684	James Robb/377-4564	Jose Rivera/647-9763
Sierra Leone	Ronald Trigg/647-3395	Philip Michelini/377-4388	Rudolph Thomas/647-7985
Singapore	Colin Helmer/647-3278	Don Ryan/377-3875	Karl Schwartz/647-9240
Solomon Islands	Stanley Ifshin/647-3546	Gary Bouck/377-3647	Helene Kaufman/647-9137
Somalia	Dale Dean/647-5684	James Robb/377-4564	Deborah Mendelson/647-8145
South Africa	Mark Bellamy/647-8433	Davis Coale/377-5148	Jonathan Conly/647-4230
Soviet Union	Robert Clarke/647-9370	Jack Brougher/377-4655	**
Spain	George Chester/647-1412	Christine Sloop/377-4508	Christine Adamcyzk/647-9114
Sri Lanka	Stephen Blake/647-2351	Stan Bilinski/377-2954	David Garms/64-4516
St. Christopher and Nevis, St. Lucia, St. Vincent, and the Grenadines	Eugenia Davis/647-2621	Thomas Klotzbach/377-2527	**
Sudan	Ross Trowbridge/647-5648	James Robb/377-4564	Janice Weber/647-8145
Suriname	William Moore/647-4195	Thomas Klotzbach/377-2527	Edward Campbell/647-4105
Swaziland	John Ordway/647-8252	Fred Stokelin/377-5148	Leonard Pompa/647-4289
Sweden	George Boutin/647-5669	James Devlin/377-4414	**
Switzerland	William Millan/647-2005	Philip Combs/377-2920	**
Syria	William Jordan/647-1131	Thomas Sams/377-5767	Ben Hawley/647-9001
Taiwan	David Brown/647-7711	Dan Duvall/377-4957	**

Country	State Officer/Phone	Commerce Officer/Phone	AID Officer/Phone
Tanzania	Eunice Reddick/647-8913	James Robb/377-4564	John Rose/647-9762
Thailand	John Merante/647-7108	Donald Ryan/377-3875	Karl Schwartz/647-9240
Togo	Donald Hester/647-3391	Reginald Biddle/377-4388	Mable Meares/647-6154
Tonga	Ann Kambara/647-3546	Gary Bouck/377-3647	Helene Kaufman/647-9137
Trinidad and Tobago	Nancy Lees/647-2621	Vacant/377-2527	**
Tunisia	Rosemay O'Neill/647-3614	Simon Bensimon/377-4652	Ingrid Peters/647-9001
Turkey	Robert Pace/647-6114	Geoffrey Jackson/377-3945	**
Tuvalu	Ann Kambara/647-3546	Gary Bouck/377-3647	Helene Kaufman/647-9137
Uganda	Jim Entwistle/647-8913	James Robb/377-4564	John Rose/647-9762
United Arab Emirates	Mark Foulon/647-6562	Claude Clement/377-5545	**
United Kingdom	Howard Perlow/647-8027	Robert McLaughlin/377-3748	**
U.S. Virgin Islands	Eugenia Davis/647-2621	Ted Johnson/377-2527	**
Upper Volta (see Burkina Faso)			
Uruguay	Deborah Bolton/647-2296	Brian Hannon/377-1495	Marvin Schwartz/647-4376
Vanuatu	Stanley Ifshin/647-3546	Gary Bouck/377-3647	Chris Brown/647-9137
Vatican City	Marcie Ries/647-2453	Noel Negretti/377-2177	**
Venezuela	L. Brad Hittle/647-3338	Marie Haugen/377-1659	Helen Soos/647-4376
Vietnam	Laurence Kerr/647-3132	JeNelle Matheson/377-2462	**
Western Sahara	Anthony Benesch/647-2865	Simon Bensimon/377-4652	**
Western Samoa	Ann Kambara/647-3546	Gary Bouck/377-3647	Helene Kaufman/647-9137
Yemen Arab Republic	Kathleen Allegrone/647-6571	Cynthia Anthony/377-4652	Peter Deinken/647-9000
Yemen, People's Democratic Republic of	Kathleen Allegrone/647-6571	Cynthia Anthony/377-4652	**
Yugoslavia	John Schmidt/647-4138	Jeremy Keller/377-5373	**
Zaire	Earl Irving/647-4965	Ian Davis/377-0357	Dean Bernius/647-7884
Zambia	John Ordway/647-8252	Emily Solomon/377-5148	Robert Wrin/647-4328
Zimbabwe	Helen Weinland/647-8434	Emily Solomon/377-5148	Robert Wrin/647-4328

* Area code 202
** AID does not operate in country

KEY PERSONNEL AT U.S. EMBASSIES

Instructions for Addressing Mail to a U.S. Foreign Service Post

Correspondence to a foreign service post should be addressed to a section or position rather than to an officer by name. Normally, correspondence concerning commercial matters should be addressed "Commercial Section," followed by the name and correct mailing address of the post.

Below are the three accepted forms of addressing mail to a foreign service post using the Economic/Commercial Section of the American Embassy in Manama, Bahrain as an example:

Economic/Commercial Section   or   Economic/Commercial Section
American Embassy   Manama
FPO NY 09526   Department of State
                                               Washington, DC 20520

or

Economic/Commercial Section
American Embassy
P.O. Box 26431*
Manama, Bahrain

Key

The following abbreviations are used in this chart:

ACM	Assistant Chief of Mission
ADM	Administration
AGR	Agricultural Section (USDA/FAS)
AID	Agency for International Development
AMB	Ambassador
ATO	Agricultural Trade Office (USDA/FAS)
BO	Branch Office of Embassy
C	Consulate
CG	Consul General, Consulate General
CHG	Charge d'Affaires
COM	Commercial Section (FCS)
CON	Consul, Consular Section
DCM	Deputy Chief of Mission

*Use street address only when P.O. box is not supplied.

248

DPO   Deputy Principal Officer
E   Embassy
ECO   Economic Section
M   Mission
PO   Principal Officer
POL   Political Section
SCI   Scientific Attache
VC   Vice Consul

Description of Embassy Officers' Responsibilities

At the head of each U.S. diplomatic mission are the *Chief of Mission* (with the title of *Ambassador, Minister, or Charge d'Affaires*) and the *Deputy Chief of Mission*. These officers are responsible for all components of the U.S. mission within a country, including consular posts.

Economic/commercial officers represent the entire spectrum of U.S. economic and commercial interests within their countries of assignment. Their activities range from trade promotion to economic reporting. At larger posts, where trade volume, travel, and private investment interest are high, there are *commercial officers* who specialize in export promotion, arrange appointments with local business and government officials, and provide maximum assistance to American business.

Political officers analyze and report on political developments and their potential impact on U.S. interests.

Consular officers extend to U.S. citizens and their property abroad the protection of the U.S. government. They maintain lists of local attorneys, act as liaison with police and other officials, and have the authority to notarize documents. The State Department recommends that business representatives residing overseas register with the consular officer; in troubled areas, even travelers are advised to register.

Agricultural officers promote the export of U.S. agricultural products and report on agricultural production and market developments in their area.

Scientific attachés follow science and technology developments that are of concern to the science community and may have an impact on U.S. policies.

The *AID mission director* is responsible for AID programs, including dollar and local currency loans, grants, and technical assistance.

AFGHANISTAN

Kabul (E), Wazir Akbar Khan Mina
Tel 62230-35, 62436
Workweek: Sunday–Thursday

CHG: Jon D. Glassman
DCM/CON: Edmund McWilliams, Jr.
POL: Robert H. Mills
ECO: David K. Schollenbager
ADM: Edward T. Paukert
AID: Larry K. Crandall
    (resident in Islamabad)

ALGERIA

Algiers (E), 4 Chemin Cheich Bachir
Brahimi
B.P. Box 549 (Alger-Gare) 16000
Tel [213] (2) 601-425/255/186 Telex
66047
Workweek: Saturday–Wednesday

AMB: L. Craig Johnstone
DCM: Charles H. Brayshaw
POL: John W. Limbert
ECO: David R. Burnett
COM: Laron L. Jensen
CON: G. Gaye Maris
ADM: Walter Greenfield
ATO: Besa Kotati

Oran (C), 14 Square de Bamako
Tel [213] (6) 334509 and 335499
Telex 22310 AMCONRN
Workweek: Saturday–Wednesday

PO: George S. Dragnich
CON: Jeri S. Guthrie-Corn

ANTIGUA AND BARBUDA

St. Johns (E), FPO Miami 34054
Tel [809] 462-3505/06
Telex 2140 USEMB

AMB: Paul A. Russo
    (resident in Bridgetown)
CHG: Robert W. DuBose, Jr.
ECO: Eric Sandberg
CON: Daniel Darrach
COM: Stefan Nelgesen
    (resident in Port of Spain)

ADM: Annette J. Moore
AID: James S. Holtaway
    (resident in Bridgetown)

ARGENTINA

Buenos Aires (E), 4300 Colombia, 1425
APO Miami 34034
Tel [54] (1) 774-7611/8811/9911
Telex 18156 USICA AR

AMB: Theodore E. Gildred
DCM: John A. Bushnell
POL: Robert C. Felder
ECO: Andrew D. Sens
COM: David S. Yonker
CON: Thomas L. Holladay
ADM: Sandor Johnson
SCI: William S. Tilney
AGR: J. Dawson Ahalt

AUSTRALIA

Canberra (E), Moonah PL., Canberra,
A.C.T. 2600
APO San Fran 96404
Tel [61] (62) 705000
Telex 62104 USAEMB

AMB: Laurence W. Lane, Jr.
DCM: Richard W. Teare
POL: Richard W. Baker III
ECO: Tain P. Tompkins
CON: James M. Roth
ADM: Paul Sadler
COM: Robert Taft
    (resident in Sydney)
SCI: Russell A. LaMantia
AGR: James V. Parker

Melbourne (CG), 24 Albert Rd.
South Melbourne, Victoria 3205
APO San Fran 96405
Tel [61] (3) 697-7900
Telex 30982 AMERCON

CG: Frank C. Bennett, Jr.
COM: Donald L. Schilke
CON: Carman C. Williams
ADM: David W. Fulton

Sydney (CG), 36th FL., T&G Tower, Hyde Park Square, Park and Elizabeth Sts., Sydney 2000, N.S.W.
APO San Fran 96209
Tel [61] (2) 264-7044
Telex 74223 FCSSYD

CG: John C. Dorrance
COM: Robert Taft
CON: Robert J. Chevez
ADM: Franklin D. English

Perth (CG), 246 St. George's Ter., Perth, WA 6000
Tel [61] (9) 322-4466

CG: William H. Itoh
COM: William M. Yarmy
CON: Louis A. McCall

Brisbane (C), 383 Wickham Ter., Brisbane, Queensland 4000
Tel [61] (7) 839-8955

PO: Lewis R. Murray
DEP. COMMISS. GEN.
for EXPO 88: David Seal

AUSTRIA

Vienna (E), Boltzmanngasse 16, A-1091, Vienna
APO NY 09108
Tel [43] (222) 31-55-11
Telex 114634
Consular Section:
Gartenbaupromenade 2
4th Floor, 1010 Vienna
Tel [43] (222) 51451

AMB: Ronald S. Lauder
DCM: Michael J. Habib
POL: Michael D. Sternberg
ECO: Charles Billo
COM: Arthur J. Reichenbach
CON: Thomas J. Rice
ADM: Harold E. Vickers
AGR: James K. Freckmann

Salzburg (CG), Giselakai 51, A-5020 Salzburg

Tel [43] (662) 28-6-01
Telex 63-31-64
CG: Herbert S. Malin

BAHAMAS

Nassau (E), Mosmar Bldg., Queen St.
P.O. Box N-8197
Tel [809] 322-1181, 328-2206
Telex 20-138 AMEMB NS138

AMB: Carol Boyd Hallett
DCM: John D. Whiting
POL/ECO/COM: Royal M. Wharton
CON: Cecil S. Richardson
ADM: Clarke W. Allard

BAHRAIN

Manama (E), Shaikh Isa Rd.
P.O. Box 26431
FPO NY 09526
Tel [973] 714151
Telex 9398 USATO BN
Workweek: Saturday–Wednesday

AMB: Dr. Sam H. Zakhem
DCM: Charles L. Daris
POL: David Hale
ECO: Leonard J. Lange
COM: Stephen A. Good
CON: Anne Bodine
ADM: Lawrence S. Blackburn
ATO: Pitamber Devgon

BANGLADESH

Dhaka (E), Adamjee Court Bldg. (5th Fl.), Motijheel Commercial Area
G.P.O. Box 323, Ramna
Tel [88] (2) 237161-63, 235093-99, and 235081-89
Telex 642319 AEDKA BJ
Workweek: Sunday–Thursday

AMB: Willard A. De Pree
DCM: John S. Brims
POL: A. Ellen Shippy
ECO/COM: Shirley E. Panizza
CON: Charles M. Parish, Jr.
ADM: G. Brent Olson

AGR: Lyle J. Sebranek
      (resident in New Delhi)
AID: Priscilla M. Boughton

BARBADOS

Bridgetown (E), P.O. Box 302
Box B, FPO Miami 34054
Tel [809] 436-4950 thru 7
Telex 2259 USEMB BG1 WB
Canadian Imperial Bank of Commerce
Bldg.
Broad Street, Bridgetown, Barbados

AMB: Paul A. Russo
DCM: Frank M. Fulgham
POL/ECO: Robert W. Beckham
CON: Luciano Mangiafico
COM: Stephen Helgesen
         (resident in Port-of-Spain)
ADM: Ralph B. Hartwell
AGR: Lloyd Fleck
         (resident in Caracas)
AID: James S. Holtaway

BELGIUM

Brussels (E), 27 Boulevard du Regent
B-1000 Brussels
APO NY 09667
Tel [32] (2) 513-3830
Telex 846-21336

AMB: Geoffrey Swaebe
DCM: Ronald E. Woods
POL: Thomas H. Gewecke
ECO: Lange Schermerhorn
COM: James Winkelman
CON: Brian M. Flora
ADM: Earl W. Bellinger
AGR: Roger S. Lowen

Antwerp (CG), Rubens Center,
Nationalestraat 5, B-2000 Antwerp
APO NY 09667
Tel [32] (3) 225-0071
Telex 31966

CG: Thomas G. Martin
ECO/COM: James J. Porter
CON: Dan M. Miller
POL: Alison Pentz

SHAPE (Belgium) B-7010
APO NY 09088
Tel [32] (65) 445-000

POLAD: Herbert D. Gelber

BELIZE

Belize City (E), Gabourel Lane and
Hutson St.
P.O. Box 286
Tel [501] 7161, 62, 63
Telex 213 AMCONSUL BZ

AMB: Robert G. Rich, Jr.
DCM: Keith Guthrie
POL: Leonard F. Scensny
ECO/COM: John Dyson
CON: Gerald R. Toney
ADM: Jacquelyn O. Briggs
AID: Neboysha R. Brashich
AGR: Robert R. Anlauf
          (resident in Guatemala)

BENIN

Cotonou (E), Rue Caporal Anani Bernard
B.P. 2012
Tel [229] 30-06-50

AMB: Walter E. Stadtler
ECO/COM: John G. Fox
CON: Nicholas Banks
ADM: Samuel A. Rubino
AID: Mark Wentling
          (resident in Lome)

BERMUDA

Hamilton (CG), Vallis Bldg., Front St.,
P.O. Box 325, Hamilton 5
AMCON FPO NY 09560
Tel [809] 295-1342

CG: James M. Medas
CON: Lili Ming
ADM: Herbert T. Mitchell, Jr.
POL/ECO: David A. Denny

BOLIVIA

La Paz (E), Banco Popular Del Peru
Bldg., Corner of Calles Mercado and
Colon

P.O. Box 425 La Paz
APO Miami 34032
Tel [591] (2) 350251, 350120
Telex AMEMB BV 3268

AMB: Edward M. Rowell
DCM: David N. Greenlee
POL: James C. Cason
ECO/COM: Ralph M. Buck
CON: Gerald R. Lueders
ADM: Russell F. King
AGR: Gary C. Groves
(resident in Lima)
AID: Reginald Van Raalte

BOTSWANA

Gaborone (E), P.O. Box 90
Tel [267] (3) 5398 2/3/4
Telex 2554 AMEMB BD

AMB: Natale H. Bellocchi
DCM: Johnnie Carson
POL/ECO: Trudie E. Thompson
CON/COM: Charles Neary
ADM: Frederick B. Cook
AGR: Roger F. Puterbaugh
(resident in Pretoria)
AID: John P. Hummon

BRAZIL

Brasilia (E), Avenida das Nocoes, Lote 3
APO Miami 34030
Tel [55] (61) 223-0120
Telex 061-1091

AMB: Harry W. Shlaudeman
DCM: James Ferrer, Jr.
POL: James F. Creagan
ECO: Paul L. Lease
COM: W. Kelly Joyce, Jr. (Acting)
(resident in Rio de Janeiro)
CON: Terry D. Hansen
ADM: Thomas J. Fitzpatrick
SCI: James W. Chamberlin
AGR: Robert J. Wicks
AID: (Vacancy)

Rio De Janeiro (CG), Avenida Presidente
Wilson, 147
APO Miami 34030
Tel [55] (21) 292-7117

Telex AMCONSUL 21-22831
USIS Telex 21-21466

CG: Alfonso Arenales
POL: Edward A. Torre
ECO: Stephen B. Watkins
COM: W. Kelly Joyce, Jr.
CON: Kenneth F. Sackett
ADM: Everard S. Taylor
AGR: Marcus E. Lower

Sao Paulo (CG), Rua Padre Joao Manoel,
933
P.O. Box 8063
APO Miami 34030
Tel [55] (11) 881-6511
Telex 11-31574
USIS Telex 21-21466

CG: Stephen F. Dachi
POL: Donald J. Hrinak
ECO: James H. Cheatham
COM: Arthur D. Trezise
CON: Joan E. Garner
ADM: Arnold N. Munoz
AGR: Jospeh F. Somers

Porto Alegre (C), Rua Coronel Genuino,
421 (9th Fl.)
APO Miami 34030
Tel [55] (512) 26-4288/4697
Telex 051-2292 CGEU BR

PO: George C. Lannon
CON: Pedro G. Griviti

Recife (C), Rua Goncalves Maia, 163
APO Miami 34030
Tel [55] (81) 221-1412
Telex 081-1190

PO: Donald E. Stader, Jr.
CON: Dennis L. Curry
BPAO: Carlos Bakota

U.S. Trade Center
Edificio Eloy Chaves
Avenida Paulista, 2439
Sao Paolo
APO Miami 34040
Tel (11) 853-2011/2411/2778
Telex 011-25274

Director: Arthur Trezise

BRUNEI

Bandar Seri Begawan (E), P.O. Box 2991
Tel [673] (2) 29670
Telex BU 2609 AMEMB
Workweek: Monday–Thursday and
Saturday

AMB: Thomas C. Ferguson
DCM: John Hoover
CON/ADM: Douglas V. Ellice
AGR: Peter Kurz
         (resident in Singapore)

BULGARIA

Sofia (E), 1 A. Stamboliski Blvd.
APO NY 09213
Tel [359] (2) 88-48-01 to 05
Telex 22690 BG

AMB: Sol Polansky
DCM: Jonathan B. Rickert
POL/ECO: Oscar W. Clyatt, Jr.
ECO/COM: George A. Flowers, Jr.
CON: Kevin A. Zerrusen
ADM: Bohdan Y. Paschyn
AGR: Steve Washenko
         (resident in Belgrade)

BURKINA FASO

Ouagadougou (E), B.P. 35
Tel [226] 30-67-23/24/25
Telex AEMB 5290 BF

AMB: David H. Shinn
DCM: Charles H. Twining
POL/ECO/COM: Edward D. Keeton
CON: (Vacancy)
ADM: Walter Greenfield
AID: Herbert N. Miller

BURMA

Rangoon (E), 581 Merchant St., (GPO
Box 521) AMEMBASSY, Box B, APO
San Francisco 96346
Tel 82055 or 82181
Telex 21230 AIDRGN BM

AMB: Burton Levin
DCM: Christopher J. Szymanski

POL/ECO: James H. Hall
COM: Gary C. Couey
CON: Aloysius M. O'Neill III
ADM: Leonard J. Porter
AID: Earl J. Young

BURUNDI

Bujumbura (E), B.P. 1720, Avenue du
Zaire
Tel 234-54 thru 56

AMB: James Daniel Phillips
DCM: Dennis K. Hays
POL: (Vacancy)
ECO: Cornelia P. J. Miller
COM: Easton C. Warner
ADM: Connie A. Wagner
CON: James M. Warrick
AID: Donald F. Miller

CAMEROON

Yaounde (E), Rue Nachtigal
B.P. 817
Tel [237] 234014
Telex 8223KN

AMB: Mark L. Edelman
DCM: Dennis A. Sandberg
POL: Roger J. Moran
ECO/COM: Brian J. Blood
CON: Frank C. Turley
ADM: Marshall F. Atkins
AGR: Thomas Pomeroy
         (resident in Lagos)
AID: Jay P. Johnson

Douala (C), 21 Avenue du General De
Gaulle
B.P. 4006
Tel [237] 425331, 423434
Telex 5233KN

PO: William R. Gaines
COM: (Vacancy)
ADM: Stephanie S. Sullivan

CANADA

Ottawa, Ontario (E), 100 Wellington St.,
K1P 5T1, P.O. Box 5000, Ogdensburg,
NY, 13669

Tel (613) 238-5335
Telex 0533582

AMB: Thomas M. T. Niles
DCM: Dwight N. Mason
POL: Robert J. Montgomery
ECO: James R. Tarrant
COM: James L. Blow
CON: Brooke C. Holmes
SCI: Francis M. Kinnelly
ADM: Dempsey B. Mizelle
AGR: Larry F. Thomasson

Calgary, Alberta (CG), Suite 1000, 615 Macleod Trail, S.E., Calgary, Alberta, Canada T2G 4T8
Tel (403) 266-8962
Telex 038-21332

CG: Bruce T. Howe
CON: John R. Nay
COM: Thomas K. Roesch

Halifax, Nova Scotia (CG), Suite 910, Cogswell Tower, Scotia Sq., Halifax, NS, Canada B3J 3K1
Tel (902) 429-2480-1
Telex 019-23566

CG: James D. Walsh
CON: Barabara J. Baden

Montreal, Quebec (CG), P.O. Box 65, Postal Station Desjardins, H5B 1G1
P.O. Box 847, Champlain, NY 12919-0847
Tel (514) 281-1886
Telex 05-268751

CG: Robert W. Maule
ECO: Frederick C. McEldowney
COM: Gregory D. Stoloff
CON: Michael M. Mahoney
ADM: Thomas W. Mears, Jr.

Quebec, Quebec (CG), 2 Place Terrasse, C.P. 939, G1R 4T9
Tel (418) 692-2095
Telex 051-2275

CG: Robert M. Maxim
CON: Mary B. Marshall

Toronto, Ontario (CG), 360 University Ave., M5G 1S4

P.O. Box 135, Lewiston, NY 14092
Tel (416) 595-1700
Telex 065-24132

CG: J. Donald Blevins
ECO: Hallock R. Lucius
COM: Kevin C. Brennan
CON: Ralph L. Nider
ADM: Ronald W. Mortensen

Vancouver, British Columbia (CG), 1075 West Georgia St., V6E 4E9
P.O. Box 5002, Point Roberts, WA 98281-5540
Tel (604) 685-4311
Telex 04-55673

CG: Samuel C. Fromowitz
ECO: Jeffrey R. Cunningham
COM: Thomas K. Roesch
       (resident in Calgary)
CON: David P. Bocskor

REPUBLIC OF CAPE VERDE

Praia (E), Rua Hojl Ya Yenna 81
C.P. 201
Tel [238] 614-363 or 614-253
Telex 6068 AMEMB CV

AMB: Vernon D. Penner, Jr.
CON: Louise A. Scott
ADM: Samuel V. Brock
AID: Thomas Luche

CENTRAL AFRICAN REPUBLIC

Bangui (E), Avenue President Dacko B.P. 924
Tel 61-02-00, 61-25-78, 61-43-33
Telex 5287 RC

AMB: David C. Fields
DCM: Frederick E. V. La Sor
POL: Wanda M. Miska
ECO/COM: Hugh I. Smith
CON: Sarah F. Drew
ADM: Robert L. Lane

CHAD

N'Djamena (E), Ave. Felix Eboue, B.P. 413

Tel [235] (51) 32-69, 35-13, 28-62,
23-29, 32-29, 30-94, 28-47
Telex 5203 KD

AMB: John Blane
DCM: Robert S. Ayling
POL/CON: (Vacancy)
ECO/COM: Eric Allison
ADM: Kathleen Chisholm
AID: Bernard Wilder

CHILE

Santiago (E), Codina Bldg., 1343
Agustinas
APO Miami 34033
Tel [56] (2) 710133/90 and 710326/75
Telex 240062-USIS-CL

AMB: Harry G. Barnes, Jr.
DCM: George F. Jones
POL: John F. Keane
ECO: Wendell L. Belew
COM: Richard R. Ades
CON: William H. Barkell
ADM: E. Lloyd Davis
AGR: W. John Child

CHINA*

Beijing (E), Xiu Shui Bei Jie 3
Dept of State, Wash. D.C. 20520
FPO San Fran 96655
Tel [86] (1) 532-3831
Telex AMEMB CN 22701

AMB: Winston Lord
DCM: Peter Tomsen
POL: Darryl Johnson
ECO: Kent Wiedemann
COM: Richard Johnston
CON: Elizabeth Raspolic
ADM: E. Parks Olmon
SCI: Pierre M. Perrolle
AGR: David M. Schoonover
ATO: Philip A. Skull

Guangzhou (CG), Dong Fang Hotel
Box 100, FPO San Fran 96659
Tel [86] (20) 669900 (ext. 1000)
Telex GZDFHCN 44439

———————
*See Taiwan, page 284

CG: Mark S. Pratt
POL: Herbert S. Thomas III
ECO: Stephen Schlaikjer
CON: Bruce McKenzie
COM: Nora Sun
ADM: C. Scott Thompson
ATO: Larry Senger

Shanghai (CG), 1469 Huai Hai Middle
Rd. Box 200,
FPO San Fran 96651
Tel [86] (21) 336-880
Telex USCGCN 33383

CG: Charles T. Sylvester
POL: Lawrence K. Robinson
ECO: Matthew P. Ward, Jr.
COM: Barbara Slawecki
CON: Keith Powell II
ADM: Stuart L. Spoede II

Shenyang (CG), 40 Lane 4, Section 5,
Sanjing St., Heping District
Box 45, FPO San Fran 96655
Tel [86] (24) 290000
Telex 80011 AMCS CN

CG: C. Eugene Dorris
POL: Blaine D. Benedict
ECO: Lawrence A. Walker
COM: William Center
CON: Charles A. Ray
ADM: Wade P. Leahy

Chengdu (CG), Jinjiang Hotel, 180
Renmin Rd., Chengdu, Sichuan
Tel. [86] (1) 24481
Telex ACGCH CN 60128

CG: William W. Thomas
POL: John Cook
ECO: (Vacancy)
CON: Mary F. Witt
ADM: John E. Witt

COLOMBIA

Bogota (E), Calle 38, No. 8-61
APO Miami 34038
Tel [57] (1) 285-1300/1688
Telex 44843

AMB: Charles A. Gillespie, Jr.
DCM: Michael M. Skol

POL: Jerome L. Hoganson
ECO: John P. Spillane
COM: Peter T. Noble
CON: David L. Hobbs
ADM: Christopher H. Swenson
AGR: Laurence R. Fouchs
AID: James F. Smith

Barranquilla (C), Calle 77 Carrera 68,
Centro Comerical Mayorista
APO Miami 34038
Tel [57] (5) 45-7088/7560
Telex 33482 AMCO CO

PO: Ross E. Benson
ADM/CON: Mary Ann Kekich

COMOROS

Moroni (E), Boite Postale 1318
Tel 73-12-03
Telex 257 AMEMB KO

AMB: Patricia Gates Lynch
(resident in Antananarivo)
CHG: Karl I. Danga
ADM/CON: William Carlson

PEOPLE'S REPUBLIC OF THE CONGO

Brazzaville (E), Avenue Amilcar Cabral
B.P. 1015; Box C, APO NY 09662
Tel 83-20-70, 83-26-24
Telex 5367 KG

AMB: Leonard G. Shurtleff
DCM: Joseph C. Wilson IV
CON: Victor L. Russillo
ECO: Alexander G. Andrews, Jr.
COM: Nikki Brajevich
ADM: Michael L. Bajek
AID: Tanya Perkins

COSTA RICA

San Jose (E), Avenida 3 and Calle 1
APO Miami 34020
Tel [506] 33-11-55

AMB: Dean R. Hinton
CHG: James L. Tull
POL: Joseph F. Becelia
ECO: Bonnie M. Lincoln
COM: Judith Henderson

CON: Kirk-Patrick Kotula
ADM: (Vacancy)
AGR: Lana Bennett
AID: Carl H. Leonard

COTE D'IVOIRE
(formerly Ivory Coast)

Abidjan (E), 5 Rue Jesse Owens
01 B.P. 1712
Tel [225] 32-09-79
Telex 23660

AMB: Dennis Kux
DCM: Vincent J. Farley
ECO/POL: Paul H. Blakeburn
COM: Andrew Grossman
CON: John A. Heffern
ADM: Peter F. Spalding
AGR: Richard J. Blabey
AID/REDSO: Laurance W. Bond

African Development Bank/Fund, Ave.
Joseph Anoma
01 B.P. 1387 Abidjan 01
Tel [225] 33-14-34

EXEC DIR: Donald R. Sherk
ALT DIR: Stephen P. Donovan

CUBA

Havana (USINT), Swiss Embassy,
Calzada entre L & M, Vedado Seccion
Tel 320551, 320543
Telex 512206

PO: John J. Taylor
DPO: John M. Joyce
POL: Clayton L. Cowart
CON: William J. Brencick
ADM: Robert B. Nolan

CYPRUS

Nicosia (E), Therissos St. and Dositheos
St.
FPO NY 09530
Tel [357] (2) 465151
Telex 4160 AME CY

AMB: Vacant
DCM: John U. Nix

POL: Ann Korky
ECO/COM: Robert C. Friel
CON: Marie D. Burke
ADM: Robert J. McAnneny
AGR: Robert E. Haresnape
(resident in Athens)

CZECHOSLOVAKIA

Prague (E), Trziste 15-12548 Praha
Amembassy Prague, c/o Amcongen,
APO NY 09213 (PRG)
Tel [42] (2) 53 6641/9
Telex 121196 AMEMBC

AMB: Julian M. Niemczyk
DCM: Carl W. Schmidt
POL: Randolph Bell
ECO: Clifford G. Bond
COM: Richard H. Appleton
CON: Frederick Polasky
ADM: Steven J. White
AGR: James K. Freckmann
(resident in Vienna)

DENMARK

Copenhagen (E), Dag Hammarskjolds
Alle 24
2100 Copenhagen O or APO NY 09170
Tel [45] (1) 42 31 44
Telex 22216

AMB: Terence A. Todman
DCM: Ronald D. Flack
POL: Ward C. Thompson
ECO: Frank P. Wardlaw
COM: Max Miles
CON: Dean Dizikes
ADM: Richard Smyth
AGR: Alexander Bernitz

REPUBLIC OF DJIBOUTI

Djibouti (E), Plateau du Serpent, Blvd.
Marechal Joffre
B.P. 185
Tel [253] 35-38-49-, 35-39-95, 35-29-16/
17
Workweek: Sunday–Thursday

AMB: (Vacancy)
CHG: John E. McAteer

POL: Mark D. Dembro
ECO/COM: Thomas J. Innamorato
ADM/CON: Sharon A. Lavorel
AID: John A. Lundgren

DOMINICAN REPUBLIC

Santo Domingo (E), Corner of Calle Cesar
Nicolas Penson & Calle Leopoldo
Navarro
APO Miami 34041
Tel [809] 541-2171
Telex 3460013

AMB: Lowell C. Kilday
DCM: Joseph D. McLaughlin
POL: Arlen R. Wilson
ECO: Robert J. Smolik
COM: Lawrance Eisenberg
CON: James L. Ward
ADM: A. Lucille Thomas
AGR: Lloyd S. Harbert
AID: Thomas W. Stukel

ECUADOR

Quito (E), Avenida 12 de Octubre y
Avenida Patria
P.O. Box 538
APO Miami 34039
Tel [593] (2) 562-890
Telex: 02-2329 USICAQ ED

AMB: Fernando E. Rondon
DCM: Robert B. Morley
POL: Linda M. Pfeifle
ECO: Gordon Jones
COM: Peter B. Alois
CON: Michael McCamman
ADM: David B. Langhaug
AGR: Cleveland H. Marsh
AID: Frank Almaguer

Guayaquil (CG), 9 de Octubre y Garcia
Moreno
APO Miami 34039
Tel [593] (4) 323-570
Telex: 04-3452 USICAG ED

CG: Ralph T. Jones
CON: Charles F. Keil
ADM: Bernard E. Gross II

EGYPT (ARAB REPUBLIC OF)

Cairo (E), 5 Sharia Latin America
FPO NY 09527
Tel [20] (2) 355-7371
Telex 93773 AMEMB
Workweek: Sunday–Thursday

AMB: Frank G. Wisner
DCM: Jock P. Covey
POL: Ryan Crocker
ECO: Peter Lande
COM: Frederic Gaynor
CON: Conrad Drescher
ADM: Nicholas S. Baskey
AGR: Guy Haviland
AID: Marshall Brown
SCI: Francis X. Cunningham

Alexandria (CG), 110 Ave. Horreya
FPO NY 09527
Tel [20] (4) 821911, 825607
Workweek: Sunday–Thursday

CG: Mark Hambley
CON/POL: Ronald L. Schlicher
ADM: (Vacancy)
AID: Paul Rusby

EL SALVADOR

San Salvador (E), 25 Avenida Norte No.
1230
APO Miami 34023
Tel [503] 26-7100

AMB: Edwin G. Corr
DCM: David Dlouhy
POL: Charles S. Shapiro
ECO/COM: John H. Curry
CON: Robert Chevez
ADM: Walter M. Notheis
AGR: Robert R. Anlauf
       (resident in Guatemala)
AID: Robin L. Gomez

EQUATORIAL GUINEA

Malabo (E), Calle de Los Ministros
P.O. Box 597
Tel 2406, 2507
Workweek: Monday–Friday

AMB: Chester E. Norris, Jr.
POL/ECO: Carl F. Troy
ADM/CON: George W. Indyke, Jr.
AID: Jay P. Johnson
       (resident in Yaounde)

ETHIOPIA

Addis Ababa (E), Entoto St.
P.O. Box 1014
Tel 110-666/117/129
Telex 21282

CHG: James R. Cheek
DCM: Louis F. Janowski
ECO/POL: Sharon K. Mercurio
ADM: Domonic Vallese
AID: Frederick E. Machmer, Jr.

FIJI

Suva (E), 31 Loftus St.
P.O. Box 218
Tel [679] 314-466, 314-069
Telex 2255 AMEMBASY FJ

CHG: Edric Sherman
POL: Robert A. Benzinger
ECO: Donald J. Nicol
CON: Micaela A. Cella
ADM: Richard A. Johnson
AID: William E. Paupe

FINLAND

Helsinki (E), Itainen Puistotie 14ASF-
00140
APO NY 09664
Tel [358] (0) 171931
Telex 121644 USEMB SF
Commercial Section Telex 125541

AMB: Rockwell A. Schnabel
DCM: Michael Durkee
POL: Paul Hacker
ECO: Lawrence E. Butler
COM: Kenneth L. Norton
CON: Elo-Kai Ojamaa
ADM: Ruth L. Willow
AGR: Shackford Pitcher
       (resident in Stockholm)

FRANCE

Paris (E), 2 Avenue Gabriel, 75382 Paris
Cedex 08
APO NY 09777
Tel [33] (1) 42-96-12-02, 42-61-80-75
Telex 650-221

AMB: Joe M. Rodgers
DCM: Mark C. Lissfelt
POL: Peter Semler
ECO: William H. Edgar
COM: James A. Moorhouse
CON: Robert E. Ezelle
ADM: Bruce W. Clark
SCI: Allen L. Sessons
AGR: Herbert F. Rudd

Bordeaux (CG), 22 Cours du Marechal
Foch, 33080 Bordeaux Cedex
Tel [33] (56) 56-52-65-95
Telex 540918F

CG: Judith M. Heimann
CON: Robert M. Holley

Lyon (CG), 7 Quai General Sarrail
69454 Lyon CEDEX 3
Tel [33] (7) 78-24-68-49
Telex USCSUL 380597F

CG: Stanislaus R. P. Valerga
CON: David W. Merrell

Marseille (CG), 12 Boulevard Paul
Peytral, 13286 Marseille Cedex
Tel [33] (91) 549 200

CG: Edmund Van Gilder
CON: Jay T. Smith
ECO/COM: (Vacancy)

Strasbourg (CG), 15 Ave. D'Alsace
67082 Strasbourg CEDEX or APO NY
09777-5620
Tel [33] (88) 88-35-31-04
Telex 870907

CG: Victor D. Comras

FRENCH CARIBBEAN DEPARTMENT

Martinique (CG), 14 Rue Blenac
B.P. 561, Fort-de-France 97206

Tel [596] 63-13-03
Telex 912670; 912315 MR

PO: Mary Dell Palazzolo
CON: Lisa R. Layne
POL/ECO: Louis Mazel
ADM: Michael S. Hoza

GABON

Libreville (E), Blvd. de la Mer
B.P. 4000
Tel 762003/4, 761337, 721348, 740248
Telex 5250 GO

AMB: Warren Clark, Jr.
DCM: Kenneth M. Scott, Jr.
POL: J. Wayne Jacobs
ECO/COM: William J. McGlynn, Jr.
CON: Mark R. Jensen
ADM: Paul Rowe

THE GAMBIA

Banjul (E), Fajara (East), Kairaba Ave.
P.M.B. No. 19, Banjul
Tel Serrekunda [220] 92856 or 92858,
91970, 91971
Telex 2229 AMEMB GV

AMB: Herbert E. Horowitz
ADM: Mark M. Boulware
POL/ECO/COM/CON: Linda Thomas-
Greenfield
AID: Jimmie Stone

GERMAN DEMOCRATIC REPUBLIC

Berlin (E), 1080 Berlin, Neustaedtische
Kirchstrasse 4-5
USBER Box E, APO NY 09742
Tel [37] (2) 2202741
Telex 112479 USEMB DD

AMB: Francis J. Meehan
DCM: Alan R. Thompson
POL: Jonathan G. Greenwald
ECO/COM: Reno L. Harnish
CON: Mary Rose Brandt
ADM: Warren P. Nixon
AGR: William P. Huth

FEDERAL REPUBLIC OF GERMANY

Bonn (E), Deichmanns Ave., 5300 Bonn 2
APO NY 09080
Tel [49] (228) 3391
Telex 885-452

AMB: Richard R. Burt
DCM: James F. Dobbins, Jr.
POL: Olaf Grobel
ECO: Richard H. Imus
COM: John W. Bligh, Jr.
CON: Lillian P. Mullin
ADM: Charles R. Bowers
SCI: Edward M. Malloy
AGR: Gerald W. Harvey

Berlin (M), Clayallee 170, D-1000 Berlin
33 (Dahlem)
APO NY 09742
Tel [49] (30) 83240 87
Com. Unit: Tel [49] (30) 819-7561
Telex 183-701 USBER-D

ACM: Harry J. Gilmore
DEP: James A. Williams
POL: Richard A. Smith, Jr.
ECO: A. Elizabeth Jones
COM: Edward B. O'Donnell, Jr.
CON: Sandra N. Humphrey
ADM: Michael J. McLaughlin, Jr.

Dusseldorf (CG), Emmanual Lutz Str. 1B,
4000 Duesseldorf 11
Tel 0211-596798/99, 596790
Telex 8584246

CG: David K. Edminster

Frankfurt Am Main (CG),
Siesmayerstrasse 21, 6000 Frankfurt
APO NY 90213
Tel [49] (69) 75305-0 or 75304-0 After
hours: Tel [49] (69) 75305-500 or
56002-700
Telex 412589 USCON-D

CG: Alexander L. Rattray
DPO: Merle E. Arp
COM: Thomas L. Boam
CON: Donald E. Mudd
ADM: Thomas M. Widenhouse

Hamburg (CG), Alsterufer 27/28, 2000
Hamburg 36
APO NY 09125 Tel [49] (40) 44 1061
Telex 213777
US Agricultural Trade Office:
Grosse Theaterstrasse 42
Tel [49] (40) 441061, after hours
441067
Agriculture Trade Office: Tel [49] (40)
341207
Telex 02163970 ATO D

CG: James C. Whitlock, Jr.
COM: Stephen Kaminski
CON: Karl H. Sprick
POL/CON: Russell L. Frisbie
ADM: Anne W. Patchell
ATO: Dale L. Good

Munich (CG), Koeniginstrasse 5, 8000
Muenchen 22
APO NY 09108
Tel [49] (89) 23011
Telex 5-22697 ACGM D

CG: David J. Fischer
POL: Robert W. Becker
COM: Dale Slaght
CON: Patricia L. Hall
ADM: Donald E. Huth

Stuttgart (CG), Urbanstrasse 7,7000
Stuttgart
APO NY 09154
Tel [49] (711) 21 02 21
Telex 07-22945

CG: Philip J. Griffin
COM: Catherine Houghton
CON: Jane Whitney
ADM: Donald S. Bryfogle

GHANA

Accra (E), Ring Road East
P.O. Box 194
Tel (Chancery) 775347/8/9
Tel (Annex) 776601/2, 776008

AMB: Stephen R. Lyne
DCM: Arlene Render
POL/ECO: Eric E. Svendsen

ECO/COM: H. Lee Graham
CON: Louis Russell
ADM: Thomas Cross
AGR: Thomas Pomeroy
(resident in Lagos)
AID: F. Gary Towery

GREECE

**Athens (E), 91 Vasilissis Sophias Blvd.,
10160 Athens or APO NY 09253
Tel [30] (1) 721-2951 or 721-8401
Telex 21-5548**

AMB: Robert V. Keeley
DCM: Edward M. Cohen
POL/MIL: Angel M. Rabasa
ECO: H. Clay Black
COM: Jerry Mitchell
CON: James F. Myrick
ADM: Perry Linder
AGR: Robert E. Haresnape

**Regional Trade Development Office, 91
Vasilissis Sophias Blvd. (c/o Embassy)**

**Thessaloniki (CG), 59 Leoforos Nikis,
GR-546-22 Thessaloniki
APO NY 09693
Tel [30] (31) 266-121**

CG: Donald A. Bramante
ECO/COM: Ronald Cinal
POL: Judith Jones
CON/ADM: Suzanne Payne

GRENADA

**St. George's (E), Ross Point Inn
P.O. Box 54, St. George's, Grenada,
W.I.
Tel [440] 1731/4**

CHG: John C. Leary
DCM: J. Peter Becker
POL: Philip C. French
ECO: Eugene Tuttle
COM: Edward P. Kemp
(resident in Bridgetown)
CON: Frank W. Skinner
ADM: Lester W. Klotzbach
AID: William Erdahl

GUATEMALA

**Guatemala (E), 7-01 Avenida de la
Reforma, Zone 10
APO Miami 34024
Tel [502] (2) 31-15-41**

AMB: James H. Michel
CHG: Gerald P. Lamberty
POL: Alexander Sleght
ECO: Larry C. Thompson
COM: Carlos A. Poza
CON: Dora Trujillo
ADM: Robert D. Austin, Jr.
AGR: Robert R. Anlauf
AID: Anthony J. Cauterucci

GUINEA

**Conakry (E), 2d Blvd. and 9th Ave.
B.P. 603
Tel 44-15-20 thru 24**

AMB: Samuel E. Lupo
DCM: William C. Mithoefer, Jr.
POL/ECO: Christopher R. Davis
ECO/COM: Patrick Syring
CON: Carla G. Wells
ADM: Gerald L. Hanisch
AGR: Richard J. Blabey
(resident in Abidjan)
AID: (Vacancy)

GUINEA-BISSAU

**Bissau (E), Avenida Domingos Ramos
C.P. 297
Tel [245] 212816/7**

AMB: John Dale Blacken
ADM: (Vacancy)
POL/ECO/CON: John W. Davison
AID: (Vacancy)

GUYANA

**Georgetown (E), 31 Main St.
Tel [592] (02) 54900-9
Telex 213 AMEMSY GY**

AMB: Theresa A. Tull
DCM: David C. McGaffey

POL: Augusto Recinos
ECO/COM: Helen Greely Recinos
CON: Judith A. Schmidt
ADM: Roy Sullivan
AGR: Lloyd Fleck
(resident in Caracas)

HAITI

**Port-Au-Prince (E), Harry Truman Blvd.,
P.O. Box 1761
Tel [509] (1) 20354, 20368, 20200,
20612**

AMB: Brunson McKinley
DCM: Genta Hawkins Holmes
POL: Lawrence G. Rossin
ECO/COM: Aubrey Hooks
CON: Thomas M. Murphy
ADM: Alton R. Baysden
AGR: Lloyd Harbert
(resident in Santo Domingo)
AID: Gerald Zaar

THE HOLY SEE

**Vatican City (E), Villino Pacelli, Via
Aurelia 294, 00165 Rome
APO NY 09794
Tel [396] 639-0558
Telex 622322 AMBRMC**

AMB: Frank Shakespeare
DCM: Peter K. Murphy
POL: Craig A. Kelly
ADM: Douglas B. Leonnig

HONDURAS

**Tegucigalpa (E), Avenido La Paz
APO Miami 34022
Tel [504] 32-3120**

AMB: Everett Ellis Briggs
DCM: Robert S. Pastorino
POL: William A. Moffitt
ECO: James B. Magnor
COM: Daniel DeVito
CON: James Curtis Struble
ADM: Cristobal Orozco

AGR: Robert R. Anlauf
(resident in Guatemala)
AID: John A. Sanbrailo

HONG KONG

**Hong Kong (CG), 26 Garden Rd.
Box 30, FPO San Fran 96659
Tel [852] (5) 239011
Telex 63141 USDOC HX**

CHG: Donald M. Anderson
DPO: Arthur L. Kobler
POL/ECO: Kaarn J. Weaver
COM: Lyn W. Edinger
CON: John H. Adams
ADM: D. Thomas Linville
AGR: Philip Holloway

HUNGARY

**Budapest (E), V. Szabadsag Ter 12
Am Embassy
APO NY 09213
Tel [36] (1) 126-450
Telex 18048 224-222
Commercial Devel Ctr
Telex 227136 USCDC H**

AMB: Mark Palmer
DCM: Donald B. Kursch
POL: Thomas A. Lynch
ECO: Sandra A. Dembski
COM: Stephan Wasylko
CON: Elizabeth Barnett
ADM: Wayne K. Logsdon
AGR: James K. Freckmann
(resident in Vienna)
SCI: Thomas A. Schlenker

ICELAND

**Reykjavik (E), Laufasvegur 21, FPO NY
09571
Tel [354] (1) 29100
Telex USEMB IS3044**

AMB: L. Nicholas Ruwe
DCM: James K. Connell
POL: Richard H. Zorn
ECO/COM: Jay L. Dehmlow

CON: Fredericka Schmadel-Heard
ADM: Joseph R. Manzanares

INDIA

New Delhi (E), Shanti Path,
Chanakyapuri 110021
Tel [91] (11) 600651
Telex 031-65269 USEM IN
USIS Tel 331-6841

AMB: John G. Dean
DCM: Gordon L. Streeb
POL: Stanley T. Escudero
ECO: Duane C. Butcher
COM: Edward R. Stumpf
CON: Leo Wollemborg
ADM: James McGunnigle
SCI: Syed Ahmed Meer
AGR: Lyle J. Sebranek
AID: Robert N. Bakley

Bombay (CG), Lincoln House, 78
Bhulabhai Desai Rd. 400026
Tel [91] (022) 822-3611
Telex 011-75425 ACON IN

CG: John Eddy
POL/ECO: Jeffery Castelli
COM: David Hughes
CON: Nancy C. Abell
ADM: James L. Williams

Calcutta (CG), 5/1 Ho Chi Minh Sarani,
Calcutta 700071
Tel [91] (033) 44-3611/6
Telex 021-2483

CG: Kenneth C. Brill
POL/ECO: James F. Cole
ECO/COM: (Vacancy)
CON: Laura Livingston
ADM: Jorge Cintron

Madras (CG), Mount Rd. 600006
Tel [91] (44) 473-040/477-542

CG: John D. Stempel
POL/ECO: Nancy C. Johnson
ECO/COM: (Vacancy)
CON: Elizabeth Bowen
ADM: Robert E. Jacobson

INDONESIA

Jakarta (E), Medan Merdeka Selatan 5
APO San Fran 96356
Tel [62] (21) 360-360
Telex 44218 AMEMB JKT

AMB: Paul D. Wolfowitz
DCM: Michael V. Connors
POL: Timothy M. Carney
ECO: Bruce F. Duncombe
COM: Paul T. Walters
CON: Richard P. Livingston
ADM: Bert C. Moore
AID: David N. Merrill
AGR: Kenneth L. Murray

Medan (C), Jalan Imam Bonjol 13
APO San Fran 96356
Tel [62] (61) 322200
Telex 51764

PO: Donald K. Holm
ECO/CON: Joseph Y. Yun
COM: Luis A. Fisher
ADM/CON: Kathryn Berck

Surabaya (C), Jalan Raya Dr. Sutomo 33
APO San Fran 96356
Tel [62] (31) 69287/8
Telex 031-334

PO: Lee O. Coldren
ADM/CON: John Mohanco
ECO/COM: John E. Roberts

IRAQ

Baghdad (E), Opp. For. Ministry Club
(Masbah Quarter)
P.O. Box 2447 Alwiyah, Baghdad, Iraq
Tel [964] (1) 719-6138/9, 718-1840,
719-3791
Telex 212287 USINT IK, 213966
USFCS IK
Workweek: Sunday–Thursday

AMB: David G. Newton
DCM: Stephen W. Buck
POL: Haywood Rankin
ECO: Robert F. Cekuta
COM: (Vacancy)

CON: Judith A. Wood
ADM: Richard P. Collins
ATO: Larry L. Panasuk

IRELAND

Dublin (E), 42 Elgin Rd., Ballsbridge
Tel Dublin [353] (1) 688777
Telex 93684

AMB: Margaret M. O. Heckler
DCM: Thomas H. Gewecke
POL: Stephen W. Worrel
ECO: Algirdas J. Rimas
CON: Joan V. Smith
ADM: John L. Caruso
AGR: Rolland E. Anderson, Jr.
       (resident in London)
COM: John W. Avard

ISRAEL

Tel Aviv (E), 71 Hayarkon St.
APO NY 09672
Tel [972] (3) 654338
Telex 333376 or 371386 US FCS IL

AMB: Thomas R. Pickering
DCM: Arthur H. Huges
POL: Roger C. Harrison
ECO: William R. Brew
COM: Michael J. Mercurio
CON: Wayne S. Leininger
ADM: Adriaen M. Morse
SCI: Anthony Rock
AGR: Robert E. Haresnape
       (resident in Athens)

ITALY

Rome (E), Via Veneto 119/A, 00187-
Rome
APO NY 09794
Tel [39] (6) 46741
Telex 622322 AMBRMA. USIS: Via
Boncompagni 2, 00187-Rome
Telex 625847 USISRM.

AMB: Maxwell M. Rabb
DCM: John W. Holmes
POL: Robert D. Collins
ECO: Daniel P. Serwer

COM: Emilio Iodice
CON: Dudley Sipprelle
ADM: Harold W. Geisel
SCI: Gerald J. Whitman
AGR: Mattie R. Sharpless

Genoa (CG), Banca d'America e d'Italia
Bldg., Piazza Portello, 6-16124 GENOA
Tel [39] (10) 282-741 thru 5
Telex 270324 AMCOGE I

CG: Richard J. Higgins
CON: Edward E. Milburn

Milan (CG), Via Principe Amedeo, 2/10-
20121 Milano
c/o U.S. Embassy, Box M, APO NY
09794
Tel [39] (2) 652-841 thru 5.
Commercial Section: Centro
Cooperazione Internazionale, Piazzale
Giulio Cesare Largo Africa 1, 20145
Milano
Tel [39] (2) 498-2241/2/3

CG: John A. Boyle
POL/ECO: Alan W. Barr
COM: Thomas C. Moore
ECO: John F. Fogarty
CON: Marilyn Jackson
ADM: Robert I. Weisberg
AGR: Richard B. Helm

Naples (CG), Piazza della Repubblica
80122 Naples
Box 18, FPO NY 09521
Tel [39] (81) 660966
Telex ICA NAPLES 720442 ICANA

CG: Louis P. Goelz
POL/ECO/COM: Kenneth R. Audrove
CON: James J. Reid
ADM: Suneta Lyn Halliburton
AID: Hugh L. Dwelley

Palermo (CG), Via Vaccarini 1, 90143
APO NY 09794 (c/o AmEmbassy
Rome-P)
Tel [13] (91) 291532-35
Telex 910313 USACON I

CG: Katherine Shirley
POL/ECO: Ellen Cosgrove

CON: Joseph B. Torres
ADM: Richard C. Weston

Florence (CG), Lungarno Amerigo
   Vespucci 38
   APO NY 09019
   Tel [39] (55) 298-276
   Telex 570577 AMCOFII

CG: Diane Dillard
POL/ECO/COM: Eugene P. Sweeny
CON: Virginia Morris
ADM: Patricia Hollin

Turin (C), via Pomba 23 (2d Fl.) 10123
   Turin
   APO NY 09794 (c/o Amembassy Rome)
   Tel [39] (11) 517437
   Telex 224102 AMCOTO I

IVORY COAST—See Côte d'Ivoire

JAMAICA

Kingston (E), Jamaica Mutual Life
   Center, 2 Oxford Rd., 3d Fl
   Tel [809] 929-4850

AMB: Charles G. Maguire
DCM: Stephen R. Gibson
POL: James P. Nach
ECO: Dorothy J. Black
COM: Franklin J. Gilland
CON: Elizabeth A. Swift
ADM: Herbert Rathner
AGR: Lloyd S. Harbert
          (resident in Santo Domingo)
AID: William R. Joslin

JAPAN

Tokyo (E), 10-1, Akasaka 1-chome,
   Minato-ku (107)
   APO San Fran 96503
   Tel [81] (3) 583-7141
   Telex 2422118

AMB: Michael J. Mansfield
DCM: L. Desaix Anderson
POL: Rust M. Deming
ECO: Aurelia E. Brazeal

COM: (Vacancy)
CON: M. Patricia Wazer
ADM: Jose J. Cao-Gapcia
SCI: Richard W. Getzinger
AGR: Bryant H. Wadsworth
ATO: Suzanne Hale

US Export Development Office, 7th Fl.,
   World Import Mart, 1-3 Higashi
   Ikebukuro 3-chome, Toshima-ku,
   Tokyo 170
   Tel [81] (3) 987-2441
   Telex 2722446

DIR: Edward Oliver, Jr.

Naha, Okinawa (CG), 254 Nishihara,
   Urasoe City, Okinawa 901–21
   Box 40, FPO Seattle, WA 98772
   Tel [81] (98) 876-4211

CG: Karl Spence Richardson
CON: Thomas W. Callow
POL/MIL: Richard M. Gibson

Osaka-Kobe (CG), 11–15, Nishitenma 2-
   chome, Kita-ku, APO San Fran 96503
   Tel [81] (6) 3155900
   Telex 5233037 AMCONJ

CG: John R. Malott
COM: Vladimir P. Sambaiew
CON: Nancy H. Sambaiew
POL/ECO: Robert S. Hyams
ADM: Geoffrey H. Moore

Sapporo (CG), Kita 1-Jo Nishi 28-chome,
   Chuo-ku, Sapporo 064
   APO San Fran 96503
   Tel [81] (11) 641-1115/7
   Telex 935338 AMCONSJ

CG: John R. Dinger
CON: Jason P. Hyland

Fukuoka (C), 5-26 Ohori 2-chome, Chuo-
   ku, Fukuoka-810 or Box 10, FPO
   Seattle 98766
   Tel [81] (92) 751-9331/4
   Telex 725679

PO: Stephen W. Kennedy
ECO/COM: Jeffrey J. Baron
CON: Stephanie A. Weston

JERUSALEM

Jerusalem (CG), 18 Agron Rd, Jerusalem.
APO NY 09672
Tel [972] (2) 234271 (via Israel)
Consular & Cultural Sections: 27
Nablus Rd.
Tel [972] (2) 234271 (both offices via
Israel).

CG: Philip Wilcox, Jr.
DPO: Edwin P. Cubbison
POL: Mark R. Kennon
ECO/COM: Lianer Dorsey
CON: Howard C. Kavaler
ADM: Mark L. Jacobs

JORDAN

Amman (E), Jebel Amman
P.O. Box 354 or APO NY 09892
Tel [962] (6) 644371, USAID Office Tel
[962] (6) 604171
Telex 21510 USEMB JO, Comm. Off.
Telex 24070 USCOMM JO
Workweek: Sunday–Thursday

AMB: Roscoe S. Suddarth
DCM: Patrick N. Theros
POL: C. David Welch
ECO/COM: Peter V. London
CON: Donnie P. Minyard
ADM: Anne M. Hackett
AGR: Larry L. Panasuk
    (resident in Baghdad)
AID: Lewis P. Reade

KENYA

Nairobi (E), Moi/Haile Selassie Ave.
P.O. Box 30137
APO NY 09675
Tel [254] (2) 334141
Telex 22964

AMB: Elinor G. Constable
DCM: George G. B. Griffin
POL: Judith R. Johnson
ECO: Daniel F. Waterman
COM: James M. Wilson
CON: Charles L. Stephan III
ADM: Frederick H. Sheppard

AGR: Susan R. Schayes
AID: Steven W. Sinding

Mombasa (C), Palli House, Nyerere
Avenue
P.O. Box 88079
Tel [254] (11) 315101
Telex 21063 AMCONS

PO: Eugene D. Schmiel

KOREA

Seoul (E), 82 Sejong-Ro
Chongro-ku
APO San Fran 96301
Tel [82] (2) 732-2601 thru 18
Telex AMEMB 23108
US Agricultural Trade Office: 63, 1-
KA, Eulchi-Ro, Choong-ku

AMB: James R. Lilley
DCM: Thomas S. Brooks
POL: Charles Kartman
ECO: Kevin McGuire
COM: George Mu
CON: Andrew F. Antippas
ADM: Robert G. Deason
SCI: Jerome J. Bosken
AGR: James E. Ross
ATO: Laverne E. Brabant

US Trade Center, c/o US Embassy

DIR: Thomas A. Rosengren

Pusan (C), 24 2-Ka, Dacchung Dong,
Chung-ku
Tel 23-7791

PO: Doris K. Stephens
CON: John M. McCaslin

KUWAIT

Kuwait (E), P.O. Box 77 SAFAT, 13001
SAFAT, Kuwait
Tel [965] 242-4151 thru 9
Workweek: Saturday–Wednesday
Telex 22039 HILTELS KT

AMB: W. Nathaniel Howell
DCM: James R. Hooper
POL: Joseph D. Stafford

ECO: Kenneth A. Stammerman
COM: Harry V. Ryder, Jr.
CON: William A. Colwell
ADM: Georgia J. Debell
ATO: Pitamber Devgon
        (resident in Manama)

LAOS

**Vientiane (E), Rue Bartholonie
B.P. 114; Mail to: Box V, APO San
Fran 96346
Tel 2220, 2357, 2384, or 3570 and
2357 after office hours, weekends, and
holidays**

CHG: Harriet W. Isom
POL/ECO: Lisa Taylor
COM/CON: Leonard Hill
ADM: Judith Hughes

LEBANON

**Beirut (E), Antelias, P.O. Box 70-840
Tel [961] 417774, 415802/3, 402200,
403300**

AMB: John H. Kelly
DCM: Francis T. McNamara
POL: Kenneth McKune
ECO/COM: Elizabeth McKune
CON: James Soriano
ADM: Chandler P. Roland
ATO: Theodore Horoschak
        (resident in Istanbul)
AID: Gary T. Mansavage

LESOTHO

**Maseru (E), P.O. Box 333, Maseru 100
Tel [266] 312666
Telex 4506 USAID**

AMB: Robert M. Smalley
DCM: Thomas J. Burke
ADM: Mario Ruggia
CON: Robert O. Morris
AGR: Roger F. Puterbaugh
        (resident in Pretoria)
AID: Jesse L. Snyder

LIBERIA

**Monrovia (E), APO New York 09155
111 United Nations Dr.,
P.O. Box 98
Tel [231] 222991 thru 4**

AMB: James K. Bishop
DCM: Keith L. Wauchope
POL: Simeon L. Moats
ECO/COM: Herman J. Rossi III
CON: Donald E. Parker
ADM: John Garon
AGR: Richard J. Blabey
        (resident in Abidjan)
AID: Mary C. Kilgour

LUXEMBOURG

**Luxembourg (E), 22 Blvd. Emmanuel-
Servais, 2535 Luxembourg
APO NY 09132
Tel [352] 460123**

AMB: Jean B. S. Gerard
DCM: Hugh G. Hamilton, Jr.
POL: Joseph W. Wippl
ECO/COM: Kenneth B. Davis
CON: Leroy O. Smith
ADM: Adolfo A. Ramirez
AGR: Roger S. Lowen
        (resident in Brussels)

MADAGASCAR

**Antananarivo (E), 14 and 16 Rue
Rainitovo, Antsahavola
B.P. 620
Tel 212-57, 209-56, 200-89, 207-18
Telex USA EMB MG 22202, 101
ANTANANARIVO**

AMB: Patricia Gates Lynch
DCM: Robert E. Tynes
ECO/COM: Thomas F. Morrow
ECO/POL: William Kuhn
CON: Robert H. White
ADM: Alexander T. Kirkpatrick
AID: Samuel B. Rea

MALAWI

Lilongwe (E), P.O. Box 30016
Tel 730-166
Telex 4627

AMB: (Vacancy)
CHG: Dennis C. Jett
ECO/COM: Andrew Chritton
POL: Luther R. Morris
ADM: Jerry L. Baker
AID: John F. Hicks

MALAYSIA

Kuala Lumpur (E), 376 Jalan Tun Razak
50400 Kuala Lumpur
P.O. Box No. 10035, 50700 Kuala
Lumpur
Tel [6] (03) 248-9011
Telex FCSKL MA 32956

AMB: John C. Monjo
DCM: Thomas C. Hubbard
POL: Thomas P. Hamilton
ECO: Paul H. Blakeburn
COM: Jonathan Bensky
CON: Allen S. H. Kong
ADM: Patrick R. Hayes
AGR: Francis J. Tarrant

MALI

Bamako (E), Rue Testard and Rue
Mohamed V.
B.P. 34
Tel 225834
Telex 2448 AMEMB

AMB: Robert M. Pringle
DCM: John Hargraves Lewis
POL: Alfreda E. Meyers
ECO/COM: Roger E. Freeman
CON: James E. Dillon
ADM: Stanley P. Jakubowski
AID: Eugene R. Chiavaroli

MALTA

Valletta (E), 2d Fl., Development House,
St. Anne St., Floriana, Malta

P.O. Box 535, Valletta
Tel [356] 623653, 620424, 623216

AMB: Peter R. Sommer
DCM: Eric A. Kunsman
ECO/COM: Damon V. La Brie
POL/LAB: George H. Johnson
CON: Jennifer A. Gregg
ADM: Ernest J. Parkin, Jr.
AGR: Mattie R. Sharpless
        (resident in Rome)

MARSHALL ISLANDS

Majuro (U.S. Office), P.O. Box 680,
Republic of the Marshall Islands
96960
Tel 692-9-3348

US REP: Samuel B. Thomsen
POL/ECO/CON: Arnold Campbell
ADM: Martha Campbell

MAURITANIA

Nouakchott (E), B.P. 222
Tel [2222] 52660/3
Telex AMEMB 558 MTN
Workweek: Sunday–Thursday

AMB: Robert L. Pugh
DCM: John Vincent
POL/ECO/COM: Derwood K. Staeben
CON: Philip A. Bauso
ADM: Gregory L. McLarren
AID: Arthur S. Lezin

MAURITIUS

Port Louis (E), Rogers Bldg. (4th Fl.),
John Kennedy St.
Tel 082347

AMB: Ronald D. F. Palmer
DCM: Robert C. Perry
POL: Robert J. Sise, Jr.
ECO/COM/CON: F. H. Bostock, Jr.
ADM: Gerald J. Loftus

MEXICO

Mexico, D.F. (E), Paseo de la Reforma
305, Mexico 5, D.F.
Mailing: P.O. Box 3087, Laredo, TX
78044-8700
Tel [52] (5) 211-0042
Telex 017-73-091 and 017-75-685

AMB: Charles J. Pilliod, Jr.
DCM: Morris D. Busby
POL: Andrew G. Thoms, Jr.
ECO: Richard H. Morefield
COM: John D. Perkins
CON: Charles F. Brown
ADM: Jerome F. Tolson, Jr.
SCI: Reynaldo Morales
AGR: Leon G. Mears
AID: Samuel Taylor

US Export Development Office, 31
Liverpool, Mexico 6, D.F.
Tel [52] (5) 591-01-55
Telex 01773471

DIR: Rafael Fermoselle

Ciudad Juarez (CG), 924 Avenue Lopez
Mateos, P.O. Box 10545, El Paso, TX
79995-3270
Tel [52] (161) 134048
Telex 033-840

CG: Michael J. Hancock
ADM: Robert L. Scott

Guadalajara (CG), Jal.
Progreso 175
Tel [52] (36) 25-29-98, 25-27-00
Telex 068-2-860

CG: Irwin Rubenstein
POL/ECO: John R. Walson
CON: Rudolph L. Rivera
COM: James Clement
ADM: Ralph D. Chiocco
AGR: Nathaniel Perry

Monterrey (CG), N.L.
Avenida Constitucion 411 Poniente
6406

MAIL: A.P. 152, 64006 Monterrey, N.L.
Mexico
Tel [52] (83) 45-21-20
Telex 0382853

CG: John Bennett
ECO: Raymond C. Jorgenson
CON: Ruth S. Matthews
POL: Kathleen J. Croom
COM: Robert M. Shipley
ADM: Lawrence W. Coor

Tijuana (CG), B.C.
Tapachula 96
Tel [52] (66) 817400, 817700
Telex 056-6836

CG: Larry Colbert
CON: Fernando Sanchez
ADM: Odie N. Fields

Hermosillo (C), Son.
No. 139 Morelia
Tel [52] (621) 3-89-23 thru 25
Telex 58829

PO: J. Christian Kennedy

Matamoros (C), Tamps.
Ave. Primera No. 232
Tel [52] (891) 2-52-50/1/2
Telex 035-827

PO: Danny B. Root

Mazatlan (C), Sin.
6 Circunvalacion No. 6 (at Venustiana
Carranza)
Tel [52] (678) 1-29-05
Telex 066-883

PO: Steven P. Coffman

Merida (C), Yuc.
Paseo Montejo 453, Apartado Postal
130
Tel [52] (992) 5-54-09, 5-50-11
Telex 0753885 AMCONME

PO: Virginia C. Young

Nuevo Laredo (C), Tamps.
Avenida Aliende 3330, Col. Jardin
Tel [52] (871) 4-05-12, 4-06-18
Telex 036-849

PO: Manuel R. Guerra

MICRONESIA

Kolonia (U.S. Office), P.O. Box 1286,
Federated States of Micronesia 96941
Tel. 691-9-187

US REP: Michael G. Wygant
POL/ECO/CON: Steven R. Mann
ADM: Martha Campbell
     (resident in Majuro)

MOROCCO

Rabat (E), 2 Ave. de Marrakech
P.O. Box 120
APO New York 09284
Tel [212] (7) 622-65
Telex 31005

AMB: Thomas A. Nassif
DCM: John M. Hawes
POL: Arnold Schifferdecker
ECO: Daniel L. Dolan
CON: Ted Halstead
ADM: Frank Rhinehart
AGR: David W. Culver
AID: Charles W. Johnson

Casablanca (CG), 8 Blvd. Moulay
Youssef
APO NY 09284 (CAS)
Tel [212] 22-41-49

CG: Richard L. Jackson
DPO/LAB: Keith Loken
POL: S. Phillips Amerman
COM: Charles W. Buck
ECO: Michael J. Varga
CON: Sallybeth M. Bumbrey
ADM: Brian H. McIntosh

Tangier (CG), Chemin des Amoureux
Tel [212] (9) 359-04/5/6
Telex 33025

CG: Vacant
CON/COM: Jonathan Turak

Marrakech (U.S. Information Service),
Villa Saloua, Rue Chouhada,
L'Hivernage
Tel [212] (4) 327-58

MOZAMBIQUE

Maputo (E), 35 Rua Da Mesquita, 3d Fl.
P.O. Box 783
Tel 74279, 743167, 744163
Telex: 6-143 AMEMB MO

AMB: Melissa F. Wells
CHG: Michael E. Ranneberger
POL/LAB: Aubrey V. Verdun
ECO/COM: Anthony C. Newton
CON: Louis Day
ADM: Michael Smolik
AID: Alan Silva

NEPAL

Kathmandu (E), Pani Pokhari
Tel [977] 411179, 412718, 411601
Telex NP 2381 AEKTM

AMB: Melissa F. Wells
CHG: Michael E. Ranneberger
POL/LAB: Aubrey V. Verdun
ECO/COM: Anthony C. Newton
CON: Louis Day
ADM: Michael Smolik
AID: Alan Silva

NETHERLANDS

The Hague (E), Lange Voorhout 102
APO NY 09159
Tel [31] (70) 62-49-11
Telex (044) 31016

AMB: John S. Shad
DCM: John H. Rouse
POL: Alan R. McKee
ECO: Jim B. Marshall
COM: Harrison B. Sherwood
ADM: Johnny Young
AGR: John E. Montel

Amsterdam (CG), Museumplein 19
APO NY 09159
Tel [31] (20) 64-56-61 or 79-03-21
Telex 044-16176 CGUSA NL

CG: Jake Dyels
COM: George F. Ruffner
CON: George Summers

NETHERLANDS ANTILLES

Curacao (CG), St. Anna Blvd. 19
P.O. Box 158, Willemstad, Curacao
Tel [599] (9) 613066
Telex 1062 AMCON NA

CG: Martin McLean
DPO: David Dreher
CON: Richard Morgan
AGR: Lloyd J. Fleck
(resident in Caracas)

NEW ZEALAND

Wellington (E), 29 Fitzherbert Ter.,
Thorndon, Wellington
P.O. Box 1190 Wellington
FPO San Fran 96690
Tel [64] (4) 722-068
Telex NZ 3305

AMB: Paul M. Cleveland
DCM: Alphone F. LaPorta
POL: Donald L. Jameson
ECO: Raymond V. Dickey
COM: William J. Lynch
(resident in Auckland)
CON: Joseph F. Fagan
ADM: Michael J. Adams
AGR: Evans Browne III

Auckland (CG), 4th Fl., Yorkshire
General Bldg.
CNR Shortland and O'Connell Sts.,
Auckland
Private Bag, Auckland
FPO San Fran 96690
Tel [64] (9) 32-724
Telex NZ 3305

CG: Mark J. Platt
COM: William J. Lynch
CON: Linda M. Brown

NICARAGUA

Managua (E), KM. 4-1/2 Carretera Sur.
APO Miami 34021
Tel [505] (2) 66010, 66013, 66015-18,
66026-27, 66032-34

AMB: (Vacancy)

CHG: John P. Modderno
POL: John S. Boardman
ECO: John E. Hope
CON: Wayne Griffith
ADM: John W. Fuhrer
AGR: Robert R. Anlauf
(resident in Guatemala)
AID: John E. Hope
(Acting)

NIGER

Niamey (E), (No street address), B.P.
11201
Tel [227] 72-26-61 thru 4, 72-26-70
Telex EMB NIA 5444NI

AMB: Richard W. Bogosian
DCM: Joseph A. Saloom III
POL: Mark S. Massey
ECO/CON: Cynthia Akuetteh
ADM: Stephen H. King
AID: George T. Eaton

NIGERIA

Lagos (E), 2 Eleke Crescent
P.O. Box 554
Tel [234] (1) 610097
Telex 23616 EMLA NG and 21670
USATO NG

AMB: Princeton N. Lyman
DCM: David L. Blakemore
POL: Peter R. Chaveas
ECO: Richard M. Bash
COM: Norman D. Glick
CON: Bobby L. Watson
ADM: Charles G. Maguire
AGR: Thomas A. Pomeroy
ATO: Alan Hemphill
AID: Elizabeth K. MacManus

Kaduna (CG), 2 Maska Road, P.O. Box
170
Tel [234] (1) 201070, 201071, 201072

CG: Brooke C. Holmes
POL/ECO: Harry K. Thomas
COM: Daniel L. Thompson
CON: Nancy L. Corbett
ADM: Andrew Passen

NORWAY

Oslo (E), Drammensveien 18, Oslo 2, or
APO NY 09085
Tel [47] (2) 44-85-50
Telex 78470

AMB: Robert D. Stuart, Jr.
DCM: Keith C. Smith
POL: James E. Thyden
ECO: Dennis Finnerty
COM: Robert C. Fraser
CON: Edna M. Read
ADM: Steven R. Buckler
AGR: Alexander Bernitz
(resident in Copenhagen)
PAO: Brian E. Carlson

OMAN

Muscat (E), P.O. Box 966
Tel 738-231 or 738-006
ECO/COM Section: Tel [968] 703-287,
702-545
Telex 3785 AMEMBMUS ON
Defense Att. Telex 5118 USDAOMUS
ON
Workweek: Saturday–Wednesday,
7:30-4:00

AMB: G. Cranwell Montgomery
DCM: Douglas R. Keene
POL/ECO: William T. Monroe
ECO/COM: Thomas A. Cadogan
CON: Douglas H. London
ADM: Rudy G. Hall
ATO: Pitamber Devgon
(resident in Manama)

PAKISTAN

Islamabad (E), Diplomatic Enclave,
Ramna 5
P.O. Box 1048
Tel [92] (51) 8261-61 thru 79
Telex 82-5-864
Workweek: Sunday–Thursday

AMB: Arnold L. Raphel
DCM: John T. McCarthy
POL: Edward G. Abington
ECO: Lauralee M. Peters

CON: David T. Rockey
ADM: John C. Daniels
AGR: William L. Brant
AID: Eugene S. Staples

Karachi (CG), 8 Abdullah Haroon Rd.
Tel [009] (221) 515081 thru 8
Telex 82-2-611
Workweek: Sunday–Thursday

CG: Larry C. Grahl
POL/ECO: Arma J. Karaer
COM: George A. Kachmar
CON: Sandra L. Mendyk
ADM: Burton A. Allan
AID: Robert M. Traister

Lahore (CG), 50 Zafar Ali Rd., Gulberg 5
Tel [92] (42) 870221 thru 5
Workweek: Sunday–Thursday

CG: Albert A. Thibault, Jr.
POL: (Vacancy)
ECO/COM: Fredd D. Snell
CON: David C. Stewart
ADM: Thomas M. Bovaird
AID: Richard S. Stevenson

Peshawar (C), 11 Hospital Road
Tel [92] (521) 79801, 79802, 79803
Telex 52-364
Workweek: Sunday–Thursday

PO: Michael E. Malinowski
CON: Bradford E. Hanson
AID: Donald N. Melville

PANAMA

Panama (E), Apartado 6959, Panama 5,
Rep. de Panama
Box E, APO Miami 34002
Tel [507] 27-1777

AMB: Arthur H. Davis
DCM: John F. Maisto
POL: Eleanor W. Savage
ECO: David N. Miller
COM: Samuel D. Starrett
CON: James F. Hughes
ADM: John K. Ivie
AGR: Lana Bennett
(resident in San Jose)
AID: David A. Cohen

PAPUA NEW GUINEA

Port Moresby (E), Armit St.
P.O. Box 1492
Tel [675] 211-455/594/654
Telex 22189 USAEM

AMB: Everett E. Bierman
DCM: Robert M. Pringle
POL: Todd R. Greentree
ECO/COM: Robert Winship
CON: Mary A. Gorjance
ADM: Richard B. Sorg
AID: William E. Paupe
    (resident in Suva)

PARAGUAY

Asuncion (E), 1776 Mariscal Lopez Ave.,
Casilla Postal 402
APO Miami 34036
Tel [595] (21) 201-041/9

AMB: Clyde D. Taylor
DCM: James F. Mack
POL: John L. Martin
ECO/COM: Hugo Llorens
CON: Nick Hahn
ADM: Francine L. Bowman
AGR: Daniel A. Martinez
    (resident in Brasilia)
AID: Paul W. Fritz
    (resident in Montevideo)

PERU

Lima (E), Corner Avenidas Inca
Garcilaso de la Vega & Espana
APO Miami 34031
P.O. Box 1995, Lima 100
Tel [51] (14) 338-000
Telex 25212PE USEMBGSO
Consular Section: Grimaldo Del Solar
346, Miraflores Lima 18
Tel [51] (14) 44-3621
Commercial Section: Grimaldo Del
Solar 358, Miraflores Lima 18
Tel [51] (14) 44-3921
Telex 25028PE USCOMATT
USAID Tel 333-200
Telex 20335PE USAIDPR.

AMB: Alexander F. Watson

DCM: Douglas Langan
POL: John Hamilton
ECO: Robert Knickmeyer
COM: Arthur Alexander
CON: Donna Hamilton
ADM: George Lowe, Jr.
AGR: Gary C. Groves
AID: Donor Lion

PHILIPPINES

Manila (E), 1201 Roxas Blvd.
APO San Fran 96528
Tel [63] (2) 521-7116
Telex 722-27366 AME PH
Com. Off.: 395 Buendia Ave. Extension
Makati
Tel [63] (2) 818-6674
Telex 22708 COSECPH

AMB: Nicholas Platt
DCM: Kenneth M. Quinn
POL: John M. Yates
ECO: Ralph R. Moore
COM: Theodore J. Villinski
ADM: Robert A. MacCallum
CON: J. Norbert Krieg
AGR: Robert M. McConnell
AID: Frederick W. Schieck

Asian Development Bank (Manila),
2330 Roxas Blvd.
P.O. Box 789
Tel [63] (2) 807251
Telex 7425071

U.S. EXEC DIR: Victor H. Frank, Jr.
U.S. ALT EXEC DIR: (Vacancy)

Cebu (C), 3d Fl., PCI Bank Gorordo Ave.,
Lahug
APO San Fran 96528
Tel [63] (32) 52044 or 52984
Telex 712-6226 AMCON PU

PO: Blaine D. Porter
CON: Frederick L. Kupke

POLAND

Warsaw (E), Aleje Ujazdowskle 29/31
AmEmbassy Warsaw, c/o AmConGen
(WAW), APO NY 09213

Tel [48] (22) 283041-9
Telex 813304 AMEMB PL

CHG: John R. Davis, Jr.
DCM: David H. Swartz
POL: David R. Pozorski
ECO: Howard H. Lange
COM: Edgar D. Fulton
CON: Phyllis Villegoureix-Ritaud
ADM: Michael A. Boorstein
SCI: Gary R. Waxmansky
AGR: George J. Dietz

US Trade Center (Warsaw),
Ulica Wiejska 20
Tel [48] (22) 21-45-15
Telex 813934 USTDO PL

DIR: Edgar D. Fulton

Krakow (C), Ulica Stolarska 9,
31043 Krakow
AmConsul Krakow, c/o AmConGen
(KRK), APO NY 09213
Tel [48] (12) 229764, 221400, 226040,
227793
Telex 0325350

PO: Michael M. Hornblow
POL/ECO: Steven L. Blake
CON: June Heil Kunsman
ADM: Evelyn U. Putnam

Poznan (C), Ulica Chopina 4
c/o AmConGen (POZ), APO NY 09213
Tel [48] (61) 59586, 59587, 59874
Telex 041-34-74 USA PL

PO: Peter S. Perenyi
CON: Robert O. Tatge
ADM: Henry E. Kelley

PORTUGAL

Lisbon (E), Avenida das Forcas
Armadas, 1600 Lisbon
APO NY 09678
Tel [351] (1) 726-6600, 726-6659, 726-
8670, 726-8880
Telex 12528 AMEMB

AMB: (Vacancy)
CHG: Wesley W. Egan
POL: Peter Collins

ECO: John Curry
COM: Ralph D. Griffin II
CON: Harry E. Jones
ADM: John R. Baca
AGR: Omero Sabatini
AID: David C. Leibson

Oporto (C), Rua Julio Dinis 826, 3d
Floor, 4000 Oporto
Tel [351] (2) 63094 and 690008

PO: Jacklyn A. Cahill
CON: Kim M. White

Ponta Delgada, Sao Miguel, Azores (C),
Avenida D. Henrique
APO NY 09406
Tel [351] (96) 22216/7
Telex 82126 AMCNPD P

PO: Curtis M. Stewart
VC: Hollis S. Summers
VC: Rhonda L. Ferguson-Augustus

QATAR

Doha (E), Fariq Bin Omran (opp. TV
station)
P.O. Box 2399
Tel [974] 864701/2/3
Telex 4847
Workweek: Saturday–Wednesday

AMB: Joseph Ghougassian
ECO/COM: (Vacancy)
CON: Arnold Sierra
ADM: Sandra Wenner
ATO: Pitamber Devgon
(resident in Manama)

ROMANIA

Bucharest (E), Strada Tudor Arghezi 7-9,
or AmConGen (Buch), APO NY 09213
Tel [40] (0) 10-40-40
Telex 11416

AMB: Roger Kirk
DCM: Henry L. Clarke
POL: Michael E. Parmly
ECO: James H. Williamson
COM: Milton M. Rose
CON: Virginia C. Young

ADM: Mary C. Pendleton
AGR: Steve Washenko
(resident in Belgrade)

RWANDA

Kigali (E), Blvd. de la Revolution, B.P. 28
Tel [205] 75601/2/3 and 72126/7/8

AMB: Leonard H.O. Spearman, Sr.
DCM: Jan De Wilde
ECO/COM/CON: Karl Hofmann
ADM: Kathleen Austin
AID: Emerson J. Melaven

SAUDI ARABIA

Riyadh (E), Collector Road M, Riyadh
Diplomatic Quarter
APO NY 09038, International Mail:
P.O. Box 9041, Riyadh 11143
Tel [966] (1) 488-3800
Telex 406866 AMEMB SJ
USIS: P.O. Box 865
FCS Telex: 401363 USFCS SJ
Workweek: Saturday–Wednesday (all
posts)

AMB: Hume A. Horan
DCM: Edward S. Walker, Jr.
POL: Alan L. Keiswetter
ECO: Anne W. Patterson
COM: Dirck Teller (Acting)
CON: Richard R. LaRoche
ADM: Herbert D. Deremer

Dhahran (CG), Between Aramco Hqrs
and Dhahran Int'l Airport
P.O. Box 81, Dhahran Airport 31932,
or APO NY 09616
Tel [966] (3) 891-3200
Telex CONGEN: 801925 AMCON SJ

CG: Brooks Wrampelmeier
DPO: Paul H. Tyson
ECO: Christopher Kauth
CON: Edward H. Vazquez
COM: Geoffrey Walser
ADM: Lewis K. Elbinger

Jeddah (CG), Palestine Rd., Ruwais
P.O. Box 149 or APO NY 09697

Tel [966] (2) 667-0080
Telex 605175 USCONS SJ
Com. Off.: Tel [966] (2) 667-0040
Telex 601459 USFCS SJ
US Agric Trade Off: Tel [966] (2) 661-2408
Telex 604683 USATO SJ

CG: Jay P. Freres
DPO: (Vacancy)
COM: James L. Joy
CON: Justice B. Stevens
ADM: Leroy E. Beal
ATO: Jerome M. Kuhl

SENEGAL

Dakar (E), B.P. 49, Avenue Jean XXIII
Tel [221] 21-42-96
Telex 517 AMEMB SG

AMB: Lannon Walker
DCM: Jennifer C. Ward
POL: Steve Wagenseil
ECO: Joseph T. Sikes
COM: Portia E. McCollum
CON: Betsy L. Anderson
ADM: J. Michael O'Brien
AGR: Richard J. Blabey
(resident in Abidjan)
AID: Sarah Jane Littlefield

SEYCHELLES

Victoria (E), Box 148
APO NY 09030
Tel 23921/22

AMB: James Moran
POL/ECO: Jack G. Ferraro
CON: Kristine Pelz
ADM: David M. Buss
AID/REDSO: Arthur Fell
(resident in Nairobi)

SIERRA LEONE

Freetown (E), Corner Walpole and Siaka
Stevens St.
Tel 26481
Telex (989)3509 USEMBSL

AMB: Cynthia S. Perry
DCM: Gregory M. Talcott
CON: Barbara M. Johnson
ECO/COM: James Dunn
ADM: Larry L. Palmer
AGR: Richard J. Blabey
     (resident in Abidjan)
AID: James W. Habron

SINGAPORE

Singapore (E), 30 Hill St.
  Singapore 0617
  FPO San Fran 96699
  Tel [65] 338-0251

AMB: Daryl Arnold
DCM: Peter T. Higgins
ECO/POL: John F. Hoog
COM: Beaumont Lower
CON: William Moody
ADM: Philip A. King
ATO: Peter O. Kurz

Commercial Services and Library, 111 N.
  Bridge Rd. #15-05, Peninsula Plaza,
  Singapore 0617
  Tel [65] 338-9722
  Telex RS25079 (SINGTC)

US Agricultural Office, 541 Orchard
  Road, 08-04, Liat Towers Bldg.,
  Singapore 0923
  Tel [65] 7371233
  Telex RS55318 USDA

SOLOMON ISLANDS

Honiara (C), Mailing Address and Telex:
  American Embassy, Port Moresby for
  Honiara.

PO: Hal W. Pattison

SOMALIA

Mogadishu (E), Corso Primo Luglio,
  P.O. Box 574
  Tel [252] (01) 20811
  Public Telex (999) 789 AMEMB MOG
  Workweek: Sunday–Thursday

AMB: T. Frank Crigler
DCM: David P. Rawson

POL: James B. Bond
ECO: Stephen K. Keat
CON: Christopher D. Costanzo
ADM: James J. Johnston
AID: Louis A. Cohen

SOUTH AFRICA

Pretoria (E), Thibault House, 225
  Pretorius St.
  Tel [27] (12) 28-4266
  Telex 3-751

AMB: Edward J. Perkins
DCM: Richard C. Barkley
ECO/COM: Stephen H. Rogers
ADM: Andrew Jan Winter
POL/ECO: Sheila S. Gwaltney
AGR: Roger F. Puterbaugh
AID: Timothy J. Bork

Cape Town (CG), Broadway Industries
  Center, Heerengracht, Foreshore
  Tel [27] (21) 214-280/7
  Telex 522387

CG: John A. Burroughs, Jr.
POL/ECO: Gillian A. Milovanovic
ADM: Efraim A. Cohen
CON: James B. Gray

Durban (CG), Durban Bay House, 29th
  Fl., 333 Smith St., Durban 4001
  Tel [27] (31) 304-4737/8

CG: F. Allen Harris
CON: Terrence P. McCulley

Johannesburg (CG), 11th Fl., Kine Center,
  Commissioner and Krulis Sts.,
  P.O. Box 2155
  Tel [27] (11) 331-1681
  Telex 483780-SA

CG: Peter R. Chaveas
POL: Frederick J. Kaplan
ECO: Leo F. Cecchini, Jr.
COM: Benjamin N. Brown
CON: Richard F. Crehan

SPAIN

Madrid (E), Serrano 75
  APO NY 09285

Tel [34] (1) 276-3400/3600
Telex 27763

AMB: Reginald Bartholomew
DCM: Adrain A. Basora
POL: Gerald Desantillana
ECO: Pierce Bullen
COM: Robert Kohn
CON: Larry Lane
ADM: Warren E. Littrel, Jr.
AGR: Edmund L. Nichols
SCI: Ismael Lara

Barcelona (CG), Via Layetana 33
   APO NY 09286
   Tel [34] (3) 319-9550
   Telex 52672

CG: Ruth A. Davis
COM: Charles A. Ford
CON: John A. Parker
ADM: Dainel Hernandez

Bilbao (C), Avenida del Ejercito, 11-3,
   48014 Bilbao
   APO NY 09285
   Tel [43] (4) 435-8300
   Telex 32589

PO: Gary Usrey
CON: Bradford H. Johnson

SRI LANKA

Colombo (E), 210 Galle Rd., Colombo 3
P.O. Box 106
Tel [94] (1) 548007
Telex 21305 AMEMB CE
USAID and USIS—44 Galle Rd.,
Colombo 3
Tel [94] (1) 21271, 21520, 21532

AMB: James W. Spain
DCM: Edward Marks
POL: Ernestine S. Heck
ECO: Robert P. Goold
COM: James J. Barnes
ADM: Stephen T. Smith
CON: Stephen R. Pattison
AGR: Lyle J. Sebranek
       (resident in New Delhi)
AID: Peter J. Bloom

SUDAN

Khartoum (E), Sharia Ali Abdul Latif
P.O. Box 699, APO NY 09668
Tel 74700, 75680, 74611
Telex 22619 AMEM SD
Workweek: Sunday–Thursday

AMB: G. Norman Anderson
DCM: Dane F. Smith, Jr.
POL: Douglas B. Archard
ECO: Gary D. DeVight
CON: Marvin S. Brown
ADM: Gerald E. Manderscheid
AID: John W. Koehring
AGR: Guy Haviland
       (resident in Cairo)

SURINAME

Paramaribo (E), Dr. Sophie
   Redmondstraat 129
P.O. Box 1821
Tel [597] 72900, 76459
USIS: Tel [597] 75051
Telex 373 AMEMSU SN

AMB: Richard Howland
DCM: Frank Tumninia
POL: Clyde Howard
COM/ECO: Robert J. Austin
CON: Rebecca S. Replogle
ADM: Richard A. Garrison
AGR: Lloyd J. Fleck
       (resident in Caracas)

SWAZILAND

Mbabane (E), Central Bank Bldg., P.O.
   Box 199, Warner Street
   Tel 22281/2/3/4/5
   USAID Telex 2016 WD

AMB: Harvey F. Nelson, Jr.
DCM: Gerald W. Scott
POL/ECO/CON: Lee A. Brudvig
ADM: Sandra R. Smith
AGR: Roger F. Puterbaugh
       (resident in Pretoria)
AID: Robert G. Huesmann

SWEDEN

**Stockholm (E), Strandvagen 101, S-115
27 Stockholm
Tel [46] (8) 7835300
Telex 12060 AMEMB S**

AMB: Gregory J. Newell
DCM: Roland K. Kuchel
POL: Michael R. Arietti
ECO: F. Brenne Bachmann
COM: James N. May
CON: David T. Hopper
ADM: Jeffrey S. White
AGR: Shackford Pitcher

**Goteborg (CG), Sodra Hamngatan 2,
S-411 06 Goteborg
Tel [46] (31) 100590
Telex 21954 AMCON S**

SWITZERLAND

**Bern (E), Jubilaeumstrasse 93, 3005 Bern
Tel [41] (31) 437011
Telex (845) 912603**

AMB: Faith R. Whittlesey
DCM: Frederick H. Hassett
POL: Sherman N. Hinson
ECO: Richard C. Devine
COM: Daniel Taher
CON: Annette L. Veler
ADM: (Vacancy)
AGR: Robert S. Simpson

**Geneva (BO), 11, Route de Pregny, 1292
Chambesy/Geneva
1-3 Ave de la Paix, 1201 Geneva
Tel [41] (22) 335537 or 442330
Telex 22103 USMIO CH (This office
offers no commercial services.)**

CON: Sally M. Gober

**United States Trade Representative,
Botanic Bldg., 1-3 Avenue de la Paix,
Geneva
Tel [41] (22) 320970**

DCM: Warren A. Lavorel
AGR: James A. Truran

**Zurich (CG) Zolliikerstrasse 141, 8008
Zurich
Tel [41] (1) 552566
Telex 0045-53893**

CG: Louis S. Segesvary
CON: Alford W. Cooley

SYRIA

**Damascus (E), Abu Rumaneh, Al Mansur
St. No. 2; P.O. Box 29
Tel [963] (11) 333052, 332557, 330416,
332814, 332315
Telex 411919 USDAMA SY**

AMB: William L. Eagleton, Jr.
DCM: David M. Ransom
POL: R. Bruce Ehrnman
ECO/COM: Marisa R. Lino
CON: Allen J. Kepchar
ADM: Frank Rey
AGR: W. Garth Thorburn
 (resident in Ankara)
ATO: Theodore Horoschak
 (resident in Istanbul)

TANZANIA

**Dar es Salaam (E), 36 Laibon Rd. (off
Bagamoyo Rd.)
P.O. Box 9123
Tel [255] 375014
Telex 41250
AMEMB DAR**

AMB: Donald K. Petterson
DCM: Joseph M. Segars
POL: Stevenson McIlvaine
ECO/COM: Gayleatha B. Brown
CON: Barbara M. Johnson
ADM: Robert L. Kile
AGR: Harold L. Norton
 (resident in Nairobi)
AID: Howard R. Sharlach (Acting)

THAILAND

**Bangkok (E), 95 Wireless Rd.
APO SAN FRAN 96346
TEL [66] (2) 252-5040**

Com. Off and Library.: "R" Fl., Shell Bldg., 140 Wireless Rd.
Tel [66] (2) 253-4920/2
Telex 20966 FCSBKK (Commercial Section)

AMB: William A. Brown
DCM: Joseph A. B. Winder
POL: Phillip R. Mayhew
ECO: Paul K. Stahnke
COM: Robert C. Bodden
CON: Patricia Langford
ADM: George E. Knight
AGR: Weyland Beeghly
AID: John R. Eriksson

Chiang Mai (CG), Vidhayanond Rd.
   Box C, APO San Fran 96346
   Tel [66] (53) 252-629/30/31

PO: Charles S. Ahlgren
CON: William F. Davnie III
ADM: James A. Forbes

Songkhla (C), 9 Sadao Rd.
   Box S, APO San Fran 96346
   Tel [66] (2) 311-589

PO: Douglas Rasmussen

Udorn (C), 35/6 Supakitjanya Rd.
   Box UD, APO San Fran 96346
   Tel [66] (42) 221-548

PO: Margaret K. McMillion
CON: Robert Siegenthaler

TOGO

Lome (E), Rue Pelletier Caventou & Rue Vauban
   B.P. 852
   Tel [228] 21-29-91 thru 94 and 21-36-09

AMB: David A. Korn
DCM: Tibor P. Nagy, Jr.
POL: R. Eric Pound
ECO/COM: Mary E. Grandfield
ADM: Joseph Huggins
AID: Mark G. Wenting

TRINIDAD AND TOBAGO

Port-of-Spain (E), 15 Queen's Park West
   P.O. Box 752
   Tel [809] 622-6372/6, 6176

AMB: Sheldon J. Krys
DCM: C. Robert Dickerman
POL: James P. Bell, Jr.
ECO: V. Edward Olson
CON: Karla Reed
ADM: John P. Markey
COM: Stephen J. Helgesen
AGR: Lloyd J. Fleck
        (resident in Caracas)

TUNISIA

Tunis (E), 144 Ave. de la Liberte, 1002 Tunis-Belvedere
   Tel [216] (1) 782-566
   Telex 13379 AMTUN TN

AMB: Robert H. Pelletreau, Jr.
DCM: Gordon S. Brown
POL: Edmund J. Hull
ECO/COM: Lewis I. Cohen
CON: Philip S. Covington
ADM: Peter S. Flynn
ATO: Besa Kotati
        (resident in Algiers)
AID: Charles F. Weden

TURKEY

Ankara (E), 110 Ataturk Blvd.
   APO NY 09254
   Tel [90] (41) 26 54 70
   Telex 43144 USIA TR

AMB: Robert Strausz-Hupé
DCM: William F. Rope
POL: Michael I. Austrian
ECO: G. Clay Nettles
COM: Dan A. Wilson
CON: Robert E. Sorensen
ADM: Katherine L. Kemp
AGR: W. Garth Thorburn

Istanbul (CG), 104-108 Mesrutiyet Caddesi, Tepebasl
   APO NY 09380

Tel [90] (1) 151 36 02
Telex 24306 USIC TR

CG: Wiliam E. Rau
POL: Joseph E. Le Baron
ECO: Steven M. Brattain
COM: E. Scott Bozek
CON: Roger D. Pierce
ADM: Raymond M. Nowakowski
ATO: Theodore Horoschak

Izmir (CG), 92 Ataturk Caddesi (3d Fl.)
APO NY 09224
Tel [60] (51) 149426, 131369

CG: Albert N. Williams
POL: Martin Adams
ECO/CON: Robert Stephen Ford
ADM: Albert E. Schrock

Adana (C), Ataturk Caddesi
APO NY 09289

Tel [90] (711) 39106, 42145, 43774

PO: Mary Virginia Kennedy
POL/ECO: Scott F. Kilner
ADM/CON: David A. Rollman

UGANDA

Kampala (E), British High Commission
Bldg., Obote Ave.
P.O. Box 7007
Tel 259791, Chancery 259791/2/3/5

AMB: Robert G. Houdek
DCM: Charles H. Morris, Jr.
POL/CON: James C. Mellstrom
POL/ECO: Susan W. Zelle
ECO/CON: David R. Salazar
ADM: (Vacancy)
AID: Richard Podol

UNION OF SOVIET SOCIALIST REPUBLICS

Moscow (E), Ulitsa Chaykovskogo 19/21/
23, or APO NY 09862
Tel [7] (096) 252-24-51 thru 59
Telex 413160 USGSO SU

AMB: Jack F. Matlock, Jr.
DCM: Richard E. Combs, Jr.

POL: Mark Ramee
ECO: Robert F. Ober, Jr.
COM: H. Michael Mears
CON: Eugene C. Zajac
ADM: David R. Beall
SCI: John C. Zimmerman
AGR: Thomas Hamby

US Commercial Office (Moscow)
Ulitsa Chaykovskogo 15
Tel [7] (096) 255-48-48, 255-46-60
Telex 413-205 USCO SU

DIR: H. Michael Mears

Leningard (CG), Ulitsa, Petra Lavrova St.
15
Box L, APO NY 09664
Tel [7] (812) 274-8235
Telex 64-121527 AMCONSUL SU

CG: Edward Hurwitz
DPO: Thomas Maertens
CON: Joyce Marshall
POL/ECO: Robert Thomas
ADM: Matthew Burns

UNITED ARAB EMIRATES

Abu Dhabi (E), Al-Sudan St.
P.O. Box 4009
Tel [971] (2) 336691
Telex 23513 AMEMBY EM
Com. Sec: Blue Tower Bldg., 8th Floor,
Shaikh Khalifa Bin Zayed St.
Tel [971] (2) 345545
Telex 22229 AMEMBY EM
Workweek: Saturday–Wednesday

AMB: David L. Mack
DCM: Ronald Newmann
POL: John W. Chamberlin
ECO: Donald Roberts
COM: Paul Huygelen
CON: Robert Murphy
ADM: Robert A. Sarofeen

Dubai (CG), Dubai International Trade
Center
P.O. Box 9343
Tel [971] (4) 371115

Telex 98346031 BACCUS EM
Workweek: Saturday–Wednesday

CG: David C. Litt
ECO: Richard Chiarantona
COM: John L. Priamou
CON: George Brazier
ATO: Pitamber Devgon
    (resident in Manama)

UNITED KINGDOM

**London, England (E), 24/31 Grosvenor Sq., W. 1A 1AE
or Box 40, FPO NY 09509
Tel [44] (01) 499-9000
Telex 266777**

AMB: Charles H. Price II
DCM: Raymond Seitz
POL: Miles S. Pendleton
ECO: Richard M. Ogden
COM: David A. Diebold
CON: Edward Kreuser
ADM: Lawrence D. Russell
SCI: James B. Devine
AGR: Rolland E. Anderson, Jr.
ATO: Robert D. Fondahn

**Belfast, Northern Ireland (CG), Queen's House, 14 Queen St., BT1 6EQ
Tel [44] (232) 328239
Telex 747512**

CG: Robert P. Myers, Jr.
CON: Francis Scanlan
AGR: Rolland E. Anderson, Jr.
    (resident in London)

**Edinburgh, SCOTLAND (CG), 3 Regent Ter. EH 75BW
Tel [44] (31) 556-8315
Telex 727303**

CG: Douglas H. Jones
CON: Maurice Parker
AGR: Rolland E. Anderson, Jr.
    (resident in London)

URUGUAY

**Montevideo (E), Lauro Muller 1776
APO Miami 34035**

Tel [598] (2) 40-90-51 and afterhours 40-91-26

AMB: Malcolm R. Wilkey
DCM: Richard C. Brown
POL: Janet L. Crist
ECO/COM: James J. Reilly
ADM: Ned E. Morris
CON: James P. Walsh
AGR: J. Dawson Ahalt
    (resident in Buenos Aires)
AID: Paul W. Fritz

VENEZUELA

**Caracas (E), Avenida francisco de Miranda and Avenida Principal de la Floresta, P.O. Box 62291, Caracas 1060-A or APO Miami 34037
Tel [58] (2) 284-7111/6111
Telex 25501 AMEMB VE
US Agricultural Trade Office: Centro Plaza, Tower C, Piso 18, Los Palos Grandes, Caracas
Tel [58] (2) 283-2599 or 284-3264
Telex 29119 USATO VC**

AMB: Otto J. Reich
DCM: Jeffrey Davidow
POL: Claus W. Ruser
ECO: Alfred J. White
COM: Kenneth Moorefield
CON: Don E. Bean
ADM: Leon M. Johnson, Jr.
AGR: Lloyd J. Fleck
ATO: John Jacobs

**Maracaibo (C), Edificio Sofimara, Piso 3, Calle 77 Con Avenida 13, or APO Miami 34037
Tel [58] (61) 84-253/4, 52-54-55, 83-504/5
Telex 62213 USCON VE**

PO: (Vacancy)
CON: Mark Mayfield
ADM: John Bradshaw

YEMEN ARAB REPUBLIC

**Sanaa (E), P.O. Box 1088
Tel [967] (2) 271950 through 58**

Telex 2697 EMBSAN YE
Workweek: Saturday–Wednesday
Commercial Office Tel [967] (2) 272417
USAID Tel [967] (2) 231213/4/5

AMB: Charles F. Dunbar
DCM: Theodore H. Kattouf
POL: Dundas McCullough
ECO/COM: Brian L. Goldbeck
CON: Greta Holtz
ADM: Edward Harkness
ATO: Jerome M. Kuhl
    (resident in Jeddah)
AID: Kenneth H. Sherper

YUGOSLAVIA

Belgrade (E), Kneza Milosa 50
  Tel [38] (11) 645-655
  Telex 11529 AMEMBA YU
  AMCONGEN (BEG) APO NY 09213
  Workweek: Monday–Friday 7:30-4:15
  Consular Section 7:30-3:30

AMB: John D. Scanlan
DCM: Joseph A. Presel
POL: Louis D. Sell
ECO: Lloyd R. George
COM: David K. Katz
CON: William E. Ryerson
ADM: William J. Hudson
SCI: Thomas Vrebalovich
AGR: Steve Washenko

Zagreb (CG), Brace Kavurica 2
  Tel [38] (41) 444-800
  Telex 21180 YU AMCON
  AMCONGEN (ZGB) APO NY 09213

CG: James W. Swihart, Jr.
POL/ECO/COM: Daniel T. Fantozzi
CON: Lorraine W. Polik
ADM: David W. Ball

ZAIRE

Kinshasa (E), 310 Avenue des Aviateurs
  APO NY 09662
  Tel [243] (12) 25881 thru 6
  Telex 21405 US EMB ZR

AMB: Brandon H. Grove, Jr.
DCM: Marc A. Baas

POL: Michael W. Cotter
ECO/COM: Ralph E. Bresler
CON: Barbara Hemingway
ADM: Byron P. Walker
AGR: Richard J. Blabey
    (resident in Abidjan)
AID: Dennis Chandler

Lubumbashi (CG), 1029 Blvd. Kamanyola
  B.P. 1196
  APO NY 09662
  Tel 222324

CG: Jay Grahame
POL: John Bennett
ECO/COM: David Brown
AID: Bruce Spake
CON: (Vacancy)
ADM: Julie Gardner

ZAMBIA

Lusaka (E), corner of Independence and
  United Nations Aves.
  P.O. Box 31617
  Tel [2601] 214911
  Telex AMEMB ZA 41970

AMB: Paul J. Hare
DCM: H. Kenneth Hill
POL: Phillip H. Egger
ECO/COM: John J. Hartley II
CON: Paul D. Birdsall
ADM: Stanton R. Bigelow
AGR: Susan R. Schayes
    (resident in Nairobi)
AID: Ted D. Morse

ZIMBABWE

Harare (E), 172 Rhodes Ave., P.O. Box
  3340
  Tel [263] (0) 794-521
  Commercial Section: 1st Fl., Century
  House West, 36 Baker Ave.
  Tel [263] (14) 728-957
  Telex 4591 USFCS ZW

AMB: James Wilson Rawlings
DCM: Edward F. Fugit
POL/ECO: Paul B. Larsen

CON: Arthur H. Mills II
ADM: Richard A. Megica
AGR: Roger F. Puterbaugh
        (resident in Pretoria)
AID: Allison B. Herrick

TAIWAN

Unofficial commercial and other relations with the people of Taiwan are maintained through a private instrumentality, the American institute in Taiwan, which has offices in Taipei and Kaohsiung. The addresses of these offices are:

American Institute in Taiwan (Taipei Office), 7 Lane 134, Hsin Yi Road, Section 3; Tel 002 [886] (2) 709-2000 Telex 23890 USTRADE

American Institute in Taiwan (Kaohsiung Office), 88 Wu Fu 3d Road

The Taipei office of the Institute operates a trade center located at 600 Min Chuan East Road (Tel 713-2571).

For further information, contact the Washington office of the American Institute in Taiwan, 1700 N. Moore St. (17th Fl.), Arlington, VA 22209, (703) 525-8474.

Index

A

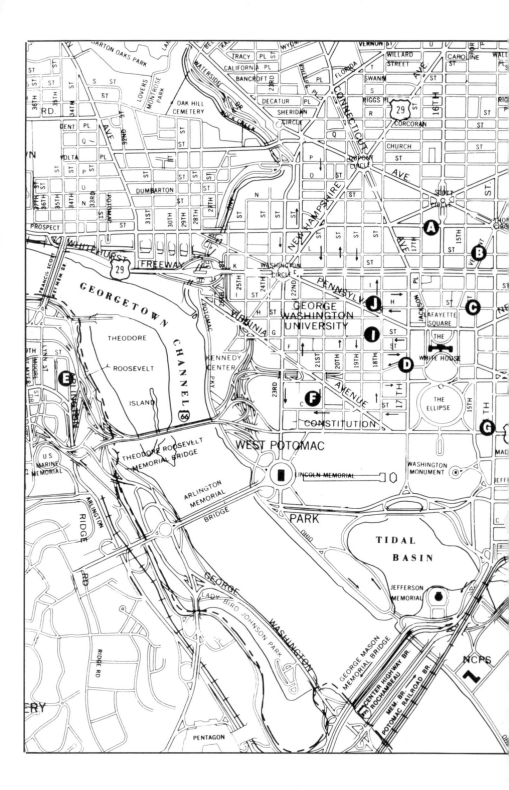